Mathematics
— LEVEL 8 —

JEAN HOLDERNESS

CAUSEWAY PRESS

Published by Causeway Press Ltd
PO Box 13, Ormskirk, Lancs L39 5HP

First published 1992

British Library Cataloguing in Publication Data
Holderness, Jean
  Mathematics: Level 8.
  1. Mathematics
  I. Title
  510

  ISBN 0-946183-87-2

Other books in this series:
Mathematics: Levels 3 & 4 by David Alcorn
Mathematics: Level 5 by Jean Holderness
Mathematics: Level 6 by Jean Holderness
Mathematics: Level 7 by Jean Holderness

Other titles by Jean Holderness published by
Causeway Press:
GCSE Maths: Higher Level
GCSE Maths: Intermediate Level
GCSE Maths: Foundation Level
Pure Maths in Practice

Typesetting by Alden Multimedia Ltd., Northampton
Printed by Alden Press, Oxford

Preface

Mathematics: Level 8 has been written for pupils in secondary schools and it follows on from the work covered in the book *Mathematics: Level 7* and the earlier books in this series. It is based mainly on the programme of study for level 8 of the National Curriculum, but it also provides consolidation for some work of earlier levels, and it is a useful introduction for some work at higher levels.

For most pupils, the book could be used as a basis for a year's work, although there is sufficient material included for it to be used for more than a year. The teacher can decide how best to use the book with a particular class. (There are some notes for teachers on page *ix*.)

As usual, my family and friends have given me support and encouragement while I have been planning and writing this book, and I would like to thank them for this. I should also like to thank those who have helped with the production of the book, Sue and Andrew, my brother Jim, and the staff at Alden Multimedia and Alden Press. From Causeway Press I have had support from everyone, and especially from David and Mike, and I thank them for all their help.

Jean Holderness

iv

Acknowledgements

Artwork, page design and cover Susan and Andrew Allen

Photography © Jim Holderness and Andrew Allen

Copyright photographs

Ed Buziak pp. 75 (middle left), 75 (bottom right), 88 (top), 93, 153 (bottom left), 183
Hulton Picture Company p. 197 (top)
Sally and Richard Greenhill pp. 19, 50 (bottom right), 74 (bottom left), 75 (top right), 75 (bottom left),
    139 (bottom), 227 (top), 227 (bottom)
The Image Bank — Kee Hwa Jeun (cover)
Topham Picture Source pp. 22, 33 (top), 33 (bottom left), 33 (bottom right),
        50 (top left), 50 (bottom left), 51, 124 (bottom right),
        125 (top right), 125 (bottom right), 134, 150, 212 (left),
        212 (right), 237, 248
Trustees of the Science Museum pp. 2 (bottom 571/63), 124 (bottom left 647/51),
        138 (64/49), 152 (2578), 276 (6/39)

Contents

Topics for Activities (included in the miscellaneous sections)

To the teacher

Mathematics: Level 8 has been planned for use in secondary schools. It follows on from the work in the book *Mathematics: Level 7* and the earlier books in the series.

It is based on the revised National Curriculum at level 8. It contains all the topics needed for the Programme of Study and the Attainment Targets, as well as linking the work to that of earlier levels where appropriate. Some topics give practice in basic ideas which can be extended into the work of higher levels.

Work at level 8 is aimed at the more able pupils who will be working at this level towards the end of Key Stage 3, and at some others who will reach it in Key Stage 4. The mathematical content in some topics is quite demanding, and there is less scope than in earlier levels to link some topics with suitable and genuine real-life applications.

The book follows the same pattern as the earlier books in the series, with the chapters arranged in an order which interlinks the various topics, to give variety. Each chapter begins with an introductory section, followed by bookwork, worked examples and straightforward exercises, and ending with a miscellaneous exercise of applications and activities.

In the straightforward exercises, there should be no need for every pupil to have to work through every part of every question. More, rather than fewer, questions have been included so that pupils who need more practice to gain confidence, particularly in new topics, have the questions available. For other pupils, a selection can be made, and the remaining questions will be available if revision is needed later on.

The book has 15 chapters, roughly 5 for each term if the book is to be used for a year. After every 5 chapters there is a miscellaneous section with aural questions, revision questions and more suggestions for activities. There are puzzle questions fitted in at the ends of chapters where there is space, and these are in no particular order, and are there to give further interest.

The teacher should be ready to link mathematics with any topics or activities which apply directly to the interests of the class, such as studies in other subjects, or current local or national issues.

Here are some notes about particular points:

Calculators. The references to calculators are based on scientific calculators. Since they do not all work in the same way or have similar keys, pupils with different types may need individual help at times. This is particularly so when using them for trigonometry questions or with standard form.

Probably, some pupils will have calculators which can calculate with fractions. Such pupils may think it is unnecessary to learn the methods for manipulating fractions (Chapter 1), so they should be warned that their calculators will not sort out the algebraic fractions of Chapter 6, and a good understanding of the methods is essential. Some pupils may have graphics calculators and if they can be helped to understand how to use these to draw graphs, these can be drawn quickly, and this should help pupils to have a clearer understanding of the graphs of different types of functions. Alternatively, graphs can be drawn on a computer screen using a graph-plotting program.

Graph paper. 2 mm graph paper with a grid 16 cm by 20 cm will be suitable for most graphs. For the regions in Chapter 4, squared paper could be used, except in the last exercise. For the cumulative frequency graphs, scales have not always been suggested, since in some cases a better graph is obtained if you are using slightly bigger paper.

Chapter 1. Fractions have been used in other books in this series but now the ideas have been gathered together.
Working with fractions and ratios gives an opportunity for revision of basic, mental arithmetic. A check by the teacher that pupils can do simple arithmetic quickly and accurately is sometimes necessary. Those pupils who have forgotten their tables and use a calculator for simple processes waste so much of their time.

Algebra. There is quite a lot of algebra in Level 8, especially in comparison with lower levels. That is why it has been included in small portions in many chapters, e.g. with work on fractions in Chapter 1. In Chapter 6, which is the main algebra chapter, rather than beginning with a large section on revision, it has been split into smaller sections, each section leading to new work.

Chapter 4, Regions. In the examples I have described the regions clearly as **not** including the boundary lines. I did not think that it was a good idea at that stage to draw all the boundary lines as dotted lines. Pupils will find it easier to be able to concentrate on drawing the correct lines and finding the correct regions, without this extra complication. It is not until the practical questions of the last exercise that pupils need to decide whether a particular boundary line is, or is not, to be included in a certain region.

Chapter 5, Statistical Investigations. I have given some suggestions of possible ways to analyse a questionnaire with multiple responses, and I hope that these are acceptable methods.
I have not included the alternative option that the pupils should design and use an experiment with several variables. This would best be linked with work in Science or some other suitable subject.

Chapters 7 and 11, Trigonometry. In the past there were extra complications with trig. tables, degrees and minutes, difference columns, tables used in reverse, log trig. tables, etc. All these problems have disappeared now that we can press a few keys on our calculators.

In Chapter 7, I have concentrated on the tangent ratio, and the pupils should find this quite straightforward. If they learn that $\tan \theta = \dfrac{\text{opp}}{\text{adj}}$ at this stage, they should not find it so difficult to learn the other two ratios later. (There is also an introduction to trigonometry on page 100.)

For practical use, answers given to an accuracy of less than 1 mm when the given measurements are in centimetres seem rather pointless. In any case, all calculations are based on measurements which are themselves subject to error. But, possibly, examination boards may still want to check accuracy to more than 1 or 2 significant figures. So in the basic exercises I have asked for answers for lengths to 3 significant figures, and for angles to 0.1°. In the practical questions I have given answers to what I judge to be a sensible degree of accuracy, e.g. I would give the height that a ladder reaches up a wall to 0.1 m rather than to the nearest centimetre.

Chapter 8. Indices and standard form. There is further work on indices in level 9. You may like to extend the work at this stage. As with the trigonometry questions, the problems of standard form are solved by pressing a few keys. But it is very desirable for pupils to understand the processes, as well as being able to use a calculator.

Chapter 12. Cumulative frequency. This chapter has been split up into sections. I think a lot of confusion is caused between cumulative frequency graphs and histograms, so histograms are not mentioned here. Also confusion is caused if pupils just write the cumulative frequency totals on an extra column of the frequency table. If they are encouraged to write out a separate table and think about the wording in the first column, it should be much clearer.

Since answers have to be obtained from the horizontal axis, it is important that the labelling on that axis uses main numbers, e.g. 3.0, 4.0, 5.0, . . . rather than 3.95, 4.95, 5.95, . . . The points can be **plotted** at 3.95, 4.95, 5.95, . . . quite easily on a scale labelled at 3.0, 4.0, 5.0, . . . (If the graph is labelled with thick lines at 3.95, 4.95, 5.95, . . . then the plotted points lie on these lines but it is very difficult to work out the values for the median and the quartiles.)

I have shown both a cumulative frequency curve and a cumulative frequency polygon. The National Curriculum asks for cumulative frequency curves. However, pupils probably find it easier to draw cumulative frequency polygons, and you might like them to start off by drawing these. Later in the chapter I have called them cumulative frequency graphs, so you may decide which type to use.

The answers have been calculated as from cumulative frequency polgons and there will be some variations in acceptable answers, especially if curves are drawn.

Chapter 14, Vectors. This is just a brief introduction to vectors, which come in more detail in level 9. The rule for addition of vectors has not been mentioned, but pupils may discover it at this stage.

Chapter 15. This is a rather miscellaneous chapter which may give pupils a chance to develop their mathematical skills.

Answers. The answers to the straightforward questions are given, but not always to questions where it is important that the pupils make their own discoveries. Therefore there are no answers for Chapter 5 or Chapter 15, for most of the 'activities' questions, or for the puzzles.
I think that at this level it will probably be appropriate for the pupils to have the answer pages, but if you do not want the class to have them, they can be cut out of the book.

I hope that you and your pupils find this book useful and interesting. Enjoy your Maths.

Jean Holderness.

Formulae

Perimeter of a rectangle $= 2 \times$ (length + breadth) $= 2(l + b)$

Circumference of a circle $= \pi \times$ diameter $= 2\pi \times$ radius $\qquad C = \pi d$
$$C = 2\pi r$$

Area of a rectangle $=$ length $\times$ breadth $= lb$
Area of a square $=$ (length)$^2 = l^2$
Area of a triangle $= \frac{1}{2} \times$ base $\times$ perpendicular height $= \frac{1}{2}bh$
Area of a parallelogram $=$ base $\times$ perpendicular height $= bh$
Area of a trapezium $= \frac{1}{2} \times$ sum of the parallel sides $\times$ the perpendicular distance between them
$$= \frac{1}{2}(a + b)h$$
Area of a circle $= \pi \times$ (radius)$^2 \qquad A = \pi r^2$
Curved surface area of a cylinder: $\qquad S = 2\pi rh$

Volume of a cuboid $=$ length $\times$ breadth $\times$ height $= lbh$
Volume of a cube $=$ (length)$^3 = l^3$
Volume of solid of uniform cross-section $=$ area of cross-section $\times$ height
Volume of a cylinder: $\qquad\qquad V = \pi r^2 h$

Pythagoras' theorem $\qquad a^2 = b^2 + c^2$

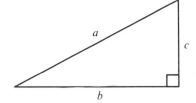

$$\text{speed} = \frac{\text{distance}}{\text{time}} \qquad \text{average speed} = \frac{\text{total distance}}{\text{total time}}$$

$$\text{mean } \bar{x} = \frac{\text{sum of the items}}{\text{number of items}} = \frac{\Sigma x}{n} \quad \text{or} \quad \frac{\Sigma fx}{\Sigma f}$$

$$\text{probability} = \frac{\text{number of successful outcomes}}{\text{number of equally likely outcomes}} = \frac{s}{n}$$

Tables

Time

60 seconds = 1 minute	52 weeks = 1 year
60 minutes = 1 hour	365 days = 1 year
24 hours = 1 day	366 days = 1 leap year
7 days = 1 week	12 months = 1 year

The Metric System   **British Units**

Length

1000 mm = 1 m	12 inches = 1 foot
100 cm = 1 m	3 feet = 1 yard
1000 m = 1 km	1760 yards = 1 mile

Area

$100 \, mm^2 = 1 \, cm^2$	144 sq. inches = 1 sq. foot
$10\,000 \, cm^2 = 1 \, m^2$	9 sq. feet = 1 sq. yard
$1\,000\,000 \, m^2 = 1 \, km^2$	
1 hectare = $10\,000 \, m^2$	1 acre = 4840 sq. yards
100 hectares = $1 \, km^2$	640 acres = 1 sq. mile

Volume

$1000 \, mm^3 = 1 \, cm^3$	1728 cu. inches = 1 cu. foot
$1\,000\,000 \, cm^3 = 1 \, m^3$	27 cu. feet = 1 cu. yard

The Metric System   British Units

Weight

$$1000\,mg = 1\,g$$
$$100\,cg = 1\,g$$
$$1000\,g = 1\,kg$$
$$1000\,kg = 1\,tonne$$

16 ounces = 1 pound
14 pounds = 1 stone
112 pounds = 1 hundredweight
8 stones = 1 hundredweight
2240 pounds = 1 ton
20 hundredweights = 1 ton

Capacity

$1000\,ml = 1\,\ell$
$100\,cl = 1\,\ell$
$1000\,\ell = 1\,kl$

1 litre = 1000 cm^3

1 litre of water weighs 1 kg
1 cm^3 of water weighs 1 g

8 pints = 1 gallon

1 pint of water weighs $1\frac{1}{4}$ lb
1 gallon of water weighs 10 lb

To change to the metric system

Length

1 inch = 2.54 cm
1 foot = 30.48 cm
1 yard = 91.44 cm = 0.9144 m
1 mile = 1.609 km

Weight

1 oz = 28.35 g
1 lb = 453.6 g
1 ton = 1016 kg = 1.016 tonne

Capacity

1 pint   = 0.568 litre
1 gallon = 4.546 litre

To change from the metric system

Length

1 cm = 0.394 in
1 m = 39.37 in = 1.094 yd
1 km = 1094 yd = 0.621 mile

Weight

1 kg   = 2.205 lb
1 tonne = 0.984 ton

Capacity

1 litre = 1.76 pints = 0.220 gallons

1 Thinking about fractions and ratios

Fractions

Until very recent times, fractions were used more often than decimals.

Using fractions

The sequence $1, \frac{1}{2}, \frac{1}{4}, \frac{1}{8}, \frac{1}{16}, \ldots,$
where each fraction is half of the
preceding one, is a familiar one in
British tables of weights and measures.

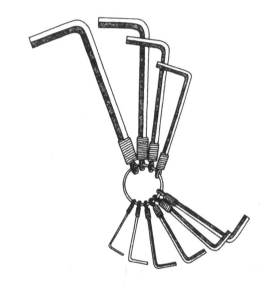

A set of weights of 4 lb, 2 lb, 1 lb, $\frac{1}{2}$ lb, $\frac{1}{4}$ lb.

A set of Allen keys, with sizes $\frac{1}{16}, \frac{5}{64}, \frac{3}{32}, \frac{1}{8}, \frac{5}{32}, \frac{3}{16}, \frac{7}{32}, \frac{1}{4}, \frac{5}{16}, \frac{3}{8}.$

What time is it ?

We can use $\frac{1}{2}$ and $\frac{1}{4}$ in the answers.

In how many different ways can you state the times shown here ?

Ratio

Direct proportion

Often we know that quantities are in direct proportion to each other.

The cost is proportional to the numbers bought, or to the weight bought.

Which of the items shown are sold by weight ?

Inverse proportion

Occasionally we recognise that quantities are in inverse proportion to each other. As one increases, the other decreases.

For the same distance, the time taken is inversely proportional to the speed.

Stagecoaches were first used by the Post Office in 1784, and their average speed was about 6 or 7 mph, rising to about 10 mph in the 1830s, as the roads improved.

Nowadays, the 200 mile journey from York to London takes about $2\frac{1}{4}$ hours by train.

1 Fractions and Ratios

Fractions

Fractions are numbers such as $\frac{1}{3}$ (one-third), $\frac{3}{4}$ (three-quarters), $\frac{7}{10}$ (seven-tenths).

The number underneath is called the **denominator**. It tells us how many smaller equal parts the whole unit is divided into.

The number on top is called the **numerator**. It tells us how many of the smaller parts are counted.

e.g. $\frac{7}{10}$.   Divide a whole unit into
10 equal parts.
Take 7 of these parts.

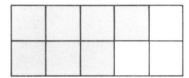

The shaded region is $\frac{7}{10}$ of the whole rectangle (and the unshaded region is $\frac{3}{10}$ of the whole rectangle).

Improper fractions and mixed numbers

Improper fractions are numbers with a greater numerator than denominator, such as $\frac{6}{5}$ and $\frac{5}{2}$.

Mixed numbers are numbers with a whole number part and a fraction part, such as $1\frac{1}{5}$ and $2\frac{1}{2}$.

Examples

1   To change $2\frac{3}{5}$ into an improper fraction.

Multiply the whole number 2 by 5 to change it into fifths.
This is 10 fifths, and another 3 fifths makes 13 fifths.

$2\frac{3}{5}$ $(=\frac{10}{5} + \frac{3}{5}) = \frac{13}{5}$

2   To change $\frac{29}{6}$ into a mixed number.

Divide 6 into 29. It goes 4 times so there are 4 whole ones.
There is a remainder 5, so there is also $\frac{5}{6}$.

$\frac{29}{6}$ $(=4 + \frac{5}{6}) = 4\frac{5}{6}$

Using fractions

3   Reduce $\frac{45}{60}$ to its lowest terms.

45 and 60 both divide by 5 so reduce the fraction by dividing both the numerator and the denominator by 5.
This process can be called **cancelling**.

$$\frac{\overset{9}{\cancel{45}}}{\underset{12}{\cancel{60}}}$$ This gives the fraction $\frac{9}{12}$ but this is still not in its lowest terms because 9 and 12 both divide by 3.
So, divide both the numerator and the denominator by 3.

$$\frac{\overset{\overset{3}{\cancel{9}}}{\cancel{45}}}{\underset{\underset{4}{\cancel{12}}}{\cancel{60}}} = \frac{3}{4}.$$ This is the fraction in its lowest terms.

4   Change $\frac{7}{8}$ into a fraction with denominator 24.

To change the denominator 8 into denominator 24 we must multiply by 3, so multiply both the numerator and the denominator by 3.

$$\frac{7}{8} \quad (=\tfrac{7 \times 3}{8 \times 3}) \quad = \quad \frac{21}{24}$$

Addition and subtraction

5 $\frac{4}{9} + \frac{2}{9} = \frac{6}{9} = \frac{2}{3}$ (4 ninths plus 2 ninths equals 6 ninths)

6 $\frac{8}{9} - \frac{7}{9} = \frac{1}{9}$ (8 ninths minus 7 ninths equals 1 ninth)

If the fractions have different denominators, change them into fractions with the same denominator.

7 $\frac{7}{8} + \frac{5}{6}$

Change $\frac{7}{8}$ and $\frac{5}{6}$ into fractions with denominator 24, because 24 is the smallest number into which 8 and 6 both divide.

$$\frac{7}{8} = \frac{21}{24}, \qquad \frac{5}{6} = \frac{20}{24}$$

$$\frac{7}{8} + \frac{5}{6} = \frac{21}{24} + \frac{20}{24} = \frac{41}{24} = 1\frac{17}{24}$$

The step $\frac{21}{24} + \frac{20}{24}$ can be written as $\frac{21 + 20}{24}$

8 $\frac{8}{9} - \frac{5}{6} = \frac{16-15}{18} = \frac{1}{18}$

If there are mixed numbers, do the whole number part and the fraction part separately.

9 $2\frac{3}{4} + 3\frac{7}{12} = 5\frac{9+7}{12} = 5\frac{16}{12} = 5\frac{4}{3} = 6\frac{1}{3}$

10 $3\frac{7}{8} - 1\frac{2}{5} = 2\frac{35-16}{40} = 2\frac{19}{40}$

Sometimes in subtraction we have to use 1 from the whole number and change it into a fraction.

11 $1 - \frac{3}{8} = \frac{8}{8} - \frac{3}{8} = \frac{5}{8}$

12 $5\frac{2}{5} - 3\frac{7}{8} = 2\frac{16-35}{40} = 2 - \frac{19}{40} \quad (=1 + \frac{40}{40} - \frac{19}{40}) = 1\frac{21}{40}$

13 $3\frac{1}{4} - 1\frac{7}{8} + 2\frac{7}{24} = 4\frac{6-21+7}{24} = 4 - \frac{8}{24} = 4 - \frac{1}{3} = 3\frac{2}{3}$

Exercise 1.1

Work out the answers to these questions without using your calculator.

1. Reduce these fractions to their lowest terms.

1	$\frac{3}{18}$		**5**	$\frac{10}{15}$		**8**	$\frac{21}{140}$
2	$\frac{15}{20}$		**6**	$\frac{5}{25}$		**9**	$\frac{10}{16}$
3	$\frac{14}{32}$		**7**	$\frac{18}{48}$		**10**	$\frac{60}{75}$
4	$\frac{16}{40}$						

2. Change these fractions into fractions with the denominator given in brackets.

1	$\frac{7}{9}$	(18)	**5**	$\frac{2}{3}$	(12)	**8**	$\frac{7}{11}$	(44)
2	$\frac{6}{7}$	(21)	**6**	$\frac{8}{9}$	(27)	**9**	$\frac{4}{5}$	(30)
3	$\frac{3}{8}$	(40)	**7**	$\frac{1}{2}$	(20)	**10**	$\frac{1}{4}$	(24)
4	$\frac{1}{6}$	(36)						

3.   Change these mixed numbers to improper fractions.

   1 $6\frac{1}{4}$ **5** $5\frac{1}{6}$ **8** $3\frac{5}{12}$

   2 $1\frac{9}{10}$ **6** $2\frac{5}{11}$ **9** $6\frac{8}{9}$

   3 $3\frac{2}{3}$ **7** $4\frac{4}{7}$ **10** $5\frac{5}{8}$

   4 $2\frac{4}{5}$

4.   Change these improper fractions to mixed numbers.

   1 $\frac{11}{8}$ **5** $\frac{35}{8}$ **8** $\frac{100}{75}$

   2 $\frac{21}{5}$ **6** $\frac{57}{9}$ **9** $\frac{58}{11}$

   3 $\frac{33}{10}$ **7** $\frac{41}{12}$ **10** $\frac{20}{16}$

   4 $\frac{11}{6}$

5.   Find the values of the following.

   1 $\frac{5}{8} + \frac{1}{8}$ **5** $1\frac{1}{2} + 2\frac{3}{8}$ **9** $2\frac{1}{3} + \frac{7}{15}$

   2 $\frac{1}{4} + \frac{1}{5}$ **6** $3\frac{1}{4} + 2\frac{7}{10}$ **10** $3\frac{5}{6} + 1\frac{3}{8}$

   3 $3\frac{5}{16} + \frac{3}{16}$ **7** $\frac{3}{4} + \frac{5}{8}$ **11** $3\frac{2}{5} + 2\frac{3}{4} + 1\frac{9}{10}$

   4 $\frac{3}{4} + \frac{1}{6}$ **8** $\frac{5}{6} + \frac{7}{12}$ **12** $3\frac{1}{3} + 4\frac{2}{5} + \frac{1}{6}$

6.   Find the values of the following.

   1 $\frac{9}{10} - \frac{7}{10}$ **5** $\frac{7}{12} - \frac{3}{8}$ **9** $1\frac{1}{7} - \frac{11}{14}$

   2 $\frac{2}{3} - \frac{1}{4}$ **6** $3\frac{7}{8} - 2\frac{1}{4}$ **10** $3\frac{7}{10} - \frac{22}{25}$

   3 $\frac{7}{12} - \frac{2}{9}$ **7** $5 - 2\frac{2}{3}$ **11** $6\frac{5}{16} - 4\frac{3}{8}$

   4 $2\frac{5}{6} - 1\frac{1}{3}$ **8** $3\frac{1}{2} - \frac{3}{4}$ **12** $7\frac{1}{2} - 1\frac{5}{6}$

7.   Find the values of the following.

   1 $\frac{3}{4} + \frac{7}{12} - \frac{5}{8}$ **4** $9\frac{3}{4} - 3\frac{2}{3} - 4\frac{1}{2}$

   2 $1 - \frac{7}{32} - \frac{3}{16}$ **5** $7\frac{2}{5} - 3\frac{5}{8} + 8\frac{3}{4}$

   3 $5\frac{3}{4} - 1\frac{11}{24} + 1\frac{7}{8}$ **6** $2\frac{1}{2} + 6\frac{3}{7} - 1\frac{1}{14}$

Multiplication

Multiplication by a whole number

Examples

1 $\frac{4}{7} \times 5 = \frac{20}{7} = 2\frac{6}{7}$

(4 sevenths multiplied by 5 is 20 sevenths)

2 $2\frac{4}{7} \times 5 = 10 + 2\frac{6}{7} = 12\frac{6}{7}$

(multiplying the whole number part and the fraction part separately)

Alternatively, you can turn $2\frac{4}{7}$ into an improper fraction.

$2\frac{4}{7} \times 5 = \frac{18}{7} \times 5 = \frac{90}{7} = 12\frac{6}{7}$

Multiplication of two fractions or mixed numbers

Examples

3 $\frac{5}{6} \times \frac{7}{8} = \frac{35}{48}$

(Multiply the two numbers in the numerator, $5 \times 7 = 35$
multiply the two numbers in the denominator, $6 \times 8 = 48$)

Sometimes you can cancel before multiplying. This is not essential but if there is a common factor in the numerator and in the denominator you will have to cancel at some stage to get the answer in its lowest terms.

4 $\dfrac{\overset{1}{\cancel{9}}}{\underset{7}{\cancel{14}}} \times \dfrac{\overset{2}{\cancel{4}}}{\underset{3}{\cancel{27}}} = \dfrac{2}{21}$

(cancelling 9 and 27 both by 9 and cancelling 4 and 14 both by 2)

With mixed numbers, turn both numbers into improper fractions.
(You will **not** get the correct answer if you multiply the whole numbers and the fractions separately.)

5 $6\frac{1}{4} \times 1\frac{1}{15} = \dfrac{\overset{5}{\cancel{25}}}{\underset{1}{\cancel{4}}} \times \dfrac{\overset{4}{\cancel{16}}}{\underset{3}{\cancel{15}}} = \dfrac{20}{3} = 6\frac{2}{3}$

(cancelling 25 and 15 by 5 and cancelling 4 and 16 by 4)

Division involving fractions or mixed numbers

Turn all the mixed numbers into improper fractions then, instead of dividing, multiply by the reciprocal of the divisor (i.e. turn the fraction you are dividing by upside down, and multiply).

Examples

6 $3\frac{8}{9} \div 1\frac{2}{5} = \frac{35}{9} \div \frac{7}{5} = \frac{\overset{5}{\cancel{35}}}{9} \times \frac{5}{\underset{1}{\cancel{7}}} = \frac{25}{9} = 2\frac{7}{9}$

7 $1\frac{7}{9} \div 8 = \frac{\overset{2}{\cancel{16}}}{9} \times \frac{1}{\underset{1}{\cancel{8}}} = \frac{2}{9}$

8 $22 \div 1\frac{5}{6} = 22 \div \frac{11}{6} = \overset{2}{\cancel{22}} \times \frac{6}{\underset{1}{\cancel{11}}} = \frac{12}{1} = 12$

9 $5\frac{1}{2} \times 3\frac{1}{5} \div 3\frac{1}{7} = \frac{11}{2} \times \frac{16}{5} \div \frac{22}{7} = \frac{\overset{1}{\cancel{11}}}{\underset{1}{\cancel{2}}} \times \frac{\overset{4}{\cancel{8}}\,\overset{}{\cancel{16}}}{5} \times \frac{7}{\underset{\underset{1}{\cancel{2}}}{\cancel{22}}} = \frac{28}{5} = 5\frac{3}{5}$

Expressing one quantity as a fraction of another

Example

10   Express 45 minutes as a fraction of $1\frac{1}{4}$ hours.

$$\frac{45 \text{ min}}{1\frac{1}{4}\text{ h}} = \frac{45 \text{ min}}{75 \text{ min}} = \frac{\overset{3}{\cancel{45}}}{\underset{5}{\cancel{75}}} = \frac{3}{5}$$

Finding a fraction of a quantity

Example

11 Find $\frac{2}{3}$ of £2.76

$$\text{Either:} \quad \frac{2}{\cancel{3}_1} \times \cancel{276}^{\,92} \text{ pence} = 184\text{p} = \text{£1.84}$$

or: $\frac{1}{3}$ of £2.76 (=£2.76 ÷ 3) = 92p

$\frac{2}{3}$ of £2.76 = 92p × 2 = £1.84

Mixed calculations

Remember that quantities inside brackets must be worked out first.
A fraction line and a square root sign are types of brackets.
Multiplication and division must be worked out before addition and subtraction.

Exercise 1.2

Find the values of the following, without using your calculator.

1.   **1** $\frac{5}{6} \times \frac{3}{10}$ **5** $4\frac{3}{8} \times \frac{2}{25}$ **9** $\frac{4}{9} \times \frac{15}{16}$

     2 $\frac{2}{5} \times \frac{25}{32}$ **6** $4\frac{4}{9} \times \frac{6}{35}$ **10** $2\frac{1}{7} \times 6\frac{3}{10}$

     3 $\frac{5}{12} \times \frac{8}{15}$ **7** $3\frac{3}{4} \times 3\frac{1}{3}$ **11** $5\frac{5}{6} \times 3\frac{1}{7} \times \frac{3}{11}$

     4 $3\frac{3}{5} \times 5\frac{5}{9}$ **9** $4\frac{2}{3} \times 5$ **12** $4\frac{4}{7} \times \frac{1}{4} \times \frac{7}{8}$

2.   **1** $\frac{1}{3} \div \frac{5}{12}$ **5** $3\frac{5}{9} \div \frac{4}{11}$ **9** $2\frac{1}{12} \div 5\frac{5}{8}$

     2 $\frac{6}{7} \div \frac{3}{4}$ **6** $\frac{1}{6} \div 2\frac{1}{4}$ **10** $8\frac{3}{4} \div 3\frac{3}{4}$

     3 $4\frac{2}{3} \div \frac{7}{9}$ **7** $2\frac{7}{10} \div 3\frac{3}{5}$ **11** $3\frac{7}{16} \div 2\frac{3}{4}$

     4 $3\frac{3}{4} \div 4\frac{3}{8}$ **8** $12\frac{3}{8} \div 9$ **12** $1\frac{3}{4} \div 7$

3.   **1** $1\frac{2}{3} \times \frac{1}{9} \div \frac{5}{12}$ **4** $2\frac{11}{12} \times \frac{3}{5} \div 7$

     2 $2\frac{1}{2} \times 1\frac{1}{3} \div \frac{5}{8}$ **5** $2\frac{2}{3} \times 1\frac{5}{6} \div 1\frac{7}{9}$

     3 $3\frac{3}{5} \times 5\frac{5}{9} \div 2\frac{2}{11}$ **6** $2\frac{1}{2} \times 1\frac{3}{4} \div 4\frac{3}{8}$

4. **1** $(\frac{6}{11} \times 6\frac{7}{8}) - 2\frac{5}{12}$ **4** $(2\frac{1}{4} + 1\frac{5}{6}) \times 1\frac{2}{7}$

    2 $2\frac{4}{5} - (1\frac{1}{3} \times 1\frac{7}{8})$ **5** $1\frac{1}{6} \div (\frac{3}{8} - \frac{1}{3})$

    3 $(2\frac{4}{5} \div 1\frac{1}{3}) - 1\frac{5}{8}$ **6** $(\frac{1}{2} + \frac{8}{15}) \div (\frac{1}{5} - \frac{1}{6})$

5. Express the 1st quantity as a fraction of the 2nd quantity, in its lowest terms.

    1 700 m, 1 km   **4** 42 min, 1 h 10 min

    2 72 mℓ, 2.4 ℓ   **5** 55 cm, 1.32 m

    3 £2.24, £5.04

6. Find these quantities.

    1 $\frac{3}{8}$ of £2.56   **4** $\frac{7}{10}$ of 2 litres

    2 $\frac{2}{5}$ of 400 m   **5** $\frac{5}{6}$ of 1.5 kg

    3 $\frac{5}{12}$ of 2 hours

Fractions and decimals

Converting fractions to decimals

In some cases you can quickly change the fraction to one with a denominator of 10 or 100.

e.g. $\frac{3}{5} = \frac{6}{10} = 0.6$

    $\frac{1}{4} = \frac{25}{100} = 0.25$

In other cases you divide, using your calculator if necessary.
If the decimal is not exact, you must give the answer correct to a suitable number of decimal places. Probably 2 or 3 places will be sufficient.

e.g. $\frac{5}{8} = 5 \div 8 = 0.625$

    $\frac{4}{7} = 4 \div 7 = 0.57142...$

                    $= 0.571$, to 3 dec pl.

    $\frac{11}{12} = 11 \div 12 = 0.91666...$

                     $= 0.917$, to 3 dec pl.

Converting exact decimals to fractions

e.g. $0.3 = \frac{3}{10}$

    $0.8 = \frac{8}{10} = \frac{4}{5}$

    $0.15 = \frac{15}{100} = \frac{3}{20}$

    $0.375 = \frac{375}{1000} = \frac{3}{8}$

Fractions in order of size

One way of comparing fractions is to write them with the same denominator.

Example

Write $\frac{5}{12}$, $\frac{1}{3}$, $\frac{4}{9}$ in order of size, smallest first.

Write them all with denominator 36, since 36 is the smallest number into which 12, 3 and 9 all divide.

$$\frac{5}{12} = \frac{15}{36}, \qquad \frac{1}{3} = \frac{12}{36}, \qquad \frac{4}{9} = \frac{16}{36}$$

In order of size they are $\frac{12}{36}$, $\frac{15}{36}$, $\frac{16}{36}$, i.e. $\frac{1}{3}$, $\frac{5}{12}$, $\frac{4}{9}$

Another way of comparing fractions is to write them as decimals.

$$\frac{5}{12} = 0.4166...$$
$$\frac{1}{3} = 0.3333...$$
$$\frac{4}{9} = 0.4444...$$

In order of size they are 0.3333..., 0.4166..., 0.4444...

i.e. $\frac{1}{3}$, $\frac{5}{12}$, $\frac{4}{9}$, as before.

Fractions in formulae

Now that you can calculate with fractions there should be no difficulty in substituting them in expressions or formulae.

Examples

1 If $x = \frac{1}{2}$ and $y = \frac{2}{3}$,

$$3x + 6y = 3 \times \frac{1}{2} + \overset{2}{6} \times \frac{2}{\underset{1}{3}} = 1\tfrac{1}{2} + 4 = 5\tfrac{1}{2}$$

$$\frac{3x}{6y} = \frac{3 \times \frac{1}{2}}{6 \times \frac{2}{3}} = \frac{\frac{3}{2}}{4} = \frac{3}{2} \div 4 = \frac{3}{2} \times \frac{1}{4} = \frac{3}{8}$$

$$\frac{y}{3x - 1} = \frac{\frac{2}{3}}{1\frac{1}{2} - 1} = \frac{\frac{2}{3}}{\frac{1}{2}} = \frac{2}{3} \div \frac{1}{2} = \frac{2}{3} \times \frac{2}{1} = \frac{4}{3} = 1\tfrac{1}{3}$$

$$x^2 + y^2 = (\tfrac{1}{2})^2 + (\tfrac{2}{3})^2 = \frac{1}{2} \times \frac{1}{2} + \frac{2}{3} \times \frac{2}{3} = \frac{1}{4} + \frac{4}{9} = \frac{9 + 16}{36} = \frac{25}{36}$$

2   A formula used to calculate distance is $s = ut + \frac{1}{2}ft^2$.

Find the value of s when $u = 7\frac{1}{3}$, $t = \frac{3}{4}$ and $f = 8$.

$$s = 7\frac{1}{3} \times \frac{3}{4} + \frac{1}{2} \times 8 \times \left(\frac{3}{4}\right)^2$$

$$= \frac{\overset{11}{\cancel{22}}}{\underset{1}{\cancel{3}}} \times \frac{\overset{1}{\cancel{3}}}{\underset{2}{\cancel{4}}} + \frac{1}{\underset{1}{\cancel{2}}} \times \overset{\overset{1}{\cancel{2}}}{\cancel{8}} \times \frac{3}{\underset{1}{\cancel{4}}} \times \frac{3}{4}$$

$$= \frac{11}{2} + \frac{9}{4}$$

$$= 5\frac{1}{2} + 2\frac{1}{4}$$

$$= 7\frac{3}{4}$$

Equal fractions

If the fraction $\dfrac{a}{b}$ is equal to the fraction $\dfrac{c}{d}$, then

$$\frac{a}{b} = \frac{c}{d}$$

Multiplying both sides by bd

$$ad = bc$$

From this equation we can find that

$$a = \frac{bc}{d}, \quad b = \frac{ad}{c}, \quad c = \frac{ad}{b}, \quad d = \frac{bc}{a}$$

We can also rearrange the equation to give

$$\frac{a}{c} = \frac{b}{d}, \quad \frac{b}{a} = \frac{d}{c}, \quad \frac{c}{a} = \frac{d}{b}$$

We can use these fractions to find an unknown quantity.

Examples

1   If $\dfrac{x}{18} = \dfrac{2}{3}$, find the value of x.

Multiply both sides by 18

$$x = \frac{2 \times \overset{6}{\cancel{18}}}{\underset{1}{\cancel{3}}}$$

$$= 12$$

2   If $\dfrac{12}{5} = \dfrac{3.6}{y}$, find the value of y.

Multiply both sides by $5y$

$12y = 3.6 \times 5$

Divide both sides by 12

$$y = \frac{3.6 \times 5}{12}$$

$$= 1.5$$

Using your calculator

You may have a calculator which will calculate with fractions.
If so, you can learn how to use it. You must find out how to enter fractions or mixed numbers, and how to read the displayed answers. You can use it to do some of the questions of the previous exercises, checking that you get the same answers as before. Do not rely on your calculator entirely. You still need to know the methods for working out fractions.

Do not worry if your calculator does not use fractions. You will get more practice in working out fractions for yourself, and you can still use your calculator to do the additions, subtractions, multiplications and divisions.

Exercise 1.3

1.   Write these fractions as decimals. If they are not exact, write them correct to 3 decimal places.

1	$\frac{11}{20}$	**5**	$\frac{1}{12}$	**8**	$\frac{8}{11}$
2	$\frac{3}{4}$	**6**	$\frac{2}{9}$	**9**	$\frac{5}{6}$
3	$\frac{1}{8}$	**7**	$\frac{23}{30}$	**10**	$\frac{3}{7}$
4	$\frac{4}{5}$				

2.   Write these decimals as fractions in their lowest terms.

1	0.9	**4**	0.005
2	0.56	**5**	0.175
3	0.35		

3. Write these fractions in order of size, smallest first.

1 $\frac{4}{5}, \frac{9}{10}, \frac{7}{8}$ **4** $\frac{9}{14}, \frac{13}{21}, \frac{7}{12}$

2 $\frac{5}{12}, \frac{2}{5}, \frac{4}{15}$ **5** $\frac{7}{13}, \frac{5}{11}, \frac{3}{5}$

3 $\frac{1}{4}, \frac{5}{24}, \frac{1}{3}$

4. Find the value of x in these fractional equations.

1 $\dfrac{x}{4.2} = \dfrac{2}{3}$ **5** $\dfrac{x}{6.5} = \dfrac{5}{13}$ **8** $\dfrac{5}{x} = \dfrac{4}{9}$

2 $\dfrac{x}{3.6} = \dfrac{8}{9}$ **6** $\dfrac{3}{x} = \dfrac{7.2}{8}$ **9** $\dfrac{x}{10.5} = \dfrac{2.8}{4.9}$

3 $\dfrac{4}{x} = \dfrac{1}{6}$ **7** $\dfrac{5.4}{x} = \dfrac{3}{20}$ **10** $\dfrac{x}{7.5} = \dfrac{3.3}{5.5}$

4 $\dfrac{7}{x} = \dfrac{2}{11}$

5. If $a = \frac{5}{9}$ and $b = \frac{2}{3}$, find the value of

1 $\frac{1}{6}b - \frac{1}{10}a$ **4** $\dfrac{8}{b-a}$

2 $\dfrac{2a}{5b}$ **5** $\sqrt{a - b^2}$

3 $2a - \frac{1}{2}b$

6. **1** If $I = \dfrac{PRT}{100}$, find I when $P = 650$, $R = 7\frac{1}{2}$, $T = 4$.

2 If $m = \dfrac{a - b}{1 + ab}$, find m when $a = 2$ and $b = \frac{1}{2}$.

3 If $E = \frac{1}{2}mv^2$, find E when $m = 36$ and $v = \frac{1}{3}$.

4 If $y = mx + c$, find y when $x = 3$, $m = \frac{1}{2}$, $c = 2\frac{1}{2}$.

5 If $s = \dfrac{a}{1 - r}$, find s when $a = 15$ and $r = \frac{5}{8}$.

Ratio and Proportion

A ratio is a way of comparing the sizes of two quantities.
e.g. A quantity divided in the ratio 2 : 3 (read as 2 to 3)
means that the 1st share is $\frac{2}{3}$ of the 2nd share,
     and the 2nd share is $\frac{3}{2}$ times the 1st share.

Ratios have no units, they are just numbers.

Examples

1   Express the amounts of £1.40,   60p as a ratio in its simplest form.

First express them as a fraction and then write that fraction as a ratio.

$$\frac{£1.40}{60p} = \frac{140p}{60p} = \frac{\overset{7}{\cancel{140}}}{\underset{3}{\cancel{60}}} = \frac{7}{3}. \quad \text{The ratio is 7 : 3.}$$

2   Express 30 cm, 1.5 m, 2.5 m as a ratio in its simplest form.

Since there are 3 quantities we cannot write them as a fraction.

30 cm : 1.5 m : 2.5 m = 30 : 150 : 250 = 3 : 15 : 25

3   Divide 60 kg in the ratio 2 : 3.

First divide 60 kg into 5 equal parts (since 2 + 3 = 5)
60 kg ÷ 5 = 12 kg
The 1st share is 2 × 12 kg = 24 kg
The 2nd share is 3 × 12 kg = 36 kg

4   Increase 2.5 m in the ratio 11 : 10.

The new amount is $\frac{11}{10}$ of 2.5 m = $\frac{11}{\cancel{10}}$ × $\cancel{250}$ cm = 275 cm = 2.75 m.

5   Decrease 3.6 kg in the ratio 4 : 9.

The new amount is $\frac{4}{9}$ of 3.6 kg = $\frac{4}{\cancel{9}}$ × $\overset{0.4}{\cancel{3.6}}$ kg = 1.6 kg.

Exercise 1.4

1.   Express as ratios in their simplest forms:

   1   £1, 35p   **6**   5.6 kg, 3.2 kg, 1.6 kg
   2   56 km/h, 84 km/h   **7** $1\frac{1}{2}$ h, 54 min, 2 h 6 min
   3   45 min, 2 h   **8**   £3.36, £2.40, £3.84
   4   500 mℓ, 4.5 ℓ **9**   1.5 ℓ, 2.5 ℓ, 2 ℓ
   5   2.75 m, 1.5 m   **10** 55 cm, 1.1 m, 2.09 m

2.   Divide these quantities in the ratios stated.

   1   12 cm, in the ratio 3 : 7
   2   £52, in the ratio 1 : 12
   3   120 hectares, in the ratio 9 : 7
   4   £3.20, in the ratio 9 : 1
   5   7.5 cm, in the ratio 11 : 4
   6   34 cm, in the ratio 2 : 7 : 8
   7   80 kg, in the ratio 3 : 6 : 11
   8   £240, in the ratio 9 : 11 : 20
   9   15 ℓ, in the ratio 4 : 3 : 2 : 1
   10 60 m, in the ratio 1 : 3 : 5 : 6

3.   Increase these quantities in the ratios stated.

   1   £8, in the ratio 5 : 2
   2   28 kg, in the ratio 10 : 7
   3   65 p, in the ratio 8 : 5
   4   7.2 ℓ, in the ratio 11 : 8
   5   95 m, in the ratio 24 : 19

4.   Decrease these quantities in the ratios stated.

   1   £12, in the ratio 5 : 8
   2 $2\frac{1}{2}$ hours, in the ratio 2 : 3
   3   9.6 kg, in the ratio 11 : 12
   4   35 ℓ, in the ratio 5 : 7
   5   20 g, in the ratio 1 : 4

Unitary method and Proportion

The next examples are of paired quantities which are in **direct proportion**. As one quantity increases (or decreases) the other one also increases (or decreases) in the same ratio.

Examples

1 If 5 m of cloth costs £18, what will be the cost of 8 m ?

1st method   Unitary method
5 m costs £18
1 m costs £3.60   (dividing by 5)
8 m costs £28.80   (multiplying by 8)

2nd method   Proportion

The costs will be in proportion to the amounts.
The ratio of amounts, new : old, is 8 : 5
The new cost is $\frac{8}{5}$ of £18 = £$\frac{8}{5}$ × 18 = £$\frac{144}{5}$ = £28.80.

2 A train travels 126 km in 3 hours. How far will it travel in 2 hours, going at the same speed ?

Either:
In 3 hours it goes 126 km
In 1 hour it goes   42 km   (dividing by 3)
in 2 hours it goes   84 km   (multiplying by 2)

Or:
The ratio of times, new : old, is 2 : 3
The new distance is $\frac{2}{3}$ of 126 km = $\frac{2}{3}$ × 126 km = 84 km.

The next examples are of paired quantities which are in **inverse proportion**. As one increases, the other decreases.

Examples

3   If there is enough food in an emergency pack to last 12 men for 20 days, how long would it last if there were 16 men ?

Either:
For 12 men, the food will last for 20 days,
For 1 man, the food will last 240 days,
(multiplying by 12, because the food will last 12 times as long)
For 16 men, the food will last for 15 days,
(dividing by 16, because the food will last for $\frac{1}{16}$ of the time).

Or:
As the number of men increases, the time the food will last decreases.
The ratio of men, new : old, is 16 : 12.
The inverse ratio is 12 : 16, and we multiply by $\frac{12}{16}$, not $\frac{16}{12}$.
The food will last for $\frac{12}{16}$ of 20 days = $\frac{12}{16}$ × 20 days = 15 days.

4   If 7 pumps empty a water tank in 36 hours, how long would it take if there were 6 similar pumps working ?

Either:
7 pumps take 36 hours,
1 pump takes 252 hours,
6 pumps take 42 hours.

Or:
The ratio of pumps, new : old, is 6 : 7, but it will take longer with less pumps so multiply by $\frac{7}{6}$.
The time taken is $\frac{7}{6}$ of 36 hours = $\frac{7}{6}$ × 36 hours = 42 hours.

Exercise 1.5

1.   If 14 kg of potatoes cost £1.33, what will be the cost of 10 kg ?

2.   If a field of 75 hectares produced 9.0 tonnes of crops, what should a field of 45 hectares produce ?

3.   If 12 mugs can be bought for £3.96, how many can be bought for £6.93 ?

4.   If 11 loads of soil weigh 12.1 tons, what will be the weight of 7 loads ?

5. A sack of corn lasts 20 hens for
    36 days. How long would it last
    if there were 24 hens ?

6. If a team of men work for 8 hours a day, they can lay a cable in 15 days. If they
    work for 10 hours a day, how many days will it take them then ?

7. In an hour, 7 people can pick 28 kg of fruit. How much can be picked in an
    hour if there are 9 people ?

8. The average length of Kevin's pace is 65 cm and the average length of Laura's
    pace is 75 cm. When Kevin takes 60 paces, how many does Laura take ?

9. A carpet of area 20 m² costs £440. What will be the cost of a similar carpet of
    area 25 m² ?

10. A car takes $3\frac{1}{2}$ hours to do a journey, going at an average speed of 40 mph.
    How long will it take if road works reduce the average speed to 35 mph ?

11. A block of stone has a volume of 0.042 m³ and it weighs 84 kg. What is the
    volume of a similar block of stone which weighs 112 kg ?

12. Jill wishes to save money to pay for her holiday. If she takes a temporary job
    paying £3 per hour, she will have to work for 20 days to raise the money. If
    instead, she gets a job paying £4 per hour, how many days will she have to
    work to raise the same amount ?

Exercise 1.6   Applications and Activities

1. The external diameter of a pipe is
   $6\frac{5}{8}$ inches. The metal of which it is
   made is $\frac{7}{16}$ inches thick. What is the
   internal diameter ?

2. Between 9.30 am and 12.15 pm a motorist travelled $71\frac{1}{2}$ miles. What was her
   average speed ?

3. **An 8th century Hindu problem**

   A necklace was broken during a struggle. $\frac{1}{3}$ of the pearls fell to the floor, $\frac{1}{5}$ stayed
   on the couch, $\frac{1}{6}$ were found by the girl and $\frac{1}{10}$ were found by her boyfriend. Six
   pearls remained on the string. How many pearls altogether did the necklace have
   originally ?

4. Nine carat gold contains $\frac{9}{24}$ pure gold and the rest is an alloy. How much pure
   gold is there in a medal made of this gold which weighs 28.8 g ?

5. Paul spends $\frac{1}{4}$ of his money on sweets, $\frac{5}{6}$ of the remainder on a magazine, and he
   has 20p left. How much had he at first ?

6. A lorry removes 36.4 tonnes of rubble in 13 loads of equal weight. How many
   more loads will be needed to remove another 25.2 tonnes ?

7. A riding stable has enough
   food for their 40 horses for 6
   days. If 10 of the horses are
   sold, how long will the food
   last the remaining horses ?

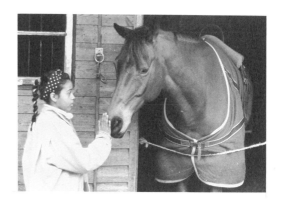

8. A metal alloy contained 2.8 kg of copper, 1.6 kg of nickel and 0.8 kg of zinc. Express these quantities as a ratio in its simplest form. If an ornament made of this alloy weighed 3.9 kg, find what weight of each metal was included.

9. The sides of a field are of lengths in the ratio 8 : 3 : 5 : 4.
    If the perimeter of the field is 500 m, find the length of each side.

10. Three men, A, B and C, invest £10 000, £12 000 and £18 000 respectively, in a business. At the end of the first year the profits were £4200. The men decide to use $\frac{5}{6}$ of this money to expand the business, and divide the remainder in proportion to their investments. How much do they each get ?

11. Copy and complete this number pattern to the line starting with $\frac{9}{10}$.

$$\frac{2}{3} - \frac{1}{2} = \frac{2 \times 2 - 3 \times 1}{3 \times 2} = \frac{1}{6}$$

$$\frac{3}{4} - \frac{2}{3} = \frac{3 \times 3 - 4 \times 2}{4 \times 3} = \frac{1}{12}$$

$$\frac{4}{5} - \frac{3}{4} = \frac{4 \times 4 - 5 \times 3}{5 \times 4} = \frac{1}{20}$$

. . .

Use the pattern to find the value of $\frac{19}{20} - \frac{18}{19}$.

12. **Ancient fractions**

    Here is an ancient formula for π, based on fractions with numerator 1. It probably dates from Hindu mathematics of about 500 BC.

    $$\pi = 4 \left(1 - \frac{1}{8} + \frac{1}{8 \times 29} - \frac{1}{8 \times 29 \times 6} + \frac{1}{8 \times 29 \times 6 \times 8}\right)^2$$

    It is not quite accurate. Use your calculator to work out the value of π to 4 decimal places, as given by this formula.

    Here is a similar formula for a different number.

    $$x = 1 + \frac{1}{3} + \frac{1}{3 \times 4} - \frac{1}{3 \times 4 \times 34}$$

    Find the value of x, to 4 decimal places.
    What is the special number for which x is the approximation ?

13. **Recurring decimals**

When you change a fraction into a decimal, it may turn into a recurring decimal.
e.g. $\frac{2}{3}$ = 0.6666666...
       $\frac{3}{11}$ = 0.27272727...

Here is a way in which you can turn a recurring decimal into a fraction.

Examples

1 Turn 0.6666666... into a fraction.

Let s = 0.6666666...   (remember these 6's go on for ever)
Multiply both sides by 10
   $10s$ = 6.6666666...   (2)
    s = 0.6666666...   (1)
Subtract (1) from (2)
    $9s$ = 6
    s = $\frac{6}{9}$ = $\frac{2}{3}$

2 Turn 0.27272727... into a fraction.

Let s = 0.27272727...
Multiply both sides by 100
(100 was chosen because there are **two** repeating figures)
   $100s$ = 27.27272727...   (2)
    s =   0.27272727...   (1)
Subtract (1) from (2)
    $99s$ = 27
    s = $\frac{27}{99}$ = $\frac{3}{11}$

Use this method to find the fractions equivalent to these recurring decimals.

1 0.5555...   **4** 0.606060...
2 0.81818181...   **5** 0.037037037...
3 0.135135135...

You can choose other recurring decimals to investigate.
What can you say about the recurring decimal 0.999999... ?

2 Thinking about using negative

Negative numbers

There are many situations where negative numbers can be used.
Can you think of some ?

Measuring from sea-level

An oil production platform is 40 m above sea-level. The sea-bed is 110 m below sea-level. This can be written as a height above sea-level of −110 m. The distance from the platform to the sea-bed is $(40 − (−110))\text{m} = 150\text{m}$.

A formula with negative numbers

Time in seconds, 0, 1, 2, 3, . . .
Times before the start of the counting, −1, −2, −3, . . .
Distance = speed × time
If an object is moving in a straight line with constant speed, then

1   if speed = 5 m/s, time = −2 s, distance = $5 × (−2)\text{m} = −10\text{m}$.
This means that 2 seconds before the start of counting the distance was 10 m from the starting point in the other direction.

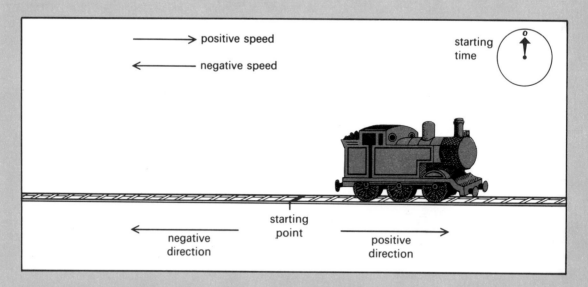

2   if speed = −4 m/s, time = 3 s, distance = $(−4) × 3\text{m} = −12\text{m}$.
This means that the particle is going in the opposite direction, and 3 seconds after starting it is 12 m in the other direction.

3   if speed = −3 m/s, time = −1 s, distance = $(−3) × (−1)\text{m} = 3\text{m}$.
This means that the particle is going in the opposite direction and 1 second before starting counting it was 3 m from the starting point in the positive direction.

numbers

Tide times

The times of high tides at Liverpool are published for each day.
For example, on one day the morning tide is at 0632 and the afternoon tide is at 1926.
The times of the tides at other places on the coast are calculated by adding these times to the time of the tide at Liverpool.

Aberystwyth	− 3 30
Blackpool	− 0 10
Chester	+ 1 05
Fishguard	− 4 00
Maryport	+ 0 24
Preston	+ 0 10
Silloth	+ 0 35
Stornoway	− 4 15

On the day stated, what are the tide times at Fishguard ?

When the Manxman was towed out of Preston Dock, it had to go out at high tide.

A negative answer in an equation

Father was 20 years old when Julie was born. Now Father is twice as old as Julie. When will he be three times as old ?

If Julie is x years old, Father is $(20 + x)$ years old.
So $20 + x = 2x$
$$x = 20$$
Now, Julie is 20, Father is 40.

In y years time, Julie will be $(20 + y)$ years old, Father will be $(40 + y)$ years old.
So $40 + y = 3(20 + y)$
$$40 + y = 60 + 3y$$
$$-20 = 2y$$
$$y = -10$$
Father will be three times as old as Julie in -10 years.
This means that Father was three times as old as Julie 10 years ago, when Julie was 10 and Father was 30.

2 Using negative numbers

Negative numbers

To add or subtract, just count up or down the number scale.

Examples

$5 + 3 = 8$

$(-5) + 3 = -2$
Start at -5 on the number scale. Go up 3 steps, getting to -2.

$(-5) + 8 = 3$
Start at -5 on the number scale. Go up 8 steps, getting to 3.

$5 - 2 = 3$

$(+5) - 7 = -2$
Start at 5 on the number scale. Go down 7 steps, getting to -2.
$(+5)$ is just another way of writing 5.

$(-5) - 1 = -6$
Start at -5 on the number scale, Go down 1 step, getting to -6.

```
8
7
6
5
4
3
2
1
0
-1
-2
-3
-4
-5
-6
-7
-8
```

If there are two signs, replace them by one sign, then you can use the number scale, as above.

$+ \ +$ is replaced by $+$
$+ \ -$ is replaced by $-$
$- \ +$ is replaced by $-$
$- \ -$ is replaced by $+$

Examples

$5 + (+3) = 5 + 3 = 8$ $(-4) + (+1) = -4 + 1 = -3$
$5 + (-6) = 5 - 6 = -1$ $(-4) + (-3) = -4 - 3 = -7$
$(+5) - (+2) = 5 - 2 = 3$ $(-4) - (+2) = -4 - 2 = -6$
$(+5) - (-1) = 5 + 1 = 6$ $(-4) - (-9) = -4 + 9 = 5$

Multiplication and division

$$(+x) \times (+y) = xy$$
$$(+x) \times (-y) = -xy$$
$$(-x) \times (-y) = xy$$

$$(+x) \div (+y) = \frac{x}{y}$$

$$(+x) \div (-y) = -\frac{x}{y}$$

$$(-x) \div (+y) = -\frac{x}{y}$$

$$(-x) \div (-y) = \frac{x}{y}$$

Examples

$$(+5) \times (+6) = 30$$
$$(+5) \times (-6) = -30$$
$$(-5) \times (+6) = -30$$
$$(-5) \times (-6) = 30$$
$$(-5) \times 6 \times (-2) = (-30) \times (-2) = 60$$
$$(-5) \times (-6) \times (-2) = 30 \times (-2) = -60$$

$$(+21) \div (+3) = 7$$
$$(+21) \div (-3) = -7$$
$$(-21) \div (+3) = -7$$
$$(-21) \div (-3) = 7$$

Mixed calculations

Remember that quantities inside brackets must be worked out first.
A fraction line and a square root sign are types of brackets.
Multiplication and division must be worked out before addition and subtraction.

Examples

$$5 \times (3 - 6) = 5 \times (-3) = -15$$

$$\frac{7 - 9}{3 - (-5)} = \frac{-2}{3 + 5} = \frac{-2}{8} = -\frac{1}{4}$$

$$\sqrt{3^2 + (-4)^2} = \sqrt{9 + (-4) \times (-4)} = \sqrt{9 + 16} = \sqrt{25} = 5$$

$$5 \times (-3) - 2 \times (-6) = -15 - (-12) = -15 + 12 = -3$$

$$3 \div (-4) + (-2) \div (-8) = -\frac{3}{4} + \frac{1}{4} = -\frac{2}{4} = -\frac{1}{2}$$

Exercise 2.1

Work out the following. Do not use your calculator.

1. **1** $(-2) - 4$ **6** $(-5) + 4 - 2$
    2 $(-4) + 6$ **7** $(-2) + 5 - 7 + 4$
    3 $(-11) + 8$ **8** $(-1) - 2 - 5$
    4 $3 - 9$ **9** $3 - 9 + 4$
    5 $(-3) - 10$ **10** $4 - 5 - 6$

2. **1** $(+2) + (-3)$ **6** $(+10) + (-8)$
    2 $(+4) - (-7)$ **7** $9 - (-9)$
    3 $(-2) + (+5)$ **8** $(-1) + (-4)$
    4 $9 - (+10)$ **9** $(-2) - (-6) + (-1)$
    5 $12 + (-12)$ **10** $(-7) + (+4) - (-3)$

3. **1** $(-2) \times (+3)$ **6** $(-42) \div (-6)$
    2 $3 \times (-4)$ **7** $0 \times (-3)$
    3 $(-7) \times (-8)$ **8** $(-20) \div (-5)$
    4 $40 \div (-5)$ **9** $(-1) \times (-6)$
    5 $(+18) \div (+3)$ **10** $(-7) \times 4$

4. **1** $2 \times 3 - 5 \times 4$ **6** $6 - (4 + 2)$
    2 $5 \times (-3) + 4 \times (-2)$ **7** $\sqrt{9 \times 5 + (-4) \times (-1)}$
    3 $(-2) - (2 - 4)$ **8** $6 \div (4 - 13)$
    4 $\dfrac{(-1) - 2}{2 + (+4)}$ **9** $2 \times (-3)^2$
                                             10 $(-3) \div (-6) + (-2) \div (+1)$
    5 $\dfrac{3 \times 2 - (-8)}{5 \times 3 + (-1)}$

Substitution in expressions or formulae

Examples

1 If $x = 4$ and $y = -3$, then

$$2x + 5y = 2 \times 4 \ + \ 5 \times (-3) = 8 - 15 = -7$$

$$\frac{3x}{5y} = \frac{3 \times 4}{5 \times (-3)} = -\frac{4}{5}$$

$$\frac{y}{x - 5} = \frac{-3}{4 - 5} = \frac{-3}{-1} = 3$$

$$x^2 - y^2 = 4^2 - (-3)^2 = 16 - 9 = 7$$

$$\sqrt{10x - 3y} = \sqrt{10 \times 4 \ - \ 3 \times (-3)} = \sqrt{40 + 9} = \sqrt{49} = 7$$

2 A formula used to calculate speeds is $v^2 = u^2 + 2as$.
Find the (positive) value of v when $u = 30$, $a = -10$ and $s = 25$.

$$\begin{aligned}
v^2 &= u^2 + 2as \\
&= 30^2 + 2 \times (-10) \times 25 \\
&= 900 - 500 \\
&= 400 \\
v &= 20
\end{aligned}$$

Using your calculator

Use the $\boxed{^+/_-}$ key to enter negative numbers.

For -3 press 3 $\boxed{^+/_-}$

To change -3 into 3, press $\boxed{^+/_-}$

Example

Use your calculator to work out the value of p, if $p = 2x^2 - 5x - 7$, when $x = -3$.

Press 2 $\boxed{\times}$ 3 $\boxed{^+/_-}$ $\boxed{x^2}$ $\boxed{-}$ 5 $\boxed{\times}$ 3 $\boxed{^+/_-}$ $\boxed{-}$ 7 $\boxed{=}$ and you will get 26.
So $p = 26$.

Use your calculator to answer some of the questions of Exercise 2.1, checking that you get the same answers as before.

Exercise 2.2

1. Find the values of the following expressions when $a = 3$, $b = -2$ and $c = -5$.

1 $2a + 5b$

2 abc

3 $4(a - b)$

4 $a^2 + b^2$

5 $\dfrac{a}{b} + \dfrac{c}{a - 1}$

6 $2c^2$

7 $(b + c)^2$

8 $\dfrac{b}{c} - a$

9 $\dfrac{3c}{2a} + b$

10 $\sqrt{2b - 8c}$

2. Find the values of the following expressions when $x = 1$, $y = -4$ and $z = 0$.

1 $2xy$

2 $x^2 - y^2$

3 $\sqrt{4x - 3y + 2z}$

4 $\dfrac{2x + 3z}{y}$

5 y^3

6 $\dfrac{5x}{z - y}$

7 $3x^2 - y$

8 $5xyz$

9 $3(y - x) + z^2$

10 $\dfrac{12}{x + y}$

3. **1** If $s = vt$, find s when $v = -4$ and $t = -\frac{1}{2}$.

   2 If $s = 4 - 2n$, find s when $n = 20$.

   3 If $I = \frac{1}{2}mv^2$, find I when $m = 30$ and $v = -10$.

   4 If $v = u - 10t$, find v when $u = 90$ and $t = -2\frac{1}{2}$.

   5 If $C = \frac{5}{9}(F - 32)$, find C when $F = -4$.

   6 If $y = mx + c$, find y when $m = -1$, $c = -5$ and $x = 3$.

   7 If $b = \dfrac{d(12 - x)}{9}$, find b when $d = -3$ and $x = 15$.

   8 If $d = \sqrt{b^2 - 4ac}$, find d when $a = 5$, $b = -2$ and $c = -3$.

   9 If $s = ut - 5t^2$, find s when $u = 7$ and $t = -2$.

   10 If $g = \dfrac{a - b}{1 + ab}$, find g when $a = -3$ and $b = 2$.

Exercise 2.3   Applications and Activities

1. When a projectile is moving in a straight line with constant acceleration f m/s², the distance s metres away from the starting point at time t seconds is given by the formula $s = ut + \frac{1}{2}ft^2$, where u is the initial velocity in m/s.

   1   If $f = -5$, $u = 10$ and $t = 2$, find the value of s.

   2   If the acceleration is 12 m/s² and the initial velocity is -30 m/s, how far is the projectile from the starting point after 6 seconds ?

2. Copy and complete this table for the values of a and b given.

a	b	a^2	b^2	$a^2 - b^2$	$a + b$	$a - b$	$(a + b)(a - b)$
6	2						32
4	−1						
0	−5						
−3	4						
−1	−9						

   Can you find a connection between the last column and one of the other columns ?

3. **Quadratic functions**

   A quadratic function has highest power x^2.

   e.g. $y = 3x^2 - 4x - 5$

   Find the values of y for this function when x has whole number values from -3 to 3, setting the working down in a table like this.

x	−3	−2	−1	0	1	2	3
x^2	9						
$3x^2$ $-4x$ -5	27 12 −5						
y	34						

   Fill in a whole row at a time before working out the next row.

   The second row is to help you to find $3x^2$.

   The last row is found by adding the last 3 numbers, for $3x^2$, $-4x$ and -5.

   Make a similar table to find the values of y for the function $y = x^2 + 3x - 6$, for whole number values of x from -4 to 2.

4.   The distance d between two points with coordinates (p, q) and (r, s) is given by
      the formula $d = \sqrt{(p - r)^2 + (q - s)^2}$.

      1   If $p = 5$, $q = -2$, $r = -1$, $s = 6$, find the value of d.
      2   If two points have coordinates $(-10, 3)$ and $(2, 8)$, find the distance
              between them.

      Maybe you would like to show that the formula is correct, by using Pythagoras'
      theorem.

5.   **Averages**

      1   The readings of a thermometer at noon each day for one week were, in
              degrees Celsius, -7, -4, -4, $+2$, -3, $+1$, $+1$.
              What was the average (mean) daily temperature for that week ?

      2   Five boys' heights were measured and their differences from a height of 1.4 m
              were noted as $+2$ cm, -4 cm, -2 cm, -7 cm and $+1$ cm. ($+2$ cm means that
              the first boy is 2 cm taller than 1.4 m.)
              What is the average of the differences ?
              What is the average height of the 5 boys ?

      3   Four loads of coal were weighed and their differences from 1 tonne were
              recorded as -30 kg, $+65$ kg, -80 kg, $+5$ kg. (-30 kg means that the first
              load weighted 30 kg less than 1 tonne.)
              What is the average weight of the 4 loads ?

PUZZLES

1.   If it is raining at midnight on Saturday, what is the probability that it will be sunny
      72 hours later ?

2.   Mary is $\frac{1}{5}$ as old as her father. Mary's father's age, when divided by 2, 3, 4, 6 or 8, leaves
      a remainder of 1 year, but when it is divided by 5, there is no remainder.
      How old is Mary ?

3.   If Edward had scored three more goals in the season, his average would have been
      4 goals per match. If he had scored three goals less than he did, his average would have
      been 3. How many goals did Edward score during the season ?

4.   The Smith's are planning a family holiday. The parents agree to pay half the cost plus
      £150, son Kevin said he would pay $\frac{1}{5}$ of the amount his parents pay, and daughter Laura
      says she can just afford the rest, which is £60.
      What is the total cost of the holiday ?

5. Use 6 matches to form 4 equilateral triangles, each one having sides equal to the length of a match.

6. If the only sister of your mother's only brother has an only child, what is that child's relationship to you ?

7. If eight volunteers can plant 16 saplings in 32 minutes, how long will it take four volunteers to plant eight saplings ?

8. When Sara asked her aunt Marie when she was born, Marie replied, 'If you write down the year of my birth, then turn the paper upside down, the date will be the same.' How old is Marie on her birthday this year ?

9. A rectangle is drawn on squared paper and a border one square wide is drawn around it. What is the size of the rectangle if the border and the rectangle have the same number of squares ?
(There are two possible answers.)

10. If $\mathbf{C}^2 = \mathbf{AT}$, and $\mathbf{AT}^2 = \mathbf{SET}$, where each letter stands for a different figure, what is the value of $\mathbf{SET}$?

11. A river is 247 m wide at the point where it is spanned by a bridge. $\frac{1}{5}$ of the bridge is on one side of the river, and $\frac{1}{6}$ of the bridge is on the other side of the river. How long is the bridge ?

12. Neil had a window in his cottage which was 1 m square, and he thought it let in too much light. He blocked up half of it, and still had a square window 1 m high and 1 m wide.
How did he do this ?

13. Mrs Roy had bought 14 dozen vases, to re-sell on her market stall. She could not remember what she had paid, except that it was within a few pence of £200. What was the cost of each vase ?

14. A water tank has three drain pipes. If the tap of the first drain is open, the water drains out in 15 minutes. If the tap of the second drain is open, the water drains out in 30 minutes, and if the tap of the third drain is open, the water drains out in 45 minutes. How long will it take to drain the water out of the tank if all three taps are opened at the same time ?

15. A team of workmen do a job for £418, and they plan to divide this money equally among themselves, each getting an exact number of £'s. However, the formeman tells them that he expects to get four times as much as each of the others. So the money has to be divided in this way, but each man still gets an exact number of £'s.
How much extra does the foreman get, using this method of sharing the money ?

16. How many tonnes of rain fall over a hectare of land when 1 cm of rain falls ?

17. Leela has discovered that she will be x years old in the year x^2. When was she born ?

18. **1** In the sequence $(1 - \frac{1}{2})$, $(1 - \frac{1}{3})$, $(1 - \frac{1}{4})$, ... , what is the product of the first hundred terms ?

    2 In the sequence $(1 - \frac{1}{2})$, $(\frac{1}{2} - \frac{1}{3})$, $(\frac{1}{3} - \frac{1}{4})$, ... , what is the sum of the first hundred terms ?

3 Thinking about similar figures

All our lives we are used to dealing
with similar figures.
They are used in scale drawings of
maps and plans.
They are used in making enlargements
or reductions of pictures, or of objects.

St Paul's Cathedral, London

Sir Christopher Wren's greatest
work; built 1675–1710, replacing
the previous church destroyed by
the Great Fire of London.

Scale of Feet

| 0 | 100 | 200 | 300 | 400 | 500 |

Plan of St Paul's Cathedral

he model village at Bourton-on-the-Water, Gloucestershire, to a scale of one-ninth.

rain of the Romney, Hythe and Dymchurch Railway,
a scale of one-third.

A model traction engine, to a scale of one-third.

3 Similar figures

Similar figures have the same shape.
All corresponding angles are equal.
All corresponding lengths are in proportion, i.e. they are in the same ratio as all other lengths.

Similar triangles

Similar cones

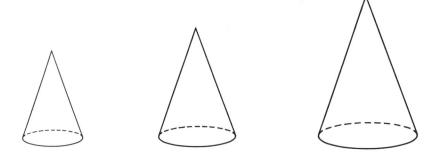

A figure and its enlargement are similar figures.

The scale factor of the enlargement is the ratio $\dfrac{\text{length of line on the enlargement}}{\text{length of line on the original}}$

Examples

1 These 2 rectangles are similar.
Find the breadth of the 2nd one.

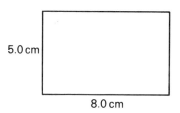

Since the rectangles are similar,
the ratio of breadths = ratio of lengths

$$\frac{x}{5.0} = \frac{9.6}{8.0}$$

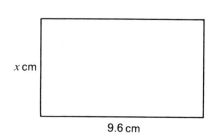

$$x = \frac{9.6 \times 5}{8} = 6$$

The breadth is 6.0 cm

Alternatively:

The scale factor of the enlargement $= \frac{9.6}{8.0} = \frac{96}{80} = \frac{6}{5}$

The new breadth $= \frac{6}{5} \times 5.0$ cm $= 6.0$ cm

2 These cylinders are similar.
What is the diameter of the smaller one ?

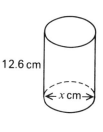
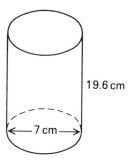

Since the cylinders are similar,
ratio of diameters = ratio of heights

$$\frac{x}{7} = \frac{12.6}{19.6}$$

$$x = \frac{12.6 \times 7}{19.6} = 4.5$$

The diameter is 4.5 cm

Alternatively:

The scale factor of the enlargement $= \frac{19.6}{12.6} = \frac{14}{9}$

The smaller diameter $= \frac{9}{14} \times 7$ cm $= 4.5$ cm

Looking for similar figures

For figures to be similar, they must have the same shape.
This means that all corresponding angles have to be equal **and** all corresponding lengths have to be in proportion.

All squares are similar to each other.
All circles are similar to each other.
All cubes are similar to each other.
All spheres are similar to each other.

But not all pairs of rectangles, parallelograms, etc. are similar.
Not all pairs of cuboids, cylinders, cones, prisms or pyramids are similar.

Examples

3

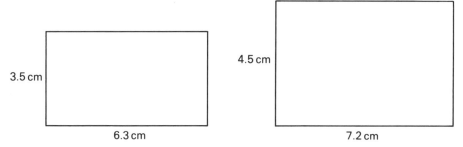

These 2 rectangles are not similar.
Although corresponding angles are equal, all 90°, corresponding lengths are not in proportion.

$$\text{Ratio of lengths} = \frac{6.3}{7.2} = \frac{63}{72} = 7 : 8$$

$$\text{Ratio of breadths} = \frac{3.5}{4.5} = \frac{35}{45} = 7 : 9$$

4

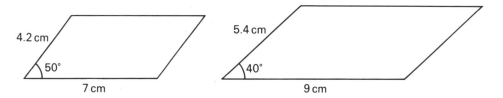

These parallelograms are not similar.
Although the corresponding sides are in proportion (7 : 9), corresponding angles are not equal.

Exercise 3.1

1. These pairs of figures are similar. Calculate the lengths of the unknown, marked sides.

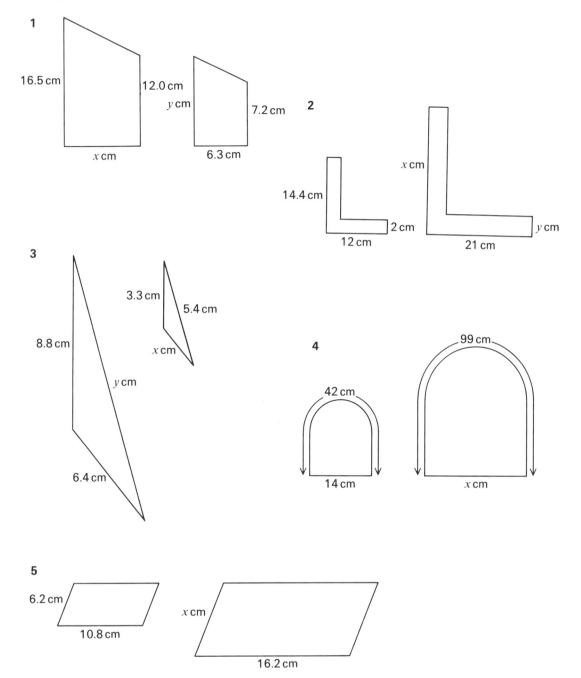

2.   These pairs of solid figures are similar. Calculate the unknown, marked lengths.

1   **2**

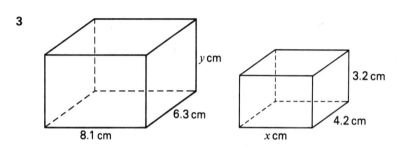

3

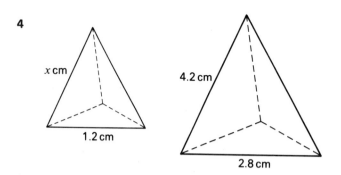

4

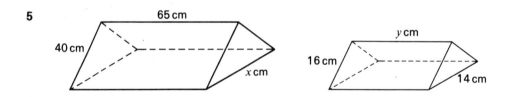

5

3. Explain why these pairs of figures are **not** similar. For each pair, sketch the figures and on your sketch alter **one** of the measurements on the 2nd figure, so that your pair of figures will be similar.

1 parallelograms

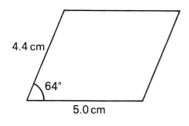

2 cuboids

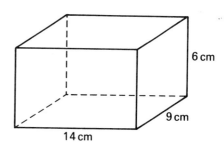

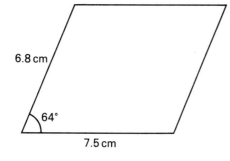

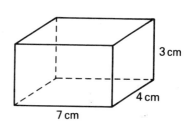

3 cylinders

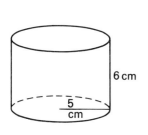
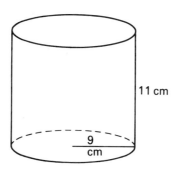

4 rhombuses

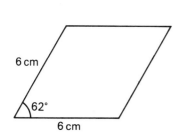
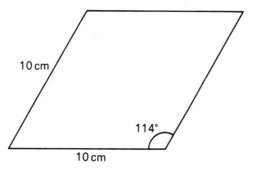

Similar triangles

For similar **triangles**, it is not necessary to know about all the sides and angles in order to show that the triangles are similar.

1. If the 3 angles of one triangle are equal to the 3 angles of a second triangle, then the triangles are similar, and therefore corresponding sides are in the same proportion.

Example

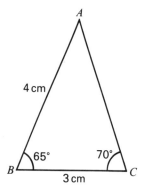
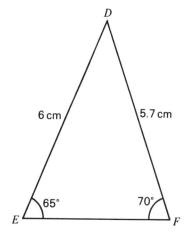

In the diagram, $\angle B = \angle E = 65°$
$\angle C = \angle F = 70°$
We can calculate $\angle A$ and $\angle D$.
$\angle A = \angle D = 45°$
Notice that it is sufficient to show that 2 pairs of angles are equal because then the 3rd pair are also equal.

These triangles can be called **equiangular** triangles.

So $\triangle ABC$ is similar to $\triangle DEF$.

Because the triangles are similar, corresponding sides are in proportion.

$$\frac{AB}{DE} = \frac{AC}{DF} = \frac{BC}{EF} \quad \left(or \; \frac{DE}{AB} = \frac{DF}{AC} = \frac{EF}{BC} \right)$$

$$\frac{AB}{DE} = \frac{4}{6} = \frac{2}{3}, \quad so \quad \frac{BC}{EF} = \frac{2}{3}.$$

i.e. $EF = \frac{3}{2} \times BC = \frac{3}{2} \times 3\,cm = 4.5\,cm$

$$\frac{AC}{DF} = \frac{2}{3},$$

$AC = \frac{2}{3} \times DF = \frac{2}{3} \times 5.7\,cm = 3.8\,cm$

2.   If the 3 sides of one triangle are proportional in turn to the 3 sides of a second triangle, then the triangles are similar and therefore corresponding angles are equal.

Example

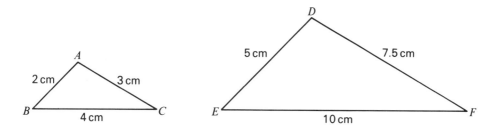

In the 1st triangle, the sides in order of size are AB, AC, BC.
In the 2nd triangle, the sides in order of size are DE, DF, EF.
Therefore, AB corresponds to DE, AC corresponds to DF, BC corresponds to EF.

$$\frac{AB}{DE} = \frac{2}{5}, \quad \frac{AC}{DF} = \frac{3}{7.5} = \frac{6}{15} = \frac{2}{5}, \quad \frac{BC}{EF} = \frac{4}{10} = \frac{2}{5}$$

So $\dfrac{AB}{DE} = \dfrac{AC}{DF} = \dfrac{BC}{EF}$

The sides are in the same ratio, so the triangles ABC, DEF are similar.

Because the triangles are similar, $\angle A = \angle D$, $\angle B = \angle E$ and $\angle C = \angle F$.

3. Sometimes you might know that 2 sides of one triangle are proportional to
    2 sides of a second triangle, and also that the angles between these sides
    (the included angles) are equal.
    Then these triangles are similar.
    The 3rd sides are also in the same proportion and the other two corresponding
    pairs of angles are equal.

Example

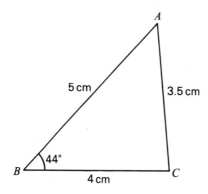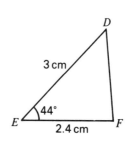

Since *AB* is longer than *BC* and *DE* is longer than *EF*, we compare the ratios of
AB : *DE* and *BC* : *EF*

$$\frac{AB}{DE} = \frac{5}{3}, \quad \frac{BC}{EF} = \frac{4}{2.4} = \frac{40}{24} = \frac{5}{3}$$

The 2 pairs of sides are proportional, the included angles ($\angle B$ and $\angle E$) are equal,
so the triangles *ABC*, *DEF* are similar.

So $\dfrac{AB}{DE} = \dfrac{BC}{EF} = \dfrac{AC}{DF}$

Then *AC* and *DF* are in the same proportion.

$$\frac{AC}{DF} = \frac{5}{3}$$

$$DF = \frac{3}{5} \text{ of } AC = \frac{3}{5} \times 3.5 \text{ cm} = 2.1 \text{ cm}$$

Also the other corresponding angles are equal, $\angle A = \angle D$ and $\angle C = \angle F$.

Summary of facts about similar triangles

If you know these facts about a pair of triangles, you can say they are similar.

1

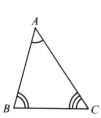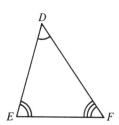

If they are equiangular,
i.e. $\angle A = \angle D$, $\angle B = \angle E$, $\angle C = \angle F$
then the triangles are similar.

2

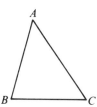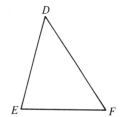

If all the sides are in the same proportion,

i.e. $\dfrac{AB}{DE} = \dfrac{BC}{EF} = \dfrac{AC}{DF}$

then the triangles are similar.

3

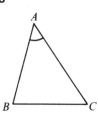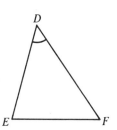

If $\dfrac{AB}{DE} = \dfrac{AC}{DF}$ and $\angle A = \angle D$

then the triangles are similar.

You will find it helpful to identify corresponding sides and angles in this way.
When you state that two triangles are similar, write down the letters in corresponding order.

e.g. If you write that $\triangle ABC$ is similar to $\triangle QRP$, you mean
that $\angle A = \angle Q$ (written first),
     $\angle B = \angle R$ (written second),
     $\angle C = \angle P$ (written last).

Also AB is proportional to QR (written 1st and 2nd)
     BC is proportional to RP (written 2nd and 3rd)
     AC is proportional to QP (written 1st and 3rd).

Exercise 3.2

1. In these questions, equal angles are marked in the same way.
   Say whether the triangles are similar and if they are, name the 3 pairs of corresponding sides, and any other equal angles.

1

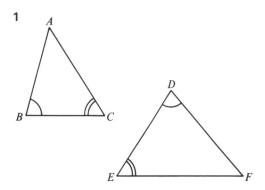

2

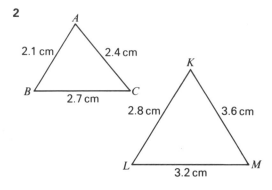

3

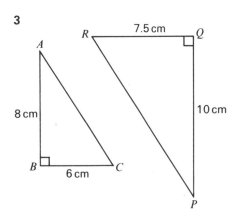

4

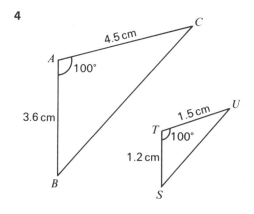

5

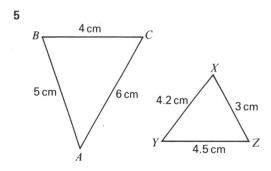

2. Explain why these triangles
    are similar.
    Calculate the lengths of PR
    and QR.

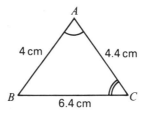
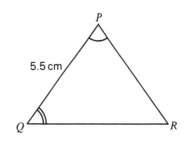

3. Triangles ABC, EDF are similar

    with $\dfrac{AB}{ED} = \dfrac{BC}{DF} = \dfrac{AC}{EF}$

    State the sizes of angles D, E
    and F.

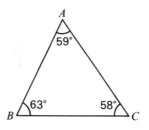
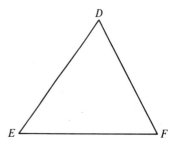

4. $\angle C = \angle Y$
    Explain why these triangles
    are similar.
    Name the angle equal to $\angle A$.
    Calculate the length of AB.

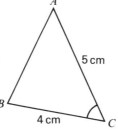
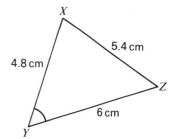

5. Explain why these triangles
    are similar.
    Name the angles equal to $\angle A$,
    $\angle B$ and $\angle C$.

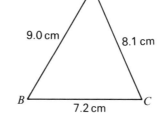
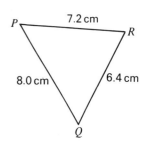

6. Explain why these triangles
    are similar.
    What is the ratio $BC : DF$?
    Name the angles equal to $\angle B$
    and $\angle C$.

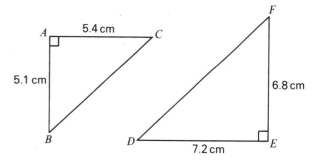

Exercise 3.3   Applications and Activities

1.   A photograph is enlarged. Its original size was 16 cm by 10 cm. On the enlargement the longer side is 20 cm. What is the length of the shorter side ?

2.   Two villages are 24 km apart. On a map this distance is measured as 8.4 cm. How far apart are two other villages, which on the same map are 7.7 cm apart ?

3.   On a drawing, a rectangle is shown as 9 cm long and 7.5 cm wide. When the drawing is reduced on a photocopier, the rectangle is 7.2 cm long. How wide will it be ?

4.   A small model figure is 14.4 cm high and 4.2 cm wide at its base. A larger, similar figure is to be made, 16.8 cm high. How wide will it be at its base ?

5.   On a photograph a building is shown as 5.5 cm long and 3.5 cm high. The length of the actual building is 66 m. How high is it ?

6.   In the diagram, *ACE* and *BCD* are straight lines, and $\angle A = \angle D$.
     Explain why $\triangle ABC$ is similar to $\triangle DEC$ and name the 3 pairs of corresponding sides.
     Calculate the lengths
     of *AB* and *CE*.

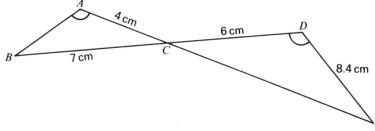

7.   *BAE* and *CAD* are straight lines.
     Explain why triangles *ABC* and *ADE* are similar.
     Find the ratio *BC* : *DE*.
     Say which angle is equal to $\angle B$.

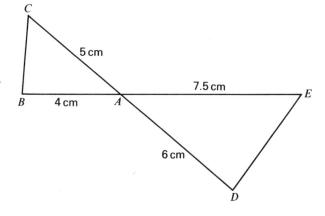

8. *ACD* and *BCE* are straight lines.
Show that these triangles are similar
and name the equal angles.
What does this prove about the
lines *AB* and *ED* ?

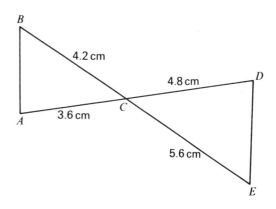

9. **Paper sizes**

Begin with 2 sheets of A4 paper.
Keep 1 sheet and label it A4.
Fold and cut the other sheet in half to make 2 sheets of A5 paper.
Keep one of these sheets and label it A5.
Fold and cut the other sheet in half to make 2 sheets of A6 paper.
You can continue the process, getting smaller sizes.
Display all your rectangles, in decreasing order of size.
Are these rectangles similar ?

10. A stick 1.5 m long is placed
vertically so that its top is in line
with the top of a building, seen
from a point on the ground 5 m
from the stick and 90 m from the
building.
How tall is the building ?

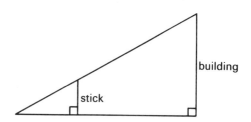

11. In the evening sunshine, a tree casts a shadow of length 190 m, and the shadow
of a man is 9.5 m. If the man is 1.75 m tall, how tall is the tree ?
(The sun is so far away that its rays form parallel lines.)

12. *AB* is a handrail on a stairway.
AC = 1 m, *BD* = 4 m and
CD = 4.5 m.
The dotted lines *PW*, *QX*, *RY*,
SZ show where vertical supports
are to be fixed. The distances
CP, *PQ*, *QR*, *RS* and *SD* are
equal.
Find the lengths of the supports.

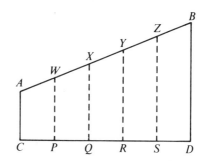

13. **Logos**

Here is a company logo, shown in several sizes. (Which company ?)

If the logo has to be used in different sizes then it has to be enlarged or reduced.

The instructions for the scale factor are given in percentage form. The instruction 150% means the scale factor is $\frac{150}{100} = 1.5 = \frac{3}{2}$. Each length on the new picture of the logo is 150% of the corresponding length on the original.

1   If the circle of the original logo has diameter 3.2 cm, what is the diameter on a new logo if the instruction given is 'reduce to 75%' ?

2   If the circle on the original logo has diameter 1.6 cm, and for a new picture the diameter has to be 3.6 cm, what is the scale factor of the enlargement, and what is this in percentage form ?

3   A school badge is in the form of a crest, 12 cm high.
If the badge has to be reproduced on notepaper, to a height of 2.7 cm, what is the scale factor of the reduction, and what is this in percentage form ?
The badge is 8 cm wide.
How wide will the reduced copy be ?

If your school has a badge or logo, see how many different sizes of it you can find, for example, on the notice board, on letter headings and on exercise books. Find the ratios of corresponding lengths on different-sized drawings.

14. Two rectangular boxes are similar in shape. The smaller one has length 15 cm, width 12 cm and height 9 cm.

    1 The larger one has height 12 cm. What are its other measurements ?

    2 Find the surface areas of the 2 boxes, and find the ratio of the surface areas, in its simplest form.

    3 Find the volumes of the 2 boxes, and find the ratio of the volumes, in its simplest form.

    4 What is the ratio of the lengths of the boxes ? Can you discover a relationship connecting the ratios of lengths, surface areas and volumes of similar boxes ?

PUZZLES

19. Adam bought some oranges. He noticed that 3 of them cost as much more than ten pence as 5 of them cost more than fifty pence.
    What was the cost of an orange ?

20. During a holiday it rained on 16 days, but when it rained in the morning the afternoon was fine, and every rainy afternoon was preceded by a fine morning. There were 12 fine mornings and 14 fine afternoons. How long was the holiday ?

21. The Terriers, United, Villa and Wanderers are the four local football teams who play each other once.

    Here is the (incomplete) table of results, in alphabetical order.

	Played	Won	Lost	Drawn	Goals for	Goals against
Terriers	3			1	0	3
United	3					3
Villa	3	3			4	
Wanderers	3					

    It is known that the result of the match between United and Wanderers was a draw (1–1), and that United have scored more than 3 goals altogether.
    Copy and complete the table and find the score in each match.

22. If it takes 20 waggonloads of bricks to build a wall round a square field which measures $\frac{1}{2}$ hectare in area, what will be the area of a square field which has a wall built round it consisting of 40 waggonloads of bricks ? (The walls are the same height and of the same thickness.)

23. Victoria drives from Pixton to Quenley, a journey of 90 km, averaging 45 km/h on the journey. At what speed must she travel on the return journey to average
    1 60 km/h, **2** 90 km/h, on the complete trip ?

4 Thinking about inequalities and

Inequalities

Often in life things are more unequal than equal. We learn to recognise this at an early age.
What inequalities can you see in these pictures ?

regions

egions of the UK.

The UK divided into regions according to the
maximum wind speed expected, figures in m/s.
This information is needed so that roofs can be
designed to stay fixed in such winds.

Netball

A netball court is divided into six regions. Depending on
which position you play in, you are only allowed to enter
certain regions.
Do you know which ones ?

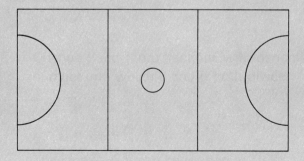

Practice for the shooter before
a match.

4 Inequalities and Regions

Inequalities

Remember the signs:

< means less than
≤ means less than or equal to
> means greater than
≥ means greater than or equal to

To solve simple inequalities, use the same methods as for solving simple equations.

You can add equal numbers to both sides,
you can subtract equal numbers from both sides,
you can multiply both sides by the same **positive** number,
you can divide both sides by the same **positive** number,

and the inequality remains true.

If you multiply or divide both sides by a **negative** number, the inequality sign must be reversed at the same time.

Examples

1 Solve the inequality $15x - 4 < 3x - 12$

Subtract $3x$ from both sides
$$12x - 4 < -12$$
Add 4 to both sides
$$12x < -8$$
Divide both sides by 12
$$x < -\tfrac{2}{3}$$

2   Solve the inequality $\frac{2}{3}x \geqslant 1 + \frac{1}{4}x$

Multiply both sides by 12, to turn the fractions into whole numbers.
($\frac{2}{3}x \times 12 = 8x$, $\frac{1}{4}x \times 12 = 3x$)
$$8x \geqslant 12 + 3x$$
Subtract $3x$ from both sides
$$5x \geqslant 12$$
Divide both sides by 5
$$x \geqslant 2\frac{2}{5}$$

3   Solve the inequality $10x + 6 > 16x + 18$

If you begin by subtracting $16x$ from both sides, you get
$$-6x + 6 > 18$$
Subtract 6 from both sides
$$-6x > 12$$
Divide both sides by -6 and reverse the inequality sign
$$x < -2$$

You could avoid dividing by a negative number by beginning by subtracting $10x$ from both sides
$$6 > 6x + 18$$
Subtract 18 from both sides
$$-12 > 6x$$
Divide both sides by 6
$$-2 > x$$
i.e. $x < -2$, the same answer as before.

4   Solve the inequality $8 - 3x \leqslant 20$

Either: Subtract 8 from both sides
$$-3x \leqslant 12$$
Divide both sides by -3 and reverse the inequality sign
$$x \geqslant -4$$

Or: Add $3x$ to both sides
$$8 \leqslant 20 + 3x$$
Subtract 20 from both sides
$$-12 \leqslant 3x$$
Divide both sides by 3
$$-4 \leqslant x$$
i.e. $x \geqslant -4$, the same answer as before.

Exercise 4.1

Solve these inequalities.

1. **1** $3x - 7 > 11$
    2 $9(7x + 2) < 81$
    3 $2x + 18 \leqslant 29$
    4 $4x + 1 \geqslant 2x - 19$
    5 $2 - 9x > 5(7 - 4x)$

    6 $\dfrac{3x}{4} < 7$
    7 $5x - 7 < 12x + 7$
    8 $4(3x + 1) \geqslant 3(9x - 2)$
    9 $30 - 7x \leqslant 3x + 10$
    10 $8 > 12 - \dfrac{x}{5}$

2. **1** $7(x - 4) - 21 > 0$
    2 $3(x - 2) + 2(x + 1) \leqslant 6$
    3 $\dfrac{4x}{5} < 8$
    4 $3(x + 2) \geqslant 5x + 6$
    5 $5(x + 2) - (x - 1) \leqslant 2$

    6 $\dfrac{x}{7} + 10 > 12 + x$
    7 $3(x - 5) + 9 \geqslant 15$
    8 $\dfrac{x}{6} + 8 \leqslant 7 - \dfrac{x}{3}$
    9 $5(1 - 4x) - 3(2x + 1) > 28$
    10 $\dfrac{x + 4}{3} < 5$

Other inequalities

Examples

1 Solve the inequality $4x^2 < 36$

Divide both sides by 4
   $x^2 < 9$

First, think of the **equation** $x^2 = 9$
There are two solutions, $x = -3$ and $x = 3$

Now, if x has any value between -3 and 3, then x^2 is less than 9
If x has any value less than -3 or greater than 3, x^2 is greater than 9

So the solution to $x^2 < 9$ is
'x lies between -3 and 3'
This is written as $-3 < x < 3$
It is shown here on a number line.

2   Solve the inequality $x^2 \geqslant 25$

This means $x^2 = 25$ or $x^2 > 25$
$x^2 = 25$ when $x = -5$ or $x = 5$
If x has any value less than -5 or greater than 5 then $x^2 > 25$

So the solution to $x^2 \geqslant 25$ is $x \leqslant -5$ or $x \geqslant 5$

This cannot be written any simpler
as it is represented by two distinct
regions on the number line.

You can check your solution mentally by trying various values.
Try a value less than -5.
If $x = -6$, then $x^2 = (-6) \times (-6) = 36$, which is greater than 25.
Try a value greater than 5.
If $x = 5\frac{1}{2}$, then $x^2 = 5\frac{1}{2}^2 = 30\frac{1}{4}$, which is greater than 25.
But then try a value between -5 and 5.
If $x = -4$, then $x^2 = (-4)^2 = 16$, which is less than 25.

Exercise 4.2

Find the values of x which satisfy these inequalities.

1.   **1** $x^2 < 16$ **4** $x^2 < 2.25$
     2 $x^2 > 1$ **5** $x^2 \geqslant \frac{1}{9}$
     3 $x^2 \leqslant 81$

2.   **1** $2x^2 \leqslant 50$ **4** $4x^2 < 3x^2 + 49$
     2 $3x^2 > 300$ **5** $\frac{1}{3}x^2 < 12$
     3 $x^2 + 9 \geqslant 73$

3.   If x is a positive whole number such that $1 \leqslant x \leqslant 10$, state the values of x
     satisfied by these inequalities.

     1 $x^2 < 30$ **4** $5x^2 > x^2 + 180$
     2 $x^2 \geqslant 50$ **5** $20 < x^2 < 40$
     3 $2x^2 + 1 \leqslant 25$

Straight-line graphs

Straight-line graphs have an equation of the form $y = mx + c$, where m and c are numbers.
You have drawn such graphs by plotting any 3 points, and joining them.
Here is a slightly different method of finding 3 points on the line, which you may prefer to use.

Gradients

The gradient of a line $= \dfrac{\text{increase in } y}{\text{increase in } x}$

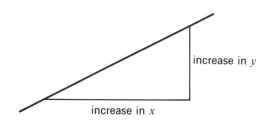

Examples

Lines with gradient 3

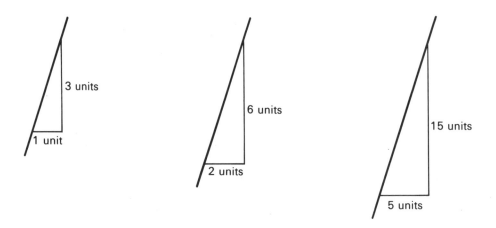

Lines with gradient 3 have equations with the coefficient of x equal to 3.
e.g. $y = 3x$
        $y = 3x + 2$
        $y = 3x - 5$, and so on.

Lines with gradient $-\frac{1}{2}$

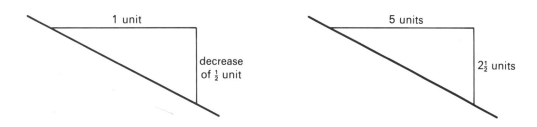

Lines with gradient $-\frac{1}{2}$ have equations with the coefficient of x equal to $-\frac{1}{2}$.

e.g. $y = -\frac{1}{2}x$

$y = -\frac{1}{2}x + 2$

$y = -\frac{1}{2}x - 5$, and so on.

(To avoid fractions, these equations may be written as $2y = -x$, $2y = -x + 4$, $2y = -x - 10$, respectively.)

If you are using different scales on the x and y axes, remember that you must count in x or y **units**, and 1 unit in the x direction will not be the same length as 1 unit in the y direction.

If you know the equation of a line, you can state its gradient. In general, the line with equation $y = mx + c$ has gradient m.

Also $(0, c)$ is the point where the line cuts the y-axis.

Examples

$y = 2x + 3$ has gradient 2 and cuts the y-axis at $(0, 3)$,

$y = 3x - 1$ has gradient 3 and cuts the y-axis at $(0, -1)$,

$y = \frac{1}{2}x$ has gradient $\frac{1}{2}$ and passes through the origin,

$y = 2\frac{1}{2} - 6x$ has gradient -6 and cuts the y-axis at $(0, 2\frac{1}{2})$,

$y = 5 - x$ has gradient -1 and cuts the y-axis at $(0, 5)$.

You can use this information to draw the line.

Example

Draw the graph of $y = 2x + 3$ from $x = -2$ to 4.

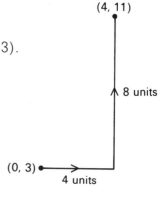

The gradient of the line is 2, and it cuts the y-axis at (0, 3).
Mark the point (0, 3) on your graph.
From (0, 3), if you increase x by
4 units you must increase y by 8 units,
because the gradient is 2.
So the point (4, 11) lies on the graph.
Mark this point.

From (0, 3), if you decrease x by 2 units
you must decrease y by 4 units.
So the point $(-2, -1)$ lies on the graph.
Mark this point.
You now have 3 points which lie on the line.
Check that they do lie on a line, then draw the line.

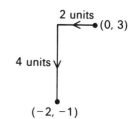

Exercise 4.3

1. On graph paper, label the x-axis from 0 to 8, and the y-axis from 0 to 10, using
    equal scales on both axes.

    Draw these lines, showing as much of the line as fits on the paper:
    1   A line with gradient 1, passing through the origin.
    2   A line with gradient 2, passing through the point (0, 3).
    3   A line with gradient -3, passing through the point (0, 8).
    4   A line with gradient $-\frac{1}{2}$, passing through the point (0, 9).

2. State the gradients of these lines and the point where each line cuts the y-axis.

    1 $y = 5x - 2$ **4** $y = 8 - x$
    2 $y = \frac{1}{2}x + 4$ **5** $y = 3x$
    3 $y = 3 - 2x$

3. On graph paper, label the x-axis from -3 to 5 and the y-axis from -3 to 7,
    taking equal scales on both axes.

    Draw these lines, showing as much of each line as fits on the paper:
    1 $y = \frac{1}{2}x + 1$ **2** $y = 6 - 2x$
    State the coordinates of the point where the lines cross each other.

4.   On graph paper, label the x-axis from -4 to 4 and the y-axis from -2 to 18, taking a scale of 2 cm to 1 unit on the x-axis and 2 cm to 2 units on the y-axis.

Draw these lines, showing as much of each line as fits on the paper:
1 $y = x + 2$ **2** $y = 11 - 3x$
State the coordinates of the point where the lines cross each other.

Regions

Here is the line $x = 4$.
This line divides the graph paper into 2 regions.
All points on the left of the line have x-coordinates less than 4.
This is the region $x < 4$.
All points on the right of the line have x-coordinates greater than 4.
This is the region $x > 4$.

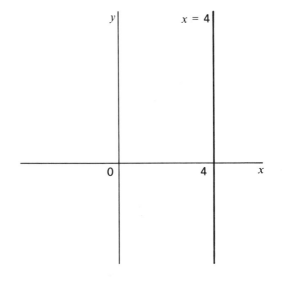

The unshaded area is the region $x < 4$, the shaded area is the region $x > 4$, the boundary line is the line $x = 4$.

Here are the regions divided by the line $y = 3$.

The shaded area is the region $y > 3$,
the unshaded area is the region $y < 3$,
the boundary line is the line $y = 3$.

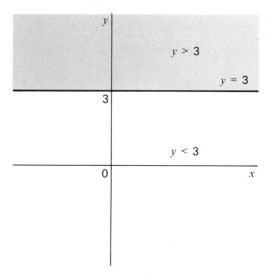

Here are the regions divided by the line $y = 2x + 3$.

The shaded area is the region
$y < 2x + 3$.
This is the part below the line
since y is less than $2x + 3$.

The unshaded area is the region
$y > 2x + 3$.
This is the part above the line
since y is greater than $2x + 3$.

The boundary line is the line
$y = 2x + 3$.

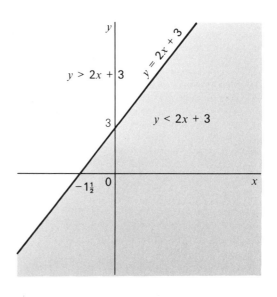

Here are the regions divided by the line $y = 15 - 3x$.

The shaded area is the region
$y > 15 - 3x$,
the unshaded area is the region
$y < 15 - 3x$,
the boundary line is the line
$y = 15 - 3x$.

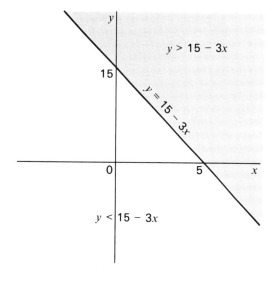

Examples

1   The shaded region is bounded by the
    lines $x = -1$ and $x = 4$ and it is the
    region $-1 < x < 4$.

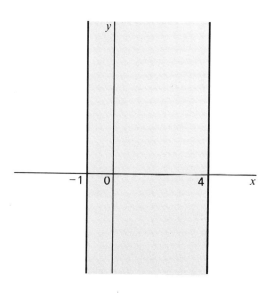

2   The shaded region is bounded by the
    lines $y = 6$ and $y = -2x$ and it is the
    region $y > 6$, $y < -2x$.

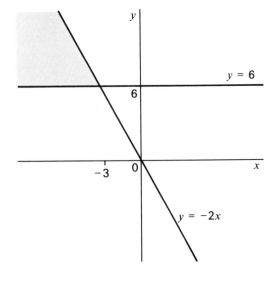

Checking the answer
You can check that for a point such as
A $(-5, 7)$ which lies within the region,
that y **is** greater than 6, and y (7) **is** less
than $-2x$ (10).

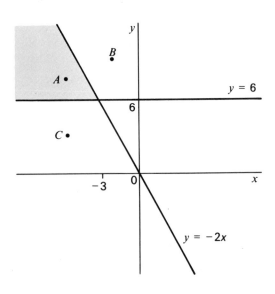

On the other hand, for a point such as
B $(-2, 8)$ which lies outside the region,
although y is greater than 6, y (8) is
not less than $-2x$ (4).

For a point C $(-5, 3)$, y is not greater
than 6, although y (3) is less than
$-2x$ (10).

If you are not sure whether you have found the correct region, first check that you
have used the correct boundary lines. Then choose a suitable point inside the
region and check that its coordinates satisfy the inequalities.
You can also check that coordinates of certain points outside the region do not
satisfy both or all the inequalities.

Exercise 4.4

1. Identify the regions A and B on these diagrams. (A is the shaded region, B is the unshaded region.)

1

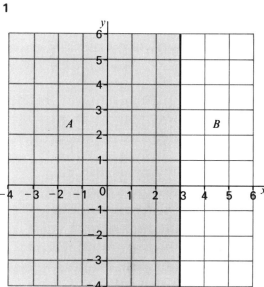

2

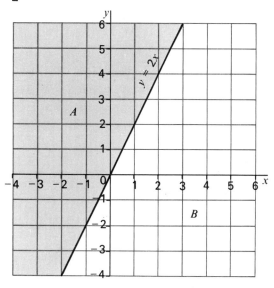

3

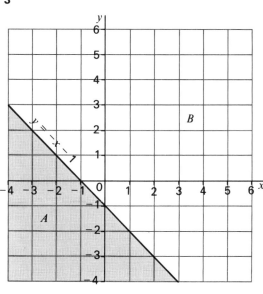

4

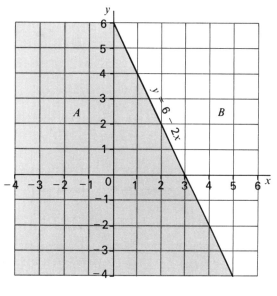

2. Draw separate small graphs on squared paper or graph paper, labelling the x and
    y axes from -4 to 6.
    Show these lines, and on the graph label the regions on either side of the line.

    1 $y = 4$ **4** $y = x + 1$
    2 $x = -3$ **5** $y = 3 - x$
    3 $y = -x$

3. Identify the shaded regions in these diagrams.

1

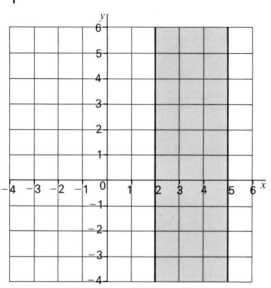

2

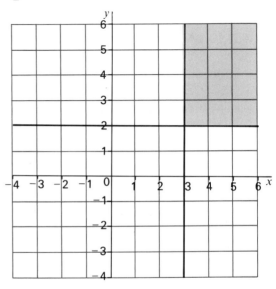

3

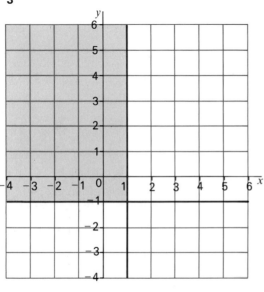

4

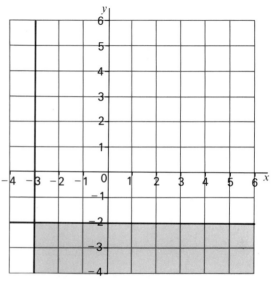

4. Draw separate small graphs on squared paper or graph paper, to show these regions.

   1 $-1 < x < 3$ **4** $x < -2, \; y > 1$
   2 $0 < y < 4$ **5** $x > 0, \; y < -2$
   3 $x > 3, \; y > -1$

5. Identify the shaded regions in these diagrams.

1

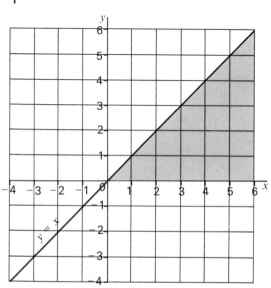

2

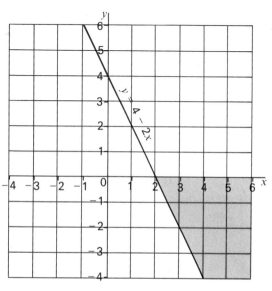

3

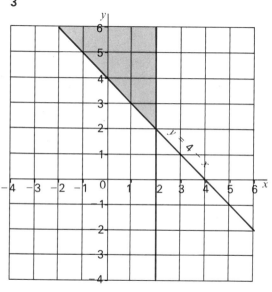

4

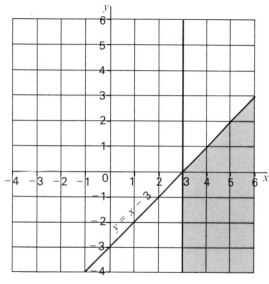

6. Draw separate small graphs on squared paper or graph paper, labelling the x and y axes from -4 to 6.

    1   Draw the line $y = 2x - 2$.
          Shade the region $y > 0$, $y < 2x - 2$.
    2   Draw the lines $y = 2$ and $y = x + 3$.
          Shade the region $y > 2$, $y < x + 3$.
    3   Draw the lines $x = 3$ and $y = 5 - x$.
          Shade the region $x < 3$, $y > 5 - x$.
    4   Draw the lines $y = -2$ and $y = -\frac{1}{2}x$.
          Shade the region $y > -2$, $y < -\frac{1}{2}x$.
    5   Draw the lines $x = 1$ and $y = x - 2$.
          Shade the region $x > 1$, $y > x - 2$.

Closed regions

Examples

1   On a graph draw the lines $x = 7$, $y = 2$ and $y = x - 2$.
       Identify the region where $x < 7$, $y > 2$ and $y < x - 2$.

       On squared paper or graph paper draw the x-axis from 0 to 8 and the y-axis from -2 to 6.
       Draw the lines $x = 7$, $y = 2$ and $y = x - 2$.

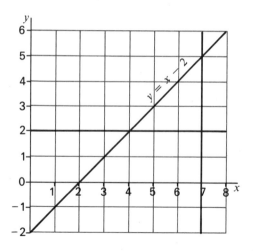

The 3 lines divide the graph into 7 regions which here we have labelled from A to G.
For the region $x < 7$, we need the area on the left of the line $x = 7$, so this excludes regions B, C and D.
For the region $y > 2$, we need the area above the line $y = 2$, so this excludes regions D (again), E and F.

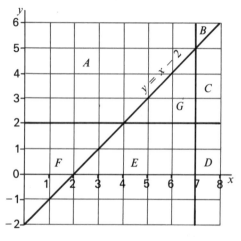

For the region $y < x - 2$, we need the area below the line $y = x - 2$, so this excludes regions F (again), A and B (again).
The only region which is left is G.
G is the region where $x < 7$, $y > 2$ and $y < x - 2$.

Normally you would not label the regions like this. You would just decide which areas were not wanted and identify the final region which satisfies all the conditions.

You may find it easier to shade the parts you do **not** want, i.e. B, C, D then F, E, D then F, A, B. This leaves the region G to be identified as the unshaded area.

You can check your answer. First, make sure that the region (G) is bounded by the 3 lines $x = 7$, $y = 2$ and $y = x - 2$. Then choose a suitable point inside the region. On the diagram, the point (6, 3) lies inside the region.
Then, for this point, x (6) **is** less than 7, y (3) **is** greater than 2 and y (3) **is** less than $x - 2$ (4).
If you check for any points outside the region their coordinates will not satisfy **all** the inequalities.

2 Identify the shaded region on the diagram.

The boundaries of the shaded area are the lines $x = 1$, $y = 3$ and $y = -2x$.

All the points in the shaded area are on the left of the line $x = 1$, so $x < 1$.
All the points in the shaded area are below the line $y = 3$, so $y < 3$.
All the points in the shaded area are above the line $y = -2x$, so $y > -2x$.

The region is the area where $x < 1$, $y < 3$ and $y > -2x$.

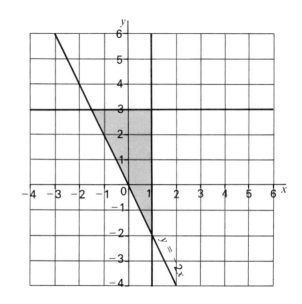

3   Identify the shaded region in the diagram.

The boundaries of the shaded area
are the lines $x = 0$ (the y-axis),
$y = x$ and $y = 3 - \frac{1}{2}x$.

All the points in the shaded area
are on the right of the y-axis, so
$x > 0$.
All the points in the shaded area
are above the line $y = x$, so $y > x$.
All the points in the shaded area
are below the line $y = 3 - \frac{1}{2}x$,
so $y < 3 - \frac{1}{2}x$.
The region is the area where
$x > 0$, $y > x$ and $y < 3 - \frac{1}{2}x$.

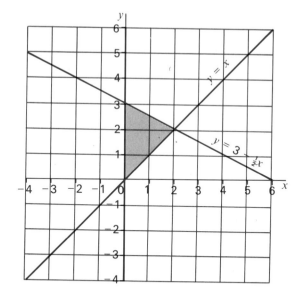

Exercise 4.5

1.   Identify the shaded areas on these diagrams.

1

2

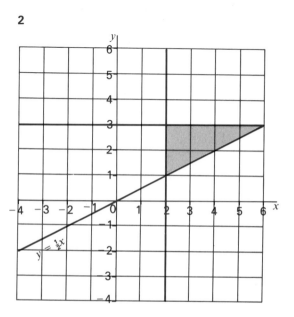

3

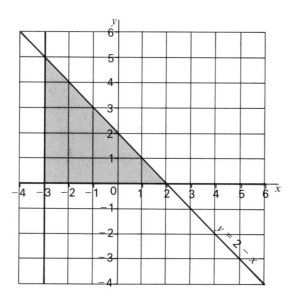

4

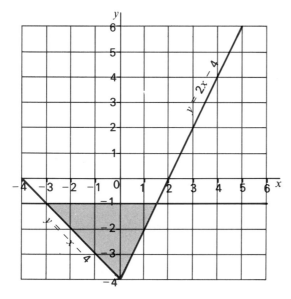

2. Draw separate graphs on squared paper or graph paper to show these regions. Draw the x and y axes from -4 to 6.

1 $x < -1$, $y < 4$, $y > -2x - 4$

2 $x > 0$, $y > 1$, $y < 2\frac{1}{2} - \frac{1}{2}x$

3 $x > 1$, $y < 5$, $y > 2x - 2$

4 $y < 4$, $y < 2x$, $y > x$

5 $x < 4$, $y < \frac{1}{2}x$, $y > -x$

Boundary lines

You need to know whether a region of points you are considering should include the boundary line or not.

e.g.   The region $x > 4$ does   The region $x \geqslant 4$ includes
       not include the line   the line $x = 4$.
       $x = 4$.

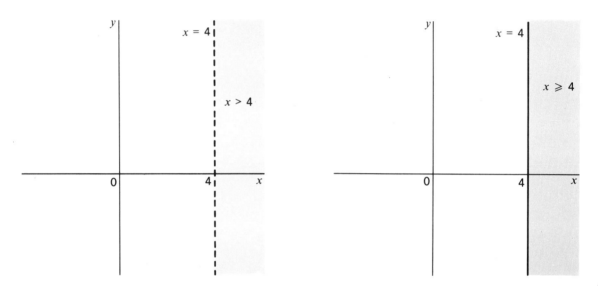

Sometimes the boundary line is dotted to show that it is not included in the region you are considering, and drawn solid if it is to be included.

However, regions are often drawn bounded by solid lines in either case, so if it is important to make it clear whether the boundary line is included or not, it is best to state this near the graph.

Exercise 4.6   Applications and Activities

1.   **Further inequalities**

     Find the values of x which satisfy these inequalities:

     1 $x^2 > 0$ **4** $x^3 > 27$
     2 $x^2 > -9$ **5** $x^3 < -8$
     3 $x^2 < -9$

2.   The formula for changing temperatures from the Celsius scale to the Fahrenheit
      scale is $y = \frac{9}{5}x + 32$, where x is the temperature in °C and y is the temperature
      in °F.
      Draw a graph of this equation. Draw the x-axis from 0 to 30 taking a scale of
      2 cm to 5 units, and the y-axis from 0 to 90, taking a scale of 2 cm to 10 units.
      Find the values of y when $x = 0$, 20 and 30 and plot corresponding points, then
      draw the line.
      An approximate rule for changing temperatures is 'Double the Celsius temperature
      and add 30, for the Fahrenheit temperature'. Express this rule as an equation in
      terms of x and y.
      Draw the graph representing this equation on the same axes as the other graph.

      What is the temperature in °C for which the approximate rule gives the exact
      value of the temperature in °F ?
      For what range of values of temperature in °C does the approximate rule give a
      lower value of temperature in °F than the true value ?
      For what range of values of temperature in °C does the approximate rule give a
      higher value of temperature in °F than the true value ?

      Do you think the approximate rule is a suitable one to use ?

3:    George has found an old map of a field, together with clues for locating a
      treasure which he hopes is buried in the field.
      All the clues are in terms of x,
      the distance in metres of the treasure
      from the edge AB of the field, and y,
      the distance in metres of the treasure
      from the edge BC.

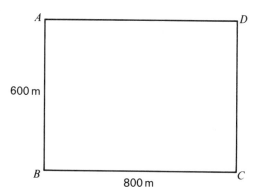

      Clues:
      1 $y \geqslant 200$
      2 $y \geqslant 600 - 2x$
      3 $y \leqslant x + 100$
      4 $y \leqslant 800 - x$

      Draw a scale drawing of the field on graph paper and use the clues to find a
      region in which the treasure must lie.

      George finds a further clue.
      5 $y = 350$
      Draw this line and mark the part of it which lies within the region on your
      drawing.
      George decides that he will dig along this line until he finds the treasure. What is
      the greatest length of line that he will have to dig ?

4. Rabia is entering a competition where she has
to design a poster.
The rules state that the poster has to be longer
than it is wide, but not twice as long.
The poster has to be between 30 cm and
60 cm wide.
The combined length + width of the poster
must be less than 130 cm.
If the width is x cm and the length is y cm, express
these rules mathematically, as inequalities.
Draw a graph with the x-axis from 0 to 80 and the
y-axis from 0 to 100, taking 2 cm to 10 units on both
axes.

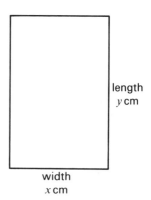

length
y cm

width
x cm

Draw the lines representing the boundaries of the inequalities on your graph, as far
as they fit on your graph paper, and identify the region of acceptable lengths and
widths.

Rabia has sheets of paper which are 76 cm long. To comply with the rules of the
competition, what is the range of widths her poster can have, if she makes it 76 cm
long ?
To make it a pleasing shape she wants the ratio width : length to be equal to
1 : 1.62 (the Golden Section Ratio).
For a length of 76 cm, what is the correct width in this ratio ?
If she chooses this width, does it comply with the competition rules ?

5. A Youth Leader wishes to buy some cans of soft drinks for her group, out on a
hike.
Lemonade costs 30p per can and orange crush costs 40p per can.
The leader cannot spend more than £12 altogether.
She needs at least twice as many cans of orange crush as cans of lemonade, and
she needs at least 30 drinks altogether.
If she buys x cans of lemonade and y cans of orange crush, write down the
statements above as inequalities in terms of x and y.
On graph paper, label the x-axis from 0 to 40 and the y-axis from 0 to 30, taking
2 cm to 5 units on both axes. Draw the lines representing the boundaries of the
inequalities and identify the region where the inequalities are satisfied.

From your graph find
1 the least number of cans of orange crush that the leader can buy,
2 the greatest number of cans of lemonade that the leader can buy.

6. A shopkeeper has two kinds of sweets
    which he wishes to mix together to make
    an assortment. The first kind costs 70p per
    quarter and the second kind costs 30p per
    quarter.
    If he mixes x quarters of the 1st sort with
    y quarters of the 2nd sort, write down an
    expression for the total cost of the sweets.
    He does not want the assorted sweets to
    be worth more than 45p per quarter.
    Write down an inequality connecting
    x and y, and show that it can be simplified
    to $y \geqslant \frac{5}{3}x$.
    The shopkeeper wants to make at least
    20 lb of the mixture but he has only 16 lb
    of the cheaper kind of sweets available.
    (4 quarters = 1 lb.)
    Write down two more inequalities satisfied
    by x and y.

On graph paper, draw the x-axis from 0 to 80 and the y-axis from 0 to 100. Draw
the 3 lines which are the boundary lines of the inequalities. Identify the region in
which x and y satisfy all the inequalities.

If the shopkeeper decides to use 15 lb of the cheaper sweets in the mixture, what
is the range of amounts of the dearer sweets he can use to mix with them ?

PUZZLES

24. A paint tin weighs $2\frac{1}{2}$ kg when half full and 2 kg when it is one-third full of paint. What is
     the weight of a full tin of paint ?

25. Bill and Ben each throw a die. What is the probability that Bill will throw a higher
     number than Ben ?

26. A farmer bought an odd number of lambs at £10 each, and also one lamb which was
     rather tiny, for which he paid less than £10. The total amount he paid was a perfect
     square.
     Although we do not know how many lambs he bought, can you say how much he paid
     for the tiny one ?

27. Which number gives the same result when it is added to $2\frac{1}{4}$ as when it is multiplied by $2\frac{1}{4}$?

5 Thinking about statistical

Making choices

What is the most popular breakfast cereal ?
A hostel caterer wants to know what
kinds of breakfast cereal to provide for
breakfasts. Discuss how you could carry
out a survey to help him decide.

What is the most popular flavour of crisps ?
What flavours of crisps should be sold at
the tuck shop ? Can you carry out a
survey to decide what flavours should be
stocked, and in what proportions ?

Adventure activities

What would be the most popular choice for an adventure holiday ?
Here are some ideas. Discuss how you could choose which holiday would be most
popular, if you could arrange it.

Abseiling

Windsurfing

nvestigations

Skiing

Pony trekking

Canoeing

Parachuting

Sailing

5 Statistical Investigations

You have used questionnaires in which answers can be classified into categories.

No	
Yes	
Don't know	

Age

Under 20	
20–under 40	
40–under 60	
60 or over	

You are now trying to analyse a more detailed questionnaire, of the kind where people put items in order of merit, order of preference, or some other order, so you cannot simply count the ticks in each group.

Example

Sam and Sally knew that the local shop sold 5 kinds of soft drinks.
We will call these drinks Poppo, Quencho, Ribbo, Squasho and Tisso.
Sam's hypothesis was that the most popular drink was Quencho, Sally's hypothesis was that the most popular drink was Tisso.
They asked 10 friends, identified here by the letters A to J, to put the drinks in order of preference, and here are the results.

1 = 1st choice, 2 = 2nd choice, etc.

	A	B	C	D	E	F	G	H	I	J
Poppo	2	3	3	3	4	3	4	5	3	3
Quencho	4	2	4	1	2	1	5	1	2	2
Ribbo	3	5	5	5	5	5	2	3	5	4
Squasho	5	4	2	2	1	4	1	4	4	1
Tisso	1	1	1	4	3	2	3	2	1	5

How would you analyse these results ?
Maybe you would like to think about this before reading further.

This is a complicated process and you might use one of several methods.

1st idea

You can see how many 1's there are for each product.

Drink	Number of 1st choices
Poppo	0
Quencho	3
Ribbo	0
Squasho	3
Tisso	4
	10

Tisso has 4 1's and this is the most popular.

However, only 4 out of 10 people voted for Tisso so you may think that this is not sufficient to say it is the best.
You might have been more sure if more than half the people had voted for it.

So you might go on to another method.

2nd idea

Count the 1st and 2nd choices.

Drink	Number of 1st choices	Number of 2nd choices	Total 1st and 2nd choices
Poppo	0	1	1
Quencho	3	4	7
Ribbo	0	1	1
Squasho	3	2	5
Tisso	4	2	6
	10	10	20

It now looks as if Quencho is the most popular, using this way of analysing the results.

3rd idea

You may think that all the choices should be taken into consideration.

You can add up all the 'scores' for each drink from the 1st table of choices.
e.g. For Poppo, 2 + 3 + 3 + 3 + 4 + 3 + 4 + 5 + 3 + 3 = 33
This gives a table like this:

Drink	Total of scores
Poppo	33
Quencho	24
Ribbo	42
Squasho	28
Tisso	23
	150

150 ← Since each column adds up to 15, this should add up to 10 × 15, and is a useful check.

Since 1 is best and 5 is worst, it is the drink with the lowest total (not the highest) which is best, so using this method it seems that Tisso is the most popular, although Quencho is a close second.

If you had asked people to give 5 marks for the best, 4 for the next best, and so on, or you had done this yourself when tabulating the results, then it would be the item with the highest total which would be considered the most popular.

You can change all the results in the table to marks in this way, and check this.

This method of scoring would be useful if, for instance, there were 10 drinks and you only asked for the 1st five to be put in order. After scores of 5, 4, 3, 2 and 1, the rest would be given marks of 0.

These methods have been suggested as possible ways in which you can come to a conclusion. Choose whichever way you want.

Perhaps you will invent your own rules to decide which item is best.

Exercise 5.1

Here are some (fictitious) results in which people A, B, C, . . . have put some products P, Q, R, . . . in order of preference.
1 = 1st choice, 2 = 2nd choice, etc.

If these were the results of surveys that you had carried out, analyse them and write down your conclusions, including saying which product you would decide is the most popular.

(Choose for yourself the methods you will use. There are no definite correct answers although some answers may be more acceptable than others.)

1.

Product	Person				
	A	B	C	D	E
P	2	1	2	4	3
Q	1	2	4	1	4
R	4	3	1	2	1
S	3	4	3	3	2

2.

Product	Person				
	A	B	C	D	E
P	1	3	3	3	3
Q	3	1	1	2	2
R	2	2	2	1	1

3.

Product	Person					
	A	B	C	D	E	F
P	1	4	3	4	3	4
Q	2	3	1	3	1	2
R	3	1	4	1	4	3
S	4	2	2	2	2	1

4.

Product	Person				
	A	B	C	D	E
P	2	1		3	3
Q			3		1
R				1	2
S	1	2	1		
T	3	3	2	2	

(People only asked for 1st 3 preferences.)

5.

Product	Person							
	A	B	C	D	E	F	G	H
P	1	2		1			1	4
Q	2	4		3		2		
R		3	2	4	1		2	1
S			4	2	3	3		
T	4	1	3		2	4	4	3
U	3		1		4	1	3	2

(People only asked for 1st 4 preferences.)

Here are the results of some (fictitious) surveys in which people were given a list of activities they could take part in, and they were asked to give their 1st 3 choices for what they wanted to do. Here are the results.

If these were surveys that you had carried out, analyse the results and write down your conclusions, including saying which one of the activities you would choose as being the one most people wanted to do.

6.

Activity	Number putting it		
	1st	2nd	3rd
P	5	7	2
Q	2	8	6
R	7	3	8
S	3	1	4
T	8	6	5

7.

Activity	Number putting it		
	1st	2nd	3rd
P	8	6	7
Q	5	6	11
R	10	8	7
S	7	10	5

8.

Activity	Number putting it		
	1st	2nd	3rd
P	8	9	7
Q	9	10	8
R	7	10	12
S	4	6	5
T	11	8	8
U	11	7	10

9.

Activity	Number putting it		
	1st	2nd	3rd
P	6	5	9
Q	7	8	5
R	7	7	6

10.

Activity	Number putting it		
	1st	2nd	3rd
P	9	10	6
Q	8	8	10
R	9	9	7
S	5	5	10
T	9	8	7

To carry out a statistical investigation

1.   Decide what you are trying to find out. This is the **aim** of the investigation, and you should write it down first of all.
In this chapter, you are going to do an investigation where people put a list of products, activities, etc. in order of preference. You could have a hypothesis that a particular one of the choices is the preferred one.

2.   Decide who you are going to ask for their opinions. It may be members of your class or other people in your school.
For some surveys you may want to ask adults, and you may choose to ask parents and friends. If you are planning to stop and ask people in the street, you should be working with friends, not alone, and your teacher should be supervising you.

3.   Design a questionnaire to provide the information you need.

Designing a questionnaire

Remember to keep the questions short,
                    keep the questions clear.
Remember not to ask questions which people may not be willing to answer,
                    not to ask questions worded unfairly.

It is a good idea to try out your questionnaire on a few people first to see if it is clear enough and likely to give you the data you need, or whether it needs improving.

4.   When you have designed your questionnaire, you have to decide whether you are going to give it to people to fill in themselves or whether you are going to ask the questions and write down the answers. Since you are asking people to put items in order of preference it may be easier for them if they have the list to fill in themselves.

5.   Having collected sufficient data, you can analyse it and make a summary of your conclusions. You may want to illustrate your results with statistical diagrams.

Here is the questionnaire which Sam and Sally used when asking their friends about soft drinks, as in the example on page 76.

Questionnaire to find the most popular soft drink

Please tick

Boy	
Girl	

Age in years

10	
11	
12	
13	

Do you usually buy soft drinks from the local shop ?

Yes	
No	

If 'Yes', in a typical week, how many would you buy ?

1–5	6–10	10–15	more than 15

Here are the five kinds of drinks sold at the shop.
Please decide on your order of preference for these drinks.

Poppo	
Quencho	
Ribbo	
Squasho	
Tisso	

Write 1 opposite your 1st choice,

2 opposite your 2nd choice,

3 opposite your 3rd choice,

4 opposite your 4th choice,

5 opposite your 5th choice.

For your 1st choice, say briefly why you like it.

— — — — — — — — — — — — — — — — —

Thank you for answering this questionnaire.

Exercise 5.2 Applications and Activities

1. Imagine you are planning a day's outing
    for a group of about ten friends. The
    possible places you can choose are the
    seaside, an amusement park, a boat trip on
    the river, a zoo or a slide-splash pool.
    (You can substitute your own ideas for
    some of these if you want to.)
    Your hypothesis would be that most
    people would prefer to go to a particular
    one of these places.
    Design a suitable questionnaire, which
    asks your friends to fill in their choices in
    order of preference. Get your friends to
    answer the questionnaire. Analyse the
    results and state your conclusions.

    Maybe you can continue the planning and, with adult help, arrange an interesting
    day out for all of you, to take place during the summer holidays.

2. There are many ideas for surveys you can do with your friends. One simple idea is
    to find about 8 or 10 cartoons from magazines or newspapers. Cut them out and
    stick them on cards and label them P, Q, R, . . .
    Then ask your friends, one by one, to put them in order of preference, or just to
    choose their 1st 3 preferences. When all your friends have given you their
    answers, analyse the results and say which is the best cartoon.
    You can do similar surveys using pictures of fashions, cars, TV personalities, pop
    groups, etc.
    You can just produce a list, without pictures, if you are asking about people's
    favourite TV series, favourite sport, favourite food, etc.
    Decide on a survey about something which interests you. Plan it and carry it out.
    Analyse the results and state your conclusions.

3.   In the Eurovision Song Content, each country puts the best 10 songs in order.
     Here, 12 points are given for 1st choice, 10 for 2nd choice, then 8, 7, 6, 5, 4, 3,
     2, 1 for choices 3rd to 10th.
     It might make a difference, if the results are very close, if the marks given were
     10, 9, 8, 7, 6, 5, 4, 3, 2, 1.
     Perhaps if you can obtain the scores for the next contest you can see if this is so.

     You can organise a contest for yourself and your friends on similar lines, with
     several judges, where you have to make your own judgements of the performers.
     For example, you could have a skateboard contest, a display of gymnastics, or of
     disco-dancing.
     Say how you are going to decide who is the winner. Then hold the competition.

PUZZLES

28.   There are 5 sacks.
      A and B together weigh 12 kg,
      B and C weigh $13\frac{1}{2}$ kg,
      C and D weigh $11\frac{1}{2}$ kg,
      D and E weigh 8 kg,
      A, C and E weigh 16 kg.
      What does each sack weigh ?

29.   There were 45 people on a coach trip. At one stop, the tourists could visit a castle, at a
      cost of £1 for adults and 75p for children.
      Two-thirds of the adults and eight-ninths of the children visited the castle. What was the
      total paid in admission fees ?

30.   The Squire needed his lawn cut for a big party he was having that evening, and it was a
      very big lawn. He sent for three men from the village. The first man said it would take
      him 6 hours to cut the whole lawn, the second man said he could do it in 4 hours, and
      the third man said he could do it in 3 hours.
      Time was getting short, so the Square decided to employ all three men.
      How long would the job take, if all three men worked together ?

31.   Can you decode this calculation, where each letter stands for a different figure ?

```
              A Y U
        ×         A
        ─────────────
          B A B Y
        +       U D
        ─────────────
          B A N D
        -       C E
        ─────────────
      U ) B U L B
        ─────────────
            N B D
```

Miscellaneous Section A

Aural Practice

Often in life you will need to do quick calculations without using pencil and paper or calculator. Sometimes you will **see** the numbers written down, and sometimes you will just **hear** the questions. These aural exercises will give you some practice in **listening** to questions.

These aural exercises, A1 and A2, should be read to you, probably by your teacher or a friend, and you should write down the answers only, doing any working out in your head. You should do the 15 questions within 10 minutes.

Exercise A1

1. A fisherman caught 8 fish, 30 fish and 10 fish on three occasions. What was his average catch ?

2. How many axes of symmetry has an equilateral triangle ?

3. A man earns £7.50 an hour. How much would he earn in a day when he worked for 8 hours ?

4. If $\frac{1}{4}x = -6$, what is the value of x ?

5. A woman bought a vase for £15 and then sold it, making a profit of 20%. How much did she sell it for ?

6. Two angles of a quadrilateral are 60° and 140°. The other two angles are equal. What is the size of one of these angles ?

7. Paula arrives at the station at 5.37 pm. How many minutes should she have to wait until the train due at 6 pm arrives ?

8. Two similar cones have heights 9 cm and 15 cm. The radius of the smaller cone is 6 cm. What is the radius of the larger one ?

9. Two men share £40 in the ratio 5 : 3. What is the smaller share ?

10. What is the fraction which is exactly half-way between $\frac{1}{4}$ and $\frac{3}{8}$?

11. The perimeter of a square is 36 cm. What is the length of one side ?

12. A car uses 24 litres of petrol for a journey of 200 miles.
How far will it go on 18 litres ?

13. A field is 351 metres long. What is this length, correct to 1 significant figure ?

14. If x is positive and x^2 is greater than 81, what can you say about x ?

15. How many cubes of edge 10 cm are there in a block 40 cm long, 30 cm wide and 20 cm high ?

Exercise A2

1. Keith bought a book which cost £2.65. How much change did he get from a £5 note ?

2. 65 sweets are shared equally by 7 children. How many sweets does each child get, and how many sweets are left over ?

3. In a right-angled triangle, if the sides next to the right angle have lengths 3 cm and 4 cm, how long is the hypotenuse ?

4. What is the area of a rectangular lawn which is 20 m long and 15 m wide ?

5. 2 litres of paraffin were mixed with 8 litres of oil. What percentage of the mixture is paraffin ?

6. The average age of 3 girls is 12 years. If 2 girls are aged 7 and 14 years, what is the age of the other girl ?

7. A rectangle has length 10 cm and breadth 8 cm. Another rectangle has length 8 cm and breadth 6 cm. Are the rectangles similar ?

8. What are the next 2 numbers in the sequence 10, 7, 4, 1 ?

9. Express the ratio 30 cm : 2 metres as a ratio in its simplest form.

10. What is the cost of five 24 pence stamps ?

11. If $3x + 8$ is greater than 8, what can you say about x ?

12. Louise spent $\frac{5}{6}$ of her money and then she had 40 pence left. How much had she at first ?

13. What word is used for the straight line from the centre of a circle to the circumference ?

14. 4 people share equally a bill for £23. How much does each one pay ?

15. There is enough food for 30 calves for 8 days. How long would it last if there were 20 calves ?

Exercise A3　Revision

1.　In a survey of trees in a park, one-third of the trees are ash, one-fifth are oak, one-sixth are beech and there are 63 other trees. How many trees are there altogether ?

2.　Write down the next 2 terms in each of these sequences.
   1　11, 8, 5, 2, . . .
   2　5, −1, $\frac{1}{5}$, −$\frac{1}{25}$, . . .
   3　−3.6, −2.8, −2.0, −1.2, . . .

3.　A cart wheel is 90 cm in diameter. How far has the cart travelled when the wheel has made 400 complete turns ?

4.   24 people went together to an exhibition. There were x adults, for whom the
      entrance fee was £8 each, and the rest were children who were charged
      £5 each.
      Find an expression for the total cost, and simplify it.
      If the total cost was £165, find how many adults and how many children there
      were.

5.   In this parallelogram, find the value of x.

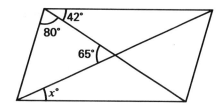

6.   If $xy = \frac{2}{3}$ and $x = \frac{20}{21}$, what is the value of y ?

7.   A straight line PQ, 45 cm long, is
      divided at R so that $PR : RQ = 5 : 4$.
      Find the length of PR.

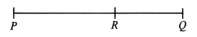

8.   Find
      1   the area of the triangular
              cross-section,
      2   the volume, of this prism.

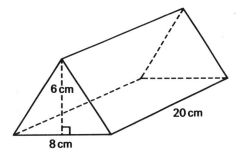

9.   Three lines have lengths $(x + 8)$ cm, $(2x - 5)$ cm and $(6x - 3)$ cm. What is the
      average length, in terms of x ?

10. Write down the next 2 lines of this pattern:

$$1^2 = 1$$
$$3^2 = 2 + 3 + 4$$
$$5^2 = 3 + 4 + 5 + 6 + 7$$

In the line beginning with 19^2,
1 how many terms will there be on the right-hand side,
2 what is the last term on the right-hand side ?

11. Solve these inequalities:
1 $\frac{1}{3}(2x + 1) > 4x - 3$
2 $x + 8 < \frac{1}{2}(4x + 3)$

3 $\dfrac{5x + 4}{2} < x - 1$

12. It is estimated that a team of 5 men can lay a pipeline in 18 days. To do the work in 10 days, how many extra men should be used ?

13. A car travels for $2\frac{1}{4}$ hours at an average speed of 60 km/h and then for $2\frac{3}{4}$ hours at an average speed of 80 km/h.
1 Find the total distance travelled.
2 Find the average speed for the whole journey.

14. Three cylinders are similar.
Cylinder A has radius 24 cm and height 40 cm.
Cylinder B has radius 36 cm. What is its height ?
Cylinder C has height 45 cm. What is its radius ?

15. Which region represents the points inside the triangle which are nearer to Q than to P and nearer to P than to R ?

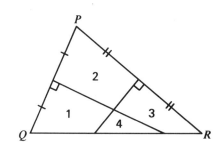

16. If $17x + 13y = 218$
    and $13x + 17y = 202$,
    find the values of
    1 $x + y$
    2 $x - y$
    3 x
    4 y

17. Which is a better buy, a 175 ml tube of cream costing £1.19 or a 225 ml tube costing £1.62 ?

18. *ABCD* is a square and *ABEFG* is a regular pentagon.
    What is the size of
    1 $\angle CBE$,
    2 $\angle BEC$?

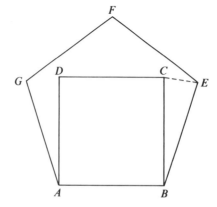

19. Tara wants to buy oranges at 18p each and grapefruits at 24p each. She has no more than £1.50 to spend. She must buy at least 2 oranges and 1 grapefruit, and her basket can hold no more than 7 fruits.
    1   Write down 4 inequalities to represent these statements, if Tara buys x oranges and y grapefruits.
    2   On graph paper draw x and y axes from 0 to 8 and draw the lines representing the boundaries of the inequalities.
    3   Identify the region on the graph where the inequalities are satisfied.
    4   If Tara decides to buy 3 oranges, what is the greatest number of grapefruits she can buy ?

20.   In a survey of 100 houses, here are the numbers of persons per house.

Persons per house	1	2	3	4	5	6	7
Number of houses	6	25	23	19	16	8	3

   1   Find the mean number of persons per house.
   2   Find the median number of persons per house.
   3   Draw a bar-line graph of the distribution.

Exercise A4   Activities

1.   **An illustrated mathematical dictionary**

   You should know many mathematical words by now. Think of words connected
   with arithmetic, algebra, geometry, statistics, probability (and possibly
   trigonometry). There are also names of famous mathematicians.
   Reduce your list to about 100 interesting words, and for each one write a
   definition, or a description about it.
   You can add further details if you want to. For many of the words you can think
   of an illustration such as a diagram or a picture which could go with the writing.

   When you have collected your ideas, put the words in alphabetical order, and
   then make your dictionary.

   Use paper smaller than A4 size, if possible. On some pages there may be only one
   or two words. Use bright colours in your illustrations (unless you intend to make
   photocopies).
   Number your pages and put a complete list of the words at the front of the book,
   with their page numbers.
   Design a suitable cover for the book.

   If everyone in the class did this activity, then you could have the dictionaries on
   display.

2. **Savings**

If you get pocket money or if you earn money from a part-time job such as a paper round, you probably wish to save some of it, rather than spending it all as soon as you get it.

Sometimes you want your savings to be safely invested so that you are not tempted to spend the money. Sometimes you may be saving up to buy something special. Sometimes you may want to keep some money at home, in case you need it quickly.

Old money boxes

Do you think it is a good idea to save some of your money ?

For what purposes would you save some money ?

Find out about, and make a list of, different places in which money can be saved, such as Banks. Consider the advantages and disadvantages of each. Decide which place would be best for your money.

When you invest money in a savings account, it will often gain interest. If you are not a tax-payer, then you can get the whole of the interest without paying any tax on it. Find the rates of interest paid in various accounts, and see which pays the most interest.

Although you may feel that you never have enough money to save any at present, if you get into the habit of saving, then when you have more money you can save more.

When you start working for a proper wage, suppose that you decide that you can save £10 per week (or another amount of your choice). How much will this amount to in 5 years' time ? You can estimate the interest that the invested money will earn, and include that in your total.

3. **Checking calculations**

A calculator can only give the correct answer if you press the right keys. Mistakes can happen, so it is wise to check that an answer seems reasonable.

Each year, in examinations, examiners point out that some very unreasonable answers are given.
e.g. The car park fee for 2 hours parking is £380. (What do you think the correct answer could have been ?)
The length of the man's stride is 1 cm.
The speed of the boat is 0.000075 mph.
The speed of the boat is 1754.386 mph.

Your teacher can probably give you further examples of answers which are probably incorrect, but which were written down without checking.

You can make a rough check of your calculations by using approximations.

Examples

1   $\dfrac{0.036 \times 0.225}{0.00375}$ is approximately $\dfrac{0.04 \times 0.2}{0.004}$

$= \dfrac{0.008}{0.004} = \dfrac{8}{4} = 2$

(The exact answer is 2.16)

2   $4 \times \pi \times 6.72^2$ is approximately $4 \times 3 \times 7^2$
$\approx 4 \times 3 \times 50 = 600$

(The exact answer is 567, to 3 sig. figs.)

By using approximate values, estimate answers for these calculations. Then you can find the correct answers, using your calculator.

1   3.95×7.01

2   $38.63 \div 12.7$

3   0.073^2

4   $0.0055 \div 0.031$

5   $\sqrt{119.9}$

6   21.3^3

7   $1783 \times 0.18 \ - \ 492 \times 0.79$

8   $\dfrac{0.085 \times 0.0042}{11.9}$

9   $5.3 \times 11.9 \ + \ 8.7 \times 18.1$

10 $2 \times \pi \times 15.2 \times 29.6$

Make rough estimates of the answers to these questions by using approximate values. Then find the correct answers, using your calculator.

11 Find the total cost of 9 bars of chocolate at 54p each and 24 bags of crisps at 16p each.

12 How many 18p stamps can be bought for £10 ?

13 Find the volume of air in a room 5.3 m long, 4.2 m wide and 2.8 m high.

14 How much change will I get from £100 if I buy 12 T-shirts at £6.99 each ?

15 If the rate of exchange is 9.52 francs to £1, how much French money can I get for £280 ?

16 If a car travels approximately $7\frac{1}{2}$ miles on 1 litre of petrol, how many litres will be needed for a journey of 240 miles, and what will be the cost of fuel, at 52p per litre ?

17 I have a 3-hour video tape and I want to record a serial programme which runs each Monday evening from 6.55 pm to 7.30 pm. How many episodes will fit on the tape ?

18 If the diameter of a circular enclosure is 78 m, what is the perimeter, and what is the area, of the enclosure ?

19 If there are 18 forms in a school with an average of 32 pupils in each form, how many pupils are there in the school ?

20 If a man earns £18 750 per year and his wife earns £16 200 per year, how much total income per week do they have ?

4. Decreasing unit fractions

On graph paper, label the x and y axes from 0 to 1, taking 1 cm to represent 0.1 unit on both axes.

Write down a sequence of unit fractions 1, $\frac{1}{2}$, $\frac{1}{3}$, $\frac{1}{4}$, $\frac{1}{5}$.

Join (1, 0) to (0, $\frac{1}{5}$) with a straight line.

Join ($\frac{1}{2}$, 0) to (0, $\frac{1}{4}$) with a straight line.

Join ($\frac{1}{3}$, 0) to (0, $\frac{1}{3}$) with a straight line.

Join ($\frac{1}{4}$, 0) to (0, $\frac{1}{2}$) with a straight line.

Join ($\frac{1}{5}$, 0) to (0, 1) with a straight line.

What do you notice ?

Repeat this with more fractions. If you use fractions up to $\frac{1}{9}$, then you begin by joining (1, 0) to (0, $\frac{1}{9}$); then ($\frac{1}{2}$, 0) to (0, $\frac{1}{8}$), and so on.

5. **Palindromic numbers**

A number is palindromic if when the digits of the number are written in reverse order the number remains unchanged. For example, 66, 171, 353 and 1441 are palindromic numbers.

In this activity you are going to investigate palindromic numbers.

Take a 2-digit number, for example, 39.
Reversing the digits of 39 gives 93.
Add 39 and 93.

```
      3 9
  +   9 3
     ─────
    1 3 2        (This is not a palindromic number, so repeat the process.
  + 2 3 1         Reverse the digits and add.)
    ─────
    3 6 3
```

The answer is a palindromic number.

Starting with the number 39, we had to reverse the digits and add twice, before we obtained a palindromic number.

Write down all the 2-figure numbers which are palindromic.

Find which 2-figure numbers are palindromic after one stage of reversing and adding.

For other 2-figure numbers find out how many times you have to repeat the process.
(If for a particular number the process seems to go on for ever, you may have to abandon your investigation of that number when it gets very big.)

When a 2-figure number has finally turned into a palindromic number, can you notice something which all these palindromic numbers have in common ?

You can also investigate 3-figure or larger numbers.

Mathematicians are investigating this problem, to see if all numbers produce palindromic numbers eventually. Using computers, larger numbers can be investigated, and very few numbers below 10 000 have not turned into palindromic numbers within 100 stages.

6. **To generate random numbers on your calculator**

Here is a method which will give you
a sequence of numbers which should
appear to be random.

On your calculator, enter any number
between 0 and 1 using all the figures
on the display.
*Multiply the number by 147.
Write down the first 4 figures after the
decimal point as your 4 random
numbers.
Subtract the whole number part from
the number on your calculator, leaving
the decimal part.
Repeat from *

e.g. Starting with 0.564428091,
Multiplying by 147 gives 82.97092938
The first 4 random numbers are 9, 7, 0, 9.
Subtract 82 then multiply by 147, getting 142.7266184
The next 4 random numbers are 7, 2, 6, 6.
Subtract 142 then multiply by 147, getting 106.8129077
The next 4 random numbers are 8, 1, 2, 9.
And so on.

If you need random numbers from 1 to 10, take the numbers singly, using
0 as 10.
If you need random numbers from 1 to 100, take the numbers in pairs,
e.g. 97, 9, 72, 66, 81, 29. Use 00 as 100.
If you go wrong with the process, just begin again with another random decimal.

When you have got 100 or more numbers, you can check whether they are really
random.
Count how many 0's, 1's, 2's, etc. there are, and show the frequencies on a
bar-line graph, and comment about them.
You can also check the balance of even and odd numbers, numbers from 0 to 4
and from 5 to 9, and so on.
You can investigate 'runs' of odd numbers, i.e. how many odd numbers come
together, and show the results on a bar-line graph. You can calculate the
probabilities of runs of 1 odd number, 2 odd numbers, 3 odd numbers, etc. and
compare your results with the theoretical probabilities.

You can find many other uses for your random numbers.

7. A regular pentagon

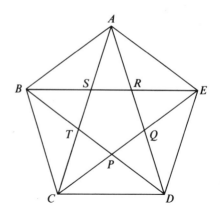

The diagram shows a regular pentagon
ABCDE with all its diagonals drawn.

1 Name a figure similar to *ABCDE*.

2 Copy the diagram and calculate the
sizes of all the angles, marking them
on your diagram.

3 Name a triangle similar to Δ*ABC*.

4 Name 2 triangles, of different sizes, similar to Δ*ACD*.

5 The second diagram shows part of
the first diagram.
We have let the side *SR* be 1 unit,
and the sides *AS* and *AR* be *x* units.
What is the length of *BS* ?

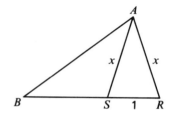

6 Explain why Δ*ARS* is similar to
Δ*BAR*, and then copy and complete
the ratio $\dfrac{AS}{..} = \dfrac{RS}{..}$

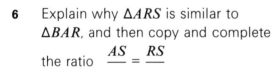

7 Hence, write down an equation involving *x*. Rearrange this equation into a
quadratic equation and solve it, using trial methods, to find the value of *x*
correct to 2 decimal places.
Do you recognise the value of the ratio *x* : 1 ?

8 If the pentagon was cut out and the line *ER* was cut, Δ*ARE* could be folded
over along the line *AR*. Where would the line *AE* then lie ? Where would
the point *E* lie ?

9 The pentagon can be used to make stars for Christmas decorations. The
craft paper which is shiny on one side and white on the other is very
suitable to use.
Draw an accurate pattern of the pentagon of a suitable size and then
transfer your pattern to the shiny paper by pricking through the points
A, B, C, D, E. On the white side, join all the lines.
Cut along the lines *AS, BT, CP, DQ, ER*.
Fold Δ*ARE* along *AR*, then Δ*BSA* along *BS*, Δ*CTB* along *CT*, Δ*DPC*
along *DP*, and finally Δ*EQD* along *EQ*, tucking its point in under the other
pieces.

(There will be a small white pentagon left uncovered in the centre of the star. You will have a spare piece of shiny paper which you can slip into this space.)

Put some cotton thread through a point of the star and hang it up. Make more stars, using other colours or other sizes, and hang them at slightly different heights.

8. **Rotating rings of tetrahedra**

Here is a little model which is not difficult to make. The net consists of equilateral triangles. If you have isometric paper then copy the net on that. If not, begin by drawing the long centre line and find the points on either side by using compasses. Triangles with edge 3 cm or 4 cm are suitable.

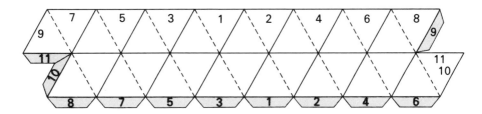

Transfer the net to cardboard by pricking through the points.
Number faintly the edges without tabs so that you will know where to stick the tabs.

Score all the lines, including the edges with tabs on, scoring the dotted lines on the other side of the cardboard. Cut out the net.
Crease all scored lines, bending them away from the side they were scored on. (Do not bend them backwards and forwards. This is important, so that you can fold the net properly.)

When you have creased all the lines properly, you should be able to bring tab 1 to meet the opposite edge at the line marked 1, and it will make a tetrahedron. Glue the tab and wait until it dries. Now do the same with tabs 2 to 7, in that order. Finally glue tabs 8, 9, 10 and 11.

Your ring of tetrahedra will rotate if you turn it gently.
Paint it so that different colours appear in turn.

This pattern has 8 tetrahedra. To make a pattern using 10 tetrahedra put 2 extra strips in the pattern, i.e. repeat the strips with tabs and edges 4 and 6 on. You can make rings with more tetrahedra in a similar way, or by taking 2 strips out you can make a ring with 6 tetrahedra, but this will not rotate.

9. **Introduction to Trigonometry**

Draw several right-angled triangles
with $\angle A = 20°$, and AB of different
lengths such as 4 cm, 5 cm, 8 cm,
10 cm, 12 cm. On large paper you can
make AB larger still.
Measure BC in each triangle and find

the ratio $\dfrac{BC}{AB}$ as a decimal, to 2 decimal

places.
Set down the results in a table.

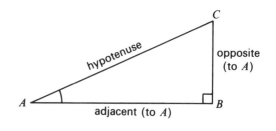

Angle $A = 20°$			
side BC	side AB	$\dfrac{BC}{AB}$ as a fraction	$\dfrac{BC}{AB}$ as a decimal
. . .	4 cm 5 cm . . .	. . .	. . .

What do you notice ? If the results in the 4th column are nearly the same, find the
average of these results, and call this number 'tan 20°'. If the results are quite
different, perhaps you should check your work again.

In relation to $\angle A$, side BC is the opposite side. AB is the side which is next to
$\angle A$, but is not the hypotenuse, and we call that the adjacent side (to $\angle A$). You

have found the value of $\dfrac{\text{opposite side}}{\text{adjacent side}}$. This ratio is referred to as the **tangent** of

$\angle A$, tan A for short.
So tan 20° = 0.364 means that if the right-angled triangle has an angle of 20°

and you find $\dfrac{\text{opposite side}}{\text{adjacent side}}$ you will always get 0.364, whatever size the triangle is.

Since this ratio is always the same, it can be printed in a book of tables, in the
table headed 'tangents', and it is stored in your calculator under the key $\boxed{\text{tan}}$.

Make sure your calculator is set to work in degrees then press 20 $\boxed{\text{tan}}$ and it will
show 0.36397... which is a more accurate value.

You will get different ratios if you change the angle A from 20° to other sizes.

Repeat your work with different triangles with $\angle A = 30°$, and then with $\angle A = 40°, 50°, 60°$ or other values. Set down the results in a table.

angle	tangent of angle
20°	0.36
30°	
40°	
. . .	

What do you notice about the value for tangent as the angle gets larger ?

You will use the tangent ratio in Chapter 7. Keep your results, to check them then.

10. **Examination marks**

This is a fictitious example, and for simplicity a class of 5 children, with exam marks in just 4 subjects, has been used.

The marks in the end-of-term exams are shown here. The form teacher should find out the average mark for each child and then write their names in order of merit.

Do this for him, copying and completing the total and average columns, and give the order of merit for the class.

	English	French	Maths	Science	Total	Average
Ali	78	35	67	30		
Babs	55	40	75	35		
Chris	40	25	90	85		
Dan	54	34	65	96		
Eve	75	80	66	10		

Class order

1st	
2nd	
3rd	
4th	
5th	

The form teacher had lost his calculator and didn't want to add up big numbers or divide by 4, so he thought he would simplify the work by placing the class in order of merit in each subject.

Here is a new table.

Orders of merit

	English	French	Maths	Science	Total of orders
Ali	1				
Babs	3				
Chris	5				
Dan	4				
Eve	2				

Copy the new table and fill in the orders of merit for French, Maths and Science. Add up the 4 numbers for each child to get the total of the orders of merit. Then use this column to make the class order that the form teacher would have got. Can you comment on the results ?

Who do you think ought to be called 'top of the class' ?

Class order

1st	
2nd	
3rd	
4th	
5th	

(In an important examination, marks can be standardized so that unfair results are avoided.)

11. Using a computer

By now, you will have had experience of using computers for various purposes, not only in Mathematics, and you will have a good idea of the use you can make of them.

For some purposes there are commercial packages available and you may have some of these. In other cases, if you are interested in programming, you can often produce a simple program to use.

You can use suitable programs to help you in maths investigations. Some ideas which link with the chapters of this book are:

Substituting numbers into formulae, including negative numbers.
Drawing straight-line graphs and regions on graphs.
Collecting and classifying the data in a statistical investigation or experiment, and analysing it.
You can use the computer to draw statistical diagrams, such as histograms and pie charts, and to work out averages.

In later chapters you can also use computer programs to help with:

Trigonometry calculations, and graphs of trigonometrical functions.
Simulations for investigating probabilities.
Graphs of quadratic functions, and other functions. You can draw several graphs on the screen and notice the differences when changes are made to the functions, e.g. the graphs of $y = x^2$, $y = x^2 + 3$, $y = x^2 - 5$, etc.
Drawing cumulative frequency graphs.
Plotting vectors.

You can think of other ideas for yourself. Do make use of a computer whenever possible.

PUZZLES

32. In this right-angled triangle, the area and the perimeter have the same numerical value. (The area is 30 square units and the perimeter is 30 units.)
Can you find another right-angled triangle, whose sides are whole numbers of units, with the same property ?

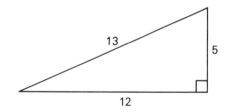

33. The postman has 4 letters to deliver, one for each of 4 flats.
If the flats are new, and not numbered, and the postman delivers one letter to each flat at random, what is the probability that
1 at least one letter has gone to the wrong flat,
2 every letter has gone to a wrong flat ?

34. A carpenter was asked to provide two wooden cubes. The edges were to be an exact number of centimetres, those of the larger cube being 8 cm longer than those of the smaller. Also the volume of the larger cube was to be 8 times that of the smaller one. What are the sizes of the cubes ?

6 Thinking about using algebra

Algebra is sometimes called 'generalized arithmetic'. Instead of using particular numbers we use letters which can represent any numbers.
The rules of algebra are very exact and logical, and easy to learn.
For example, $a + a = 2a$, and $a \times a = a^2$.

Using formulae

When we have to repeat the same kind of calculation many times, it is useful to have a formula into which we can just substitute numbers.

The distance of the horizon

This can be calculated mathematically. If the height of the eye-level of the observer is h feet, and the distance of the horizon is d miles, then

the formula is $d = \sqrt{\dfrac{3h}{2}}$.

For small heights an approximate formula, which

also allows for refraction, is $d = \dfrac{4}{3} \sqrt{h}$.

Use both formulae to find the distance of the horizon for a spectator whose eye-level is at a height of 5 feet.

Transformation of formulae

A formula can be rearranged, so that it is written in terms of any of its variables.
Here are some formulae relating to pumping water.
$H = 10.19\,P$ where H is the head of water in metres (the height of the storage tank above the pump),
and P is the pressure in bars. (1 bar = 100 000 Pa)
This formula can be rearranged to give

$P = \dfrac{H}{10.19}$, and this is approximately $P = 0.098\,H$.

The discharge from a nozzle has the formula

$L = \dfrac{2d^2}{3} \sqrt{P}$ where L is the discharge in litres/min, d is the nozzle diameter in mm, and P is the pressure in bars.

This formula can be rearranged to give

$P = \dfrac{9L^2}{4d^4}$

Removing brackets

If there are n teams in a league, then if they play each other twice (once at home and once away), then the total number of games is $n(n - 1)$.
This expression can be written as $n^2 - n$.

If the n teams play for a cup in a knock-out competition then, ignoring replays, the total number of matches to be played to find the winner is $n - 1$.

The number of extra matches to be played for a cup on a league basis rather than as a knock-out competition is
$n^2 - n - (n - 1) = n^2 - 2n + 1$.
You can show that this expression is equivalent to
$(n - 1)^2$.

Using factors

If a ball hits a floor with speed at right angles to the floor of v m/s and rebounds, then the speed of rebound is ev m/s.
e is a value between 0 and 1, depending on the elasticity of the ball, and it is called the coefficient of restitution.
The speed of the ball in the horizontal direction, u m/s, is unaltered if the ball and floor are smooth.

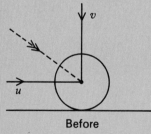

Before

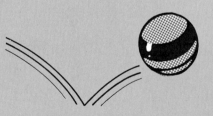

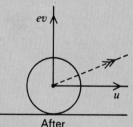

After

The fraction of energy lost on impact is $\dfrac{\frac{1}{2}mu^2 + \frac{1}{2}mv^2 - (\frac{1}{2}mu^2 + \frac{1}{2}me^2v^2)}{\frac{1}{2}mu^2 + \frac{1}{2}mv^2}$, where m is the mass of the ball, in grams.

This equals $\dfrac{\frac{1}{2}mv^2(1 - e^2)}{\frac{1}{2}m(u^2 + v^2)}$, which is $\dfrac{v^2(1 - e^2)}{u^2 + v^2}$.

Find the fraction of energy lost if $u = 8$, $v = 6$ and $e = 0.4$.

Using Algebra

Simple algebraic expressions

Addition and subtraction

Examples

$$2a + 5b + 4a - 5b = 6a$$
$$4c - 3d - 3c + 2d = c - d$$
$$5ef - 7ef = -2ef$$
$$3g^2 + g^2 = 4g^2$$
$$h^3 - h^3 = 0$$

Removing brackets (1)

A minus sign immediately in front of a bracket changes all the signs inside the bracket when the bracket is removed.

Examples

$$a - b + 2(2a - b) = a - b + 4a - 2b = 5a - 3b$$
$$3(2c + d) - 4(c + d) = 6c + 3d - 4c - 4d = 2c - d$$
$$4(e + 2f) + (e - f) = 4e + 8f + e - f = 5e + 7f$$
$$g(g + 1) - g(g - 1) = g^2 + g - g^2 + g = 2g$$
$$h(2h + 3) - 5(3h - 1) = 2h^2 + 3h - 15h + 5 = 2h^2 - 12h + 5$$

Removing brackets (2)

Examples

1 Remove the brackets from $(2x + 3)(x + 5)$
(This is sometimes called **expanding** the expression.)

You can find the answer by looking at
the rectangle, with length $2x + 3$ and
breadth $x + 5$.
The total area is $(2x + 3)(x + 5)$.
The areas of the 4 smaller rectangles give
$2x^2 + 10x + 3x + 15$, which simplifies to
$2x^2 + 13x + 15$.
So $(2x + 3)(x + 5) = 2x^2 + 13x + 15$.

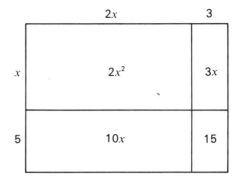

You can work this out without using the diagram in this way:

$(2x + 3)(x + 5)$ Multiply $2x$ by x. Answer $2x^2$. Write this down.

$(2x + 3)(x + 5)$ Multiply $+3$ by $+5$. Answer $+15$. Write this down leaving
a space for two more terms in front of it.

$(2x + 3)(x + 5)$ Multiply $2x$ by $+5$. Answer $+10x$.
Multiply $+3$ by x. Answer $+3x$. Write these down in
the space.

The answer so far is $2x^2 + 10x + 3x + 15$
$$= 2x^2 + 13x + 15$$

With practice you can leave out the step with separate terms $+10x$ and $+3x$ and
just write down the final answer.
We left space in the middle for the term in x because we are writing the terms in
descending order of powers, i.e. terms in x^2, then terms in x, then numbers.
Although $2x^2 + 15 + 13x$ is correct, we would not usually write the terms in that
order.

The same method can be used when the brackets contain minus signs, even though it
is not as easy to represent these on diagrams.

2   Remove the brackets from $(x + 7)(x - 9)$

$(x + 7)(x - 9)$ $x \times x = x^2$
                            $(+7) \times (-9) = -63$

$(x + 7)(x - 9)$ $x \times (-9) = -9x$
                            $(+7) \times x = 7x$

$(x + 7)(x - 9) = x^2 - 9x + 7x - 63$
$$= x^2 - 2x - 63$$

3   Remove the brackets from $(2x - 3)(x - 1)$

$$(2x - 3)(x - 1) = 2x^2 - 2x - 3x + 3$$
$$= 2x^2 - 5x + 3$$

4   Remove the brackets from $(2x + 5)^2$

$$(2x + 5)^2 = (2x + 5)(2x + 5)$$
$$= 4x^2 + 10x + 10x + 25$$
$$= 4x^2 + 20x + 25$$

5   Remove the brackets from $(3x + 4)(3x - 4)$

$$(3x + 4)(3x - 4) = 9x^2 - 12x + 12x - 16$$
$$= 9x^2 - 16$$

6   Remove the brackets from $(5 + 3x)(1 - 2x)$

$$(5 + 3x)(1 - 2x) = 5 - 10x + 3x - 6x^2$$
$$= 5 - 7x - 6x^2$$

(This is written with terms in ascending order of powers of x.)

7   Remove the brackets from $(2x + y)(5x - 2y)$

$$(2x + y)(5x - 2y) = 10x^2 - 4xy + 5xy - 2y^2$$
$$= 10x^2 + xy - 2y^2$$

Exercise 6.1

1.   Simplify these expressions.

1	$8a + a$		**6**	$6a + b + 2a - b$
2	$2b^2 + 3b^2$		**7**	$6cd - 6cd$
3	$13c - 12c$		**8**	$e - 3f + 3e - 5f$
4	$d^2 + d^2 + d^2$		**9**	$3g - 8g + 4g$
5	$7e - 4e - 3e$		**10**	$h^3 + h^3$

2.   Remove the brackets and simplify these expressions.

1    $2a(5a - 1) + a$ 6 $a(a + 1) + 3(2a + 1)$
2    $(2b + c) + (b - 2c)$ 7 $5(2b + 1) - b(b - 4)$
3    $(7d + 4e) - (2d - e)$ 8 $5c + 3d + 2 - c(4 - d)$
4    $2(5f - 6) + 3(2f + 1)$ 9 $2(3e - 5) - 3(e - 2)$
5    $3(g + 2h) + 2(2g - 3h)$ 10 $f(f^2 + 4) - f^2(f - 3)$

3.   Draw rectangles and use the areas of the whole rectangle and of separate parts to show that these statements are correct.

1    $(x + 4)(2x + 1) = 2x^2 + 9x + 4$
2    $(2x + y)(x + 2y) = 2x^2 + 5xy + 2y^2$
3    $(2x + 3)^2 = 4x^2 + 12x + 9$
4    $(x + 4y)^2 = x^2 + 8xy + 16y^2$
5    $(3x + 1)(x + 5) = 3x^2 + 16x + 5$

4.   Remove the brackets from the following expressions.

1    $(2x + 3)(x + 4)$ 6 $(x - 2)^2$
2    $(x + 2)(x - 1)$ 7 $(4x - 1)(x - 6)$
3    $(3x - 7)(x - 4)$ 8 $(x + 6)^2$
4    $(x + 5)(2x - 3)$ 9 $(2x - 3)(x + 2)$
5    $(x + 3)(x - 3)$ 10 $(1 + 3x)(1 + 4x)$

5.   Remove the brackets from the following expressions.

1    $(2x - 1)(2x + 5)$ 6 $(4x + 3)(2x + 7)$
2    $(x + 3)(2x + 3)$ 7 $(x + 8)(x - 2)$
3    $(2x + 1)(x - 5)$ 8 $(4x - 1)(2x + 3)$
4    $(x - 5)^2$ 9 $(3x - 7y)(4x - y)$
5    $(1 - 5x)(1 - 2x)$ 10 $(2x + 3y)(x - 4y)$

6.   Remove the brackets from the following expressions.

1    $(x + 4y)(x + 2y)$ 6 $(2a + 1)(2a + 5)$
2    $(x - 2y)(x + 3y)$ 7 $(1 + 2b)(5 - b)$
3    $(x + y)^2$ 8 $(4c - 3)(2c + 7)$
4    $(x + 6y)(2x - y)$ 9 $(d - 8e)(d + 2e)$
5    $(3x + 8y)(x - 5y)$ 10 $(f - 2g)^2$

Simple algebraic expressions

Multiplication

Examples

$3a \times a = 3a^2$
$bc \times 5d = 5bcd$
$4ef \times 3e = 12e^2f$
$5g^2 \times 2g^2 = 10g^4$

Division

Examples

$$14a^2 \div 2 = \frac{14a^2}{2} = 7a^2$$

$$15b^2 \div 5b = \frac{15b^2}{5b} = 3b$$

$$6c \div 9c = \frac{6c}{9c} = \tfrac{2}{3}$$

$$4 \div 8d = \frac{4}{8d} = \frac{1}{2d}$$

Common factors

Examples

1   Factorise $2xy + 6xz$

This is the opposite process to removing brackets.
The two terms $2xy$ and $6xz$ have a common factor 2 (they both divide exactly by 2),
and a common factor x.
$2xy$ divided by $2x$ leaves y
$6xz$ divided by $2x$ leaves $3z$
So $2xy + 6xz = 2x(y + 3z)$
This is the expression expressed in its factors.
It has factors 2, x and $y + 3z$.
You can check that you have the correct factors by multiplying out the bracket.

2   Factorise $x^2 - 3x$

Both terms have a common factor x
x^2 divided by x leaves x
$-3x$ divided by x leaves -3
So $x^2 - 3x = x(x - 3)$

3   Factorise $2x + 6x^2 - 18x^3$

You need a common factor of all three terms.
They all have a factor 2 and a factor x
$2x$ divided by $2x$ leaves 1
$6x^2$ divided by $2x$ leaves $3x$
$-18x^3$ divided by $2x$ leaves $-9x^2$
So $2x + 6x^2 - 18x^3 = 2x(1 + 3x - 9x^2)$

4   Factorise $6x^2y + 15xy^2$

Both terms have a factor 3, a factor x and a factor y
$6x^2y$ divided by $3xy$ leaves $2x$
$15xy^2$ divided by $3xy$ leaves $5y$
So $6x^2y + 15xy^2 = 3xy(2x + 5y)$

Normally you do not need to show the working. You can write down the expression and then the answer, finding the common factors and the remaining factor in your head.

Fractions

You can use the same methods that you have already learnt when using algebraic fractions.

Examples

Addition

$$\frac{a}{6} + \frac{a}{2} = \frac{a}{6} + \frac{3a}{6}$$

Bring to the same denominator, in this case, 6.

$$= \frac{\overset{2}{\cancel{4}a}}{\cancel{6}}$$
$$\underset{3}{}$$

$\dfrac{a}{6} + \dfrac{3a}{6}$ can be written as $\dfrac{a + 3a}{6}$

$$= \frac{2a}{3}$$

Subtraction

$$\frac{4b}{15} - \frac{b}{10} = \frac{8b - 3b}{30}$$

$$= \frac{\overset{}{5b}}{\underset{6}{30}}$$

$$= \frac{b}{6}$$

Multiplication

$$\frac{4c}{5d} \times \frac{7d}{6c^2} = \frac{\overset{2}{4c}}{5d} \times \frac{7d}{\underset{3c}{6c^2}} \qquad \text{Cancelling by 2, } c \text{ and } d.$$

$$= \frac{14}{15c}$$

Division

$$\frac{3ef^2}{8g} \div \frac{12f}{eg^2} = \frac{\overset{f}{3ef^2}}{8g} \times \frac{\overset{g}{eg^2}}{\underset{4}{12f}} \qquad \begin{array}{l}\text{Change to a multiplication question.}\\ \text{Then cancel by 3, } f \text{ and } g.\end{array}$$

$$= \frac{e^2fg}{32}$$

Equations with fractions

Examples

1 Solve the equation $\dfrac{2x}{5} + 3 = \dfrac{4x}{7}$

Multiply both sides by 35. This removes the fractions.

$$\left(\frac{2x}{\underset{}{5}} \times \overset{7}{35} = 14x, \quad \frac{4x}{\underset{}{7}} \times \overset{5}{35} = 20x \right)$$

So 14x + 105 = 20x Notice that 3 is also multiplied by 35.
Subtract 14x from both sides
           105 = 6x
Divide both sides by 6
           $x = 17\frac{1}{2}$

2 Solve the equation $\dfrac{x-4}{8} = \dfrac{3x+4}{16}$

Multiply both sides by 16

$$\left(\dfrac{x-4}{\overset{}{\underset{1}{8}}} \times \overset{2}{16} = 2(x-4)\right. \qquad \text{Notice that } x-4 \text{ is still in a bracket.}$$

$$\left.\dfrac{3x+4}{\underset{1}{16}} \times 16 = 3x+4\right)$$

So $2(x-4) = 3x+4$

$\qquad 2x - 8 = 3x + 4$

Subtract $2x$ from both sides

$\qquad -8 = x + 4$

Subtract 4 from both sides

$\qquad x = -12$

Powers and roots

If $x^2 = a$ (where a is a positive number)
Take the square root of both sides

$\qquad x = \sqrt{a}$

There is also a negative solution, $x = -\sqrt{a}$
The complete solution can be written $x = \pm\sqrt{a}$
This means x equals plus $\sqrt{a}$ or minus $\sqrt{a}$

Examples

1   If $x^2 = 25$

$\qquad x = \sqrt{25} = 5$ or $x = -\sqrt{25} = -5$

$\qquad x = \pm 5$

2   If $x^2 = 10$

$\qquad x = \sqrt{10}$ or $-\sqrt{10}$

$\qquad x = \pm 3.16$, correct to 2 dec pl.

If $x^3 = b$
Take the cube root of both sides

$\qquad x = \sqrt[3]{b}$

3   If $x^3 = 64$

      $x = \sqrt[3]{64} = 4$

(There is no negative solution.)

4   If $x^3 = 50$

      $x = \sqrt[3]{50}$

      $x = 3.68$, correct to 2 dec pl.

If $\sqrt{x} = c$

Square both sides

      $x = c^2$

5   If $\sqrt{x} = 7$

      $x = 49$

If $\sqrt[3]{x} = d$

Cube both sides

      $x = d^3$

6   If $\sqrt[3]{x} = 10$

      $x = 1000$

Exercise 6.2

1.   Simplify these expressions.

1	$5a^2 \times 4$	**5**	$4e^3 \div e$	**8**	$\dfrac{8k^2}{16k}$
2	$8b \times 7b$	**6**	$14fgh \div 7h$		
3	$27c^2 \div 3c$	**7**	$4j \times 3 \times j$	**9**	$(6m)^2$
4	$9d \times 5d^2$			**10**	$\dfrac{28p^2q}{7q}$

2.   Factorise these expressions.

1	$12 - 4a$	**5**	$3g^2 - 6gh$	**8**	$x + x^2$
2	$2b^2 - 9b$	**6**	$x^2 - 10x$	**9**	$9x^3 - 15x^2$
3	$5c^2 + 15d^2$	**7**	$14x + 35y$	**10**	$2\pi r + \pi r^2$
4	$7e + 28ef$				

3.   Factorise these expressions.

1 $a^2 + 4a$ **5** $e^2 - 16e$ **8** $7x^2 + 21xy$
2 $18b^2 - 9b$ **6** $9f^2 - 24f^3$ **9** $12y^2 - 15y$
3 $2c^2 + 8cd$ **7** $15g + 5$ **10** $2x^3 + x^2 + x$
4 $12 + 4d^2$

4.   Simplify these fractions.

1 $\dfrac{a}{2} + \dfrac{a}{3}$ **5** $\dfrac{11e}{14} - \dfrac{2e}{7}$ **8** $\dfrac{5h}{18} + \dfrac{2h}{9}$

2 $\dfrac{b}{2} + \dfrac{3b}{4}$ **6** $\dfrac{19}{24}f - \dfrac{3}{4}f$ **9** $\dfrac{2}{3}j + \dfrac{9}{10}j - \dfrac{6}{5}j$

3 $\tfrac{3}{4}c + \tfrac{1}{5}c$ **7** $\dfrac{7g}{12} - \dfrac{g}{3}$ **10** $\dfrac{7k}{18} + \dfrac{k}{3} - \dfrac{5k}{9}$

4 $\dfrac{3d}{4} - \dfrac{d}{8}$

5.   Simplify these fractions.

1 $\dfrac{3a}{5} \times \dfrac{5a}{6}$ **5** $\dfrac{3j^2}{k} \div 2jk$ **8** $\dfrac{r}{3s} \div \dfrac{4r}{s}$

2 $\dfrac{b^2}{c} \div \dfrac{1}{3}$ **6** $\dfrac{m^2}{3} \times \dfrac{12}{m^2}$ **9** $\dfrac{t^2}{3} \div \dfrac{2t^2}{9}$

3 $\dfrac{3de}{7} \times \dfrac{14d}{9e}$ **7** $\left(\dfrac{pq}{4}\right)^2$ **10** $\dfrac{6x^2}{2y} \times \dfrac{3y^2}{9x}$

4 $5fg \times 5gh \div 5fh$

6.   Solve these equations.

1 $\dfrac{x}{9} = \dfrac{2}{3}$ **4** $\dfrac{x}{4} - \dfrac{1}{4} = 1$

2 $\dfrac{4}{x} = 20$ **5** $\dfrac{9x + 2}{4} = 5$

3 $\dfrac{3x - 1}{5} = 4$

7. Solve these equations.

1 $11 - \dfrac{3}{4}x = 5$

2 $\frac{3}{4}x - \frac{2}{3}x = \frac{1}{8}$

3 $\dfrac{x}{2} - \dfrac{2x}{7} = 9$

4 $\dfrac{x - 8}{3} = \dfrac{x - 3}{2}$

5 $\dfrac{5x}{6} - \dfrac{1}{2} = \dfrac{3x}{4}$

8. Solve these equations. If the solutions are not exact, give them correct to 2 decimal places.

1 $x^2 = 81$

2 $x^3 = 64$

3 $x^2 = 1$

4 $x^2 = 1.21$

5 $x^3 = 100$

6 $x^2 = 40$

7 $\sqrt{x} = 5$

8 $\sqrt[3]{x} = 2$

9 $x^3 = 91.125$

10 $\sqrt[3]{x} = 1$

11 $\sqrt{x} = 1.2$

12 $x^2 = 0.5$

13 $\sqrt[3]{x} = 8$

14 $\sqrt{x} = 10$

15 $x^3 = 59.3$

Making formulae

Example

A closed box is l cm long, b cm wide and h cm high.
Find a formula for S, where S cm^2 is the total area of the surface.

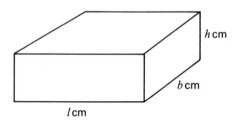

The box has 6 faces.
The area of the base and top are each lb cm^2
The area of the front and back are each lh cm^2
The area of the sides are each bh cm^2
The total area is $(2lb + 2lh + 2bh)$ cm^2
So $S = 2lb + 2lh + 2bh$

Transforming formulae

Examples

1 The formula for the area of a rectangle is $A = lb$. We can transform this formula to write it in terms of l, or b.

To write it in terms of l:
$$A = lb$$
Divide both sides of the equation by b

$$\frac{A}{b} = l$$

i.e. $l = \dfrac{A}{b}$

To write it in terms of b:
$$A = lb$$
Divide both sides of the equation by l

$$\frac{A}{l} = b$$

i.e. $b = \dfrac{A}{l}$

2 The general equation of a line drawn on a graph is $y = mx + c$.
Write this equation in terms of c.

$$y = mx + c$$
Subtract mx from both sides of the equation
$$y - mx = c$$
i.e. $c = y - mx$

Write the equation in terms of m.
$$y = mx + c$$
Subtract c from both sides of the equation
$$y - c = mx$$
Divide both sides of the equation by x

$$\frac{y - c}{x} = m$$

i.e. $m = \dfrac{y - c}{x} \quad \left(\text{or } \dfrac{y}{x} - \dfrac{c}{x} \right)$

Exercise 6.3

1. Find formulae for A, if the area of each figure is A cm^2, and all the marked lengths are in cm.

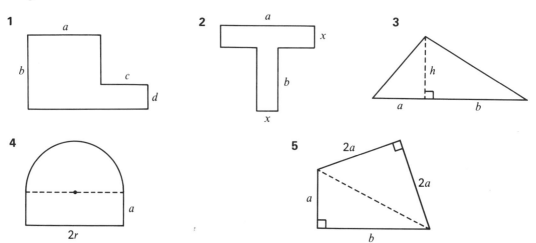

2. A formula for the area of a triangle is $A = \frac{1}{2}bh$. Write this formula in terms of h.

3. A formula for the circumference of a circle is $C = \pi d$. Write this formula in terms of d.

4. A formula for the equation of a line is $y = mx + c$. Write this formula in terms of x.

5. A formula for the average speed v in terms of distance s and time t is $v = \frac{s}{t}$. Write this formula in terms of t.

6. A formula for finding the mean is $\bar{x} = \frac{S}{n}$. Write this formula in terms of S.

7. A formula for speed when a particle has constant acceleration is $v = u + ft$. Write this formula in terms of **1** u **2** t.

8. A formula for density is $d = \frac{m}{v}$. Write this formula in terms of **1** m **2** v.

9. A formula for calculating the new price if there is a discount of 15% on the marked price is $P = \frac{17}{20}M$. Write this formula in terms of M.

10. A formula for calculating simple interest is $I = \frac{PRT}{100}$. Write this formula in terms of T.

Direct and Inverse Proportion

In Chapter 1, questions involving proportion were worked out using arithmetical methods. Quantities which are in proportion can be linked by equations.

Direct Variation

If y is directly proportional to x, i.e. y varies directly as x, then $y = kx$, where k is a positive constant number.
The word 'directly' need not be included as it is assumed that the variation is direct if the word 'inverse' is not included.

Example

1   If y is directly proportional to x and $y = 40$ when $x = 16$, find the value of y when $x = 20$.

$y = kx$
Substitute $y = 40$, $x = 16$
$40 = k \times 16$
$k = \frac{40}{16} = \frac{5}{2}$
The equation is $y = \frac{5}{2}x$
When $x = 20$, $y = \frac{5}{2} \times 20 = 50$

There are other relationships which can be expressed in a similar way.
e.g. y is proportional to x^2, has the equation $y = kx^2$.
y is proportional to the square root of x, has the equation $y = k\sqrt{x}$.

2   If y varies as x^3, and $y = 54$ when $x = 3$, find the value of y when $x = 5$.

$y = kx^3$
$54 = k \times 3^3$
$54 = k \times 27$
$k = 2$
The equation is $y = 2x^3$
When $x = 5$, $y = 2 \times 5^3 = 250$

Inverse Variation

If 2 quantities x, y are such that y is inversely proportional to x, i.e. y varies inversely as x, then $y = \dfrac{k}{x}$, where k is a constant.

3 If y varies inversely as x and $y = 20$ when $x = 4$, find the value of y when $x = 5$.

$$y = \frac{k}{x}$$

$$20 = \frac{k}{4}$$

$$k = 80$$

The equation is $y = \dfrac{80}{x}$

When $x = 5$, $y = \dfrac{80}{5} = 16$

There are other relationships which can be expressed in a similar way.

e.g. If y varies inversely as the square of x, then $y = \dfrac{k}{x^2}$.

This is called the **inverse square law**, and it has several practical applications.

4 If y is inversely proportional to the square of x, and $y = 3$ when $x = 4$, find the value of y when $x = 10$.

$$y = \frac{k}{x^2}$$

$$3 = \frac{k}{16}$$

$$k = 48$$

The equation is $y = \dfrac{48}{x^2}$

When $x = 10$, $y = \dfrac{48}{100} = 0.48$

Exercise 6.4

1. If y varies as x, and $y = 36$ when $x = 9$,
    1 write down a formula connecting x, y and k,
    2 find the value of k,
    3 find the value of y when $x = 15$,
    4 find the value of x when $y = 100$.

2. If y varies as the square of x, and $y = 75$ when $x = 5$,
    1   write down a formula connecting x, y and k,
    2   find the value of k,
    3   find the value of y when $x = 4$.

3. If y is inversely proportional to x, and $y = 15$ when $x = 6$,
    1   write down a formula connecting x, y and k,
    2   find the value of k,
    3   find the value of y when $x = 4$.

4. If y is directly proportional to the square root of x, and $y = 18$ when $x = 9$,
    1   write down a formula connecting x, y and k,
    2   find the value of k,
    3   find the value of y when $x = 49$.

5. If y is inversely proportional to the square of x, and $y = \frac{1}{2}$ when $x = 6$,
    1   write down a formula connecting x, y and k,
    2   find the value of k,
    3   find the value of y when $x = 2$.

6. **1**   If y varies as x, and $y = 5$ when $x = 6$, find the value of y when $x = 15$.
    2   If y varies as the square of x, and $y = 6$ when $x = 8$, find the value of y when $x = 12$.
    3   If y is directly proportional to the square root of x, and $y = 10$ when $x = 36$, find the value of y when $x = 16$.
    4   If y is inversely proportional to x, and $y = 8$ when $x = 9$, find the value of y when $x = 12$.
    5   If y is inversely proportional to the square of x, and $y = 5$ when $x = 3$, find the value of y when $x = 5$.

Exercise 6.5   Applications and Activities

1. The twins had 42 marbles between them. They divided these into two sorts, large ones and small ones. Derek took all the large ones and Frank took all the small ones.
    Frank said, '$\frac{8}{9}$ of the marbles I have is the same number as $\frac{2}{3}$ of the marbles you have.'
    If Frank had taken x marbles, how many had Derek got ?
    Write down an equation and solve it to find how many marbles each boy had.

2.   'Hau, its whole, its seventh, it makes 19.'
     (From an Egyptian papyrus of about 1500 BC.)
     This is an equation. Hau means the unknown, x.
     Thus $x + \frac{1}{7}x = 19$

     Solve the equation, giving the answer as a mixed number.

3.   A motorist travels b miles at an average speed of 20 mph, then $5b$ miles at
     60 mph and finally $3b$ miles at 40 mph.
     Find an expression for the total time taken.

4.   In the right-angled triangle ABC, AB is 2 cm longer than BC.
     1   Work out the brackets for $(x + 2)^2$.
     2   Write down an equation using
             Pythagoras' theorem, beginning $AB^2 =$
             Rewrite this equation in terms of x.
     3   Solve the equation to find x.
     4   State the lengths of BC and AB.

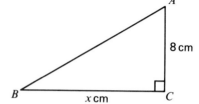

8 cm

5.   **1**   Factorise $x^2 + xy$.
     2   By substituting $x = 98$ and $y = 2$ in the factorised expression, find the
             value of $98^2 + 98 \times 2$, without using your calculator.

     Use factorising to help you to do these calculations without using a calculator.
     3 $63.5 \times 3.7 + 36.5 \times 3.7$
     4 $95 \times 26.2 - 53.3 \times 26.2 - 31.7 \times 26.2$
     5 $227^2 - 127 \times 227$

6.   Write down expressions for 5 consecutive numbers, of which the middle one
     is n.
     Prove that the sum of the squares of the 1st, 3rd and 5th of these numbers is
     $3n^2 + 8$.
     If this sum is 371, find the (positive) value of n.

7.   A, B, C are circles with radii 29 cm, 21 cm and r cm respectively.
     1   If perimeter of C = perimeter of A − perimeter of B, find the value of r.
     2   If area of C = area of A − area of B, find the value of r.
     (Do not substitute a value for π.)

8. The formula for the volume of a cone is $V = \frac{1}{3}\pi r^2 h$.
    1 Write this formula in terms of h. (Begin by multiplying both sides by 3.)
    2 Write the same formula in terms of r. (Find an expression for r^2 and then take the square root of both sides.)
    3 If $V = 565.2\,cm^3$ and $h = 15\,cm$, find the value of r, taking π as 3.14.

9. A cylinder with a base but no lid has a curved surface area of $2\pi rh$ cm² and a circular end of area πr^2 cm², when r and h are given in cm.
    1 Write an expression for the total area.
    2 Factorise this expression.
    3 Find the total surface area when the radius is 2 cm and the height is 1.5 cm, without using your calculator. Take π as 3.14.

10. In the rectangle, $AB = 5\,cm$,
    $BC = 2\,cm$.
    P is a point on DC, x cm from D.
    Express PC in terms of x.
    Use Pythagoras' theorem to find
    expressions for AP^2, PB^2 and
    $AP^2 + PB^2$, in terms of x.
    Simplify the last expression.
    If $\angle APB = 90°$, use $\triangle APB$ to write down an equation, and solve it, by trial, to find the possible values of x.
    State the two possible distances of P from D, if $\angle APB = 90°$.

11. **1** The volume of a fixed mass of gas kept at constant pressure is directly proportional to its absolute temperature. If the volume is 240 cm³ when the temperature is 280 K, what is the volume when the temperature is 700 K ? (The absolute temperature is measured on the Kelvin scale.)

    2 The weight of a solid metal sphere varies as the cube of its diameter. A sphere with diameter 12 cm weighs 8.64 kg. What is the weight of a sphere of diameter 10 cm, made with the same type of metal ?

    3 The electrical resistance of a wire of constant length varies inversely as the square of the diameter. If a wire of given length and diameter 2 mm has a resistance of 3.6 ohms, what is the resistance of a wire of the same length and material with a diameter of 3 mm ?

7 Thinking about trigonometry

What is trigonometry ?

It is a mathematical subject dealing with the relationships between the sides and angles of triangles.
(trigon . . . triangle; metron . . . measure)

Trigonometry grew out of the study of astronomy and was used by Hipparchus, who constructed the first trigonometrical tables, about 150 BC.

Three centuries later, Ptolemy wrote his great treatise, which was based on the writings of Hipparchus.

After that the ideas grew slowly, and the first purely trigonometrical textbook was written by a Persian in the 13th century. Gradually, the ideas reached Europe. Leonardo of Pisa (Fibonacci) used trigonometry in surveying in about 1220.

Modern tangent tables

A theodolite made in the late 18th century by Jesse Ramsden, the leading instrument maker of his day.
The theodolite was capable of measuring both horizontal and vertical angles to great accuracy.

A surveyor at work, using a theodolite.

Trigonometry can be used to calculate heights and distances.

The tangent ratio

$$\tan \theta = \frac{\text{opp}}{\text{adj}}$$

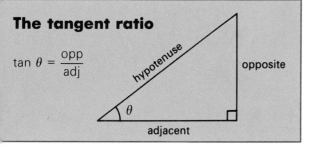

The Eiffel Tower

Distances from the Tower, which is 300 m high, can be calculated using the angles of depression. e.g. Buildings which are seen from the top of the Tower at an angle of depression of 40° are at a distance of (300 × tan 50°) metres from its foot. Find the value of this, using your calculator.

The height of the lighthouse can be calculated, using the angle of elevation at a known distance from the lighthouse.

he Eiffel Tower

A view from the Tower

7 Trigonometry (1)

Introduction

We are considering a right-angled
triangle.
In this diagram, the right angle is at **B**.
We are looking at one of the other
angles, in this case, $\angle A$.
Then the side **opposite** $\angle A$ is *BC*.
The side *AC* is the hypotenuse.

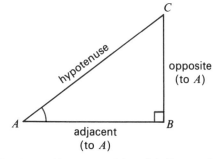

The other side next to $\angle A$ is *AB*, and we call this the **adjacent** side. ('Adjacent'
means 'next to'. When we talk of the adjacent side to an angle we mean the side next
to the angle which is not the hypotenuse.)

For any particular size of $\angle A$, if we measure the sides opposite (*CB*) and adjacent
(*AB*) and find the value of opposite ÷ adjacent, the result will always be the same.

e.g. If $\angle A = 28°$, then opposite ÷ adjacent = 0.532, to 3 decimal places.
You can check this by drawing your own diagram and measuring the sides. It does not
matter how big you make your triangle, since all such triangles will be similar.

The ratio $\dfrac{\text{opposite}}{\text{adjacent}}$ is called the **tangent** of $\angle A$, tan *A* for short.

So $\tan A = \dfrac{\text{opposite}}{\text{adjacent}}$

  $\tan 28° = 0.532$, to 3 dec pl.

All the values of tangents of different angles have been calculated, long ago. They are
published in tables.
Here is a list of tangents for angles every 5° from 0° to 85°, given to 3 decimal places.

angle	tangent	angle	tangent	angle	tangent
0°	0.000	30°	0.577	60°	1.732
5°	0.087	35°	0.700	65°	2.145
10°	0.176	40°	0.839	70°	2.747
15°	0.268	45°	1.000	75°	3.732
20°	0.364	50°	1.192	80°	5.671
25°	0.466	55°	1.428	85°	11.430

Nowadays, these values are stored in your scientific calculator.
For tan 28° press 28 [tan] and you will get 0.5317 . . .
(If you do not, perhaps your calculator is not working in degrees. Some calculators
also work in radians and grads, so you must always make sure it is in degree mode,
when using it for trigonometry. If it is not, press the [DRG] key until the display shows
DEG, then try again.)

tan θ is a **function** of θ.

(θ is the Greek letter theta and it is sometimes used for the size of an angle.)
As the angle changes, the value of tan θ changes.
From the table shown, describe how tan θ changes as θ increases from 0° to 85°.
What is tan 0° ? We cannot have a right-angled triangle with an angle of 0° but it is
useful to know this value.
What is tan 45° ? Can you explain how this value could have been calculated ?

The tangent ratio

$$\tan \theta = \frac{\text{opp}}{\text{adj}}$$

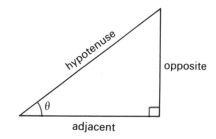

Using the tangent ratio to find the length of a side

Examples

1   To find AC

$$\tan B = \frac{\text{opp}}{\text{adj}}$$

$$\tan 28° = \frac{x}{8.3}$$

$$x = 8.3 \times \tan 28°$$

$$(= 8.3 \times 0.5317 \ldots)$$

$$= 4.413$$

$$AC = 4.4 \text{ cm, to the nearest mm.}$$

$$(AC = 4.41 \text{ cm, to 3 sig fig.})$$

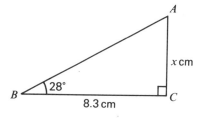

You will use your calculator to find 8.3 × tan 28°
Make sure that it is set to work in degrees.
Press 8.3 $\boxed{\times}$ 28 $\boxed{\text{tan}}$ $\boxed{=}$ and you will get 4.4131 . . .

For practical uses you would probably give the answer to the nearest mm.
However, to check that you have done a correct calculation your answer may be
wanted to 3 significant figures.

Make a rough check of the size of the answer. You can look at the shape of the
triangle, if you have a reasonable diagram.
In this triangle, since $\angle B$ is less than $\angle A$, it seems reasonable for AC to be smaller
than BC, and the answer seems acceptable.

2 To find AB

It is simpler to use the angle
opposite the side you are trying
to find, so the angle opposite
to AB is $\angle C$, and
$\angle C = 90° - 39° = 51°$

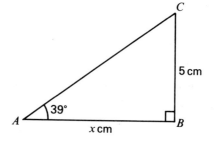

$$\tan C = \frac{\text{opp}}{\text{adj}}$$

$$\tan 51° = \frac{x}{5}$$

$$x = 5 \times \tan 51° \qquad \text{Press 5 } \boxed{\times} \text{ 51 } \boxed{\text{tan}}\,\boxed{=}$$

$$= 6.174$$

$AB = 6.2$ cm, to the nearest mm.
($AB = 6.17$ cm, to 3 sig fig.)

If you prefer to use $\angle A$, the working goes like this:

$$\tan A = \frac{\text{opp}}{\text{adj}}$$

$$\tan 39° = \frac{5}{x}$$

$$x = \frac{5}{\tan 39°} \qquad \text{Press 5 } \boxed{\div} \text{ 39 } \boxed{\text{tan}}\,\boxed{=}$$

$$= 6.174$$

$AB = 6.17$ cm, to 3 sig fig.

Finding the length of the hypotenuse

When you have found a second side you can use Pythagoras' theorem to find the hypotenuse. However, there are other trigonometrical ratios and they will be used in Chapter 11. So, in this chapter, we will use questions which do not involve the hypotenuse.

Using the tangent ratio to find an angle

Examples

3   To find $\angle A$

$$\tan A = \frac{\text{opp}}{\text{adj}}$$

$$= \frac{4}{7} \quad (= 0.5714 \ldots)$$

$\angle A = 29.7°$

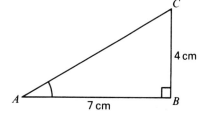

You will use your calculator to find the angle. The inverse function to tan is found by pressing $\boxed{F}$ then $\boxed{\tan}$. It is labelled $\tan^{-1}$, or maybe arctan.
We will call it inverse tan.

Press $4 \boxed{\div} 7 \boxed{=} \boxed{\text{inverse tan}}$ and you will get 29.74 . . .

It is usual to give angles in degrees correct to 1 decimal place so the answer is $\angle A = 29.7°$.

You can look at the shape of the triangle if you have a reasonable diagram, to make a rough check of the size of the answer.
Here, since CB is less than AB, $\angle A$ will be less than $\angle C$, so it will certainly be less than 45°. The answer seems acceptable.

If you also need to find the size of $\angle C$, there is no need to use the tangent ratio again.
$\angle C = 90° - \angle A = 90° - 29.7° = 60.3°$

4   To find $\angle C$

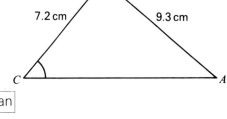

$$\tan C = \frac{\text{opp}}{\text{adj}}$$

$$= \frac{9.3}{7.2} \qquad \text{Press } 9.3 \boxed{\div} 7.2 \boxed{=} \boxed{\text{inverse tan}}$$

$\angle C = 52.3°$

(and $\angle A = 90° - \angle C = 90° - 52.3° = 37.7°$)

Exercise 7.1

1. Use your calculator to find the value of tan A, correct to 3 decimal places, if $\angle A$ equals
   1 12°   **2** 64°   **3** $37\frac{1}{2}°$ **4** 83°   **5** 6°

2. Use your calculator to find the size of $\angle B$, in degrees correct to 1 decimal place, if tan B equals
   1 2.4   **2** 0.623   **3** 3.871   **4** $\frac{10}{13}$ **5** $\frac{22}{9}$

3. Find the stated side in these right-angled triangles. Give the answers in cm, to 3 significant figures.

1

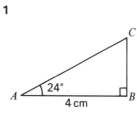

Find BC

2

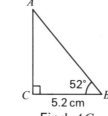

Find AC

3

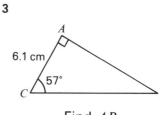

Find AB

4

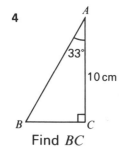

Find BC

5

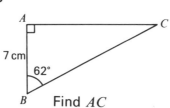

Find AC

6

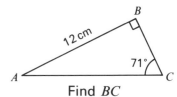

Find BC

7

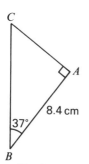

Find AC

8

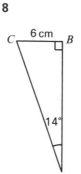

Find AB

9

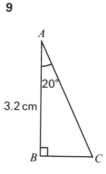

Find BC

10

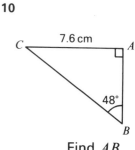

Find AB

4. Find the marked angle in these right-angled triangles, and then by subtraction find the 3rd angle of the triangle. Give the angles in degrees, correct to 1 decimal place.

1 **2** **3**

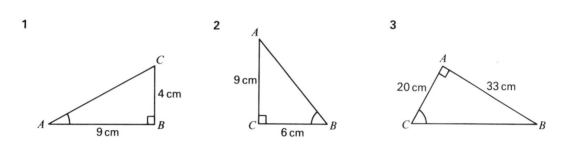

4 **5** **6**

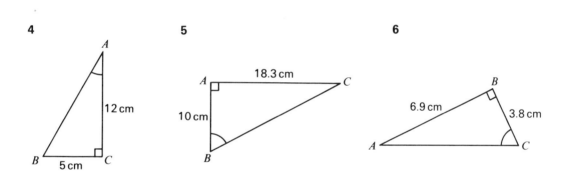

7 **8** **9** **10**

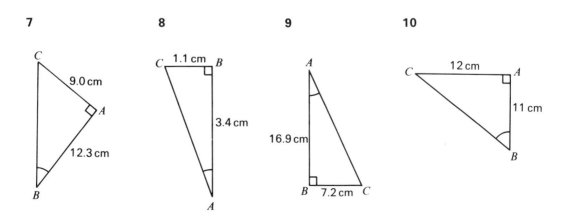

Angles of elevation and depression

Both of these angles are measured from the horizontal direction.

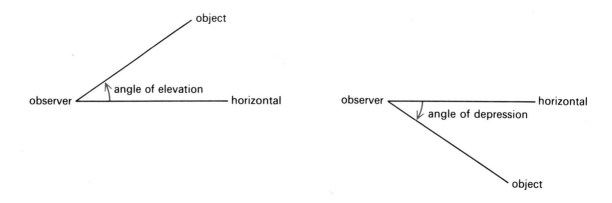

Examples

1   The top of an oak tree is at an angle of elevation of 15° when the observer is 130 m
from the foot of the tree. How tall is the tree ?

$\tan 15° = \dfrac{\text{opp}}{\text{adj}}$

$\tan 15° = \dfrac{h}{130}$

$h = 130 × \tan 15°$

$\quad = 34.8$

The tree is 34.8 m tall, or 35 m to the nearest metre.

2   A dinghy out at sea is at an angle of depression of 40° from an observer on the
edge of a cliff which is 120 m high. How far is the dinghy from the foot of the cliff ?

$\theta = 90° - 40° = 50°$

$\tan \theta = \dfrac{\text{opp}}{\text{adj}}$

$\tan 50° = \dfrac{x}{120}$

$x = 120 × \tan 50°$

$\quad = 143.0$

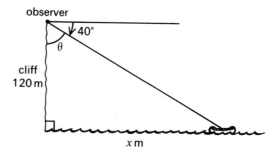

The dinghy is 143 m from the foot of the cliff, to the nearest metre.

3-figure bearings

Remember that these are measured from the North, in a clockwise direction, and are given in degrees, as 3-figure numbers.

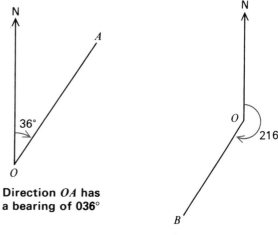

**Direction *OA* has
a bearing of 036°**

**Direction *OB* has
a bearing of 216°**

Example

3 A ship leaves a port *P* and travels 13 km due North to a point *Q*, and then 7 km due West to a point *R*. What is the bearing of *R* from *P* ?

$$\tan \theta = \frac{\text{opp}}{\text{adj}}$$

$$= \frac{7}{13}$$

$\theta = 28°$, to the nearest degree

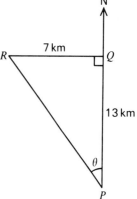

The bearing of *R* from *P* is $360° - 28° = 332°$

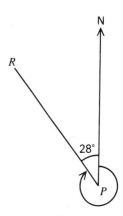

Sketch diagrams

In a practical question, begin by drawing a sketch diagram. Mark on it the sizes of any
known lengths and angles, including any right angles.
To find an unknown length or angle, look for a right-angled triangle in which you can
use the tangent ratio.

Exercise 7.2   Applications and Activities

1. From the top platform of Blackpool
    Tower, an observer noticed a ship
    out at sea, at an angle of depression
    of 12°.
    How far away was the ship, to the
    nearest 10 m ?

**Blackpool Tower
158 metres high**

2. In a local park there was a very tall poplar tree. James walked 100 m from the
    tree and from there he found that the angle of elevation of its top was 17°.
    How tall was the tree, to the nearest metre ?

3. On a mountain plateau there was a television mast. When standing 250 m from
    its base on level ground, Julie found the angle of elevation of its top to be 57°.
    How high was the mast, to the nearest metre ?

4.   Maya stood on a cliff which was 130 m high and found that the angle of
      depression of a lightship out at sea was 24°. In a direct line between the
      lightship and the foot of the cliff there was a small fishing boat, and the angle of
      depression of this boat was 33°.

      1   How far was the lightship from the foot of the cliff ?
      2   How far was the fishing boat from the foot of the cliff ?
      3   How far was the fishing boat from the lightship ?
      Give answers corrected to the nearest 10 m.

5.   A vertical pole AB is held in position by
      two supports CB and CD, as shown.
      $\angle ADC = 65°$ and $AC = 2.4$ m.

      1   Find the height of D, to the
              nearest 0.1 m.
      2   If $DB = 5$ m, find the size of
              $\angle BCA$, to the nearest degree.

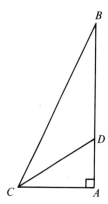

6.   Harby and Janby are two harbours, and Janby is 19 km North of Harby.
      A boat leaves Harby and sails on a bearing of 056° until it is due East of Janby.
      How far is it then from Janby, to the nearest 0.1 km ?

7. P and Q are places 3 km apart on a coastline running East–West.
      A ship S is seen out at sea. From P its bearing is 292°, and from Q it is due
      North.
      How far is the ship from Q, to the nearest 0.01 km ?

8.   From a point A on a mountain slope
      a climber measures the angle of
      elevation of the peak at B as 9°.
      On the map, with scale 1 : 50 000,
      the distance between A and B is 8 cm.
      What is the actual horizontal
      distance, AC, in km ?
      Calculate the vertical distance BC.
      The height at B is given on the map
      as 2694 m above sea level. What
      is the height above sea level at A ?

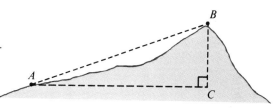

9.   **Make and use a clinometer**

This is an instrument to measure
angles of elevation and depression.
Make the main part out of cardboard.
Mark the angles as on a protractor
edge but put 0° in the centre and
90° at each end.
Fix a tube to the cardboard,
parallel to the line joining
the two 90° marks.
You can use a
straw for this, or
roll a piece of
paper to make a tube.
For the weight, a piece of lead will be
suitable, but a few washers, a pebble, or
anything you can tie to the string will do.

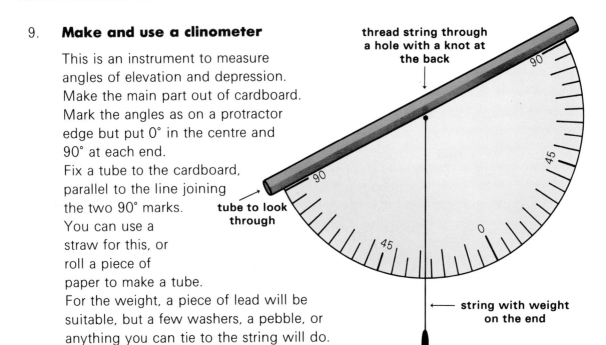

To use the clinometer to find the angle of elevation of an object, look at the
object through the tube. The weight will hang vertically and the reading, shown
where the string crosses the scale, will give the angle of elevation. A partner can
read this angle.

For an angle of depression you will tilt the clinometer downwards, and the
reading will show the angle of depression.

To use trigonometry to find a height, you need to know how far you are,
horizontally, from the object. If you have not got a suitable measuring tape, you
could make one out of rope, marking it every metre. Or you could estimate the
distance by pacing it out.
You could do several readings and calculations, standing at different distances
from the object each time. The answers should be nearly the same, and you can
take their average as your final result. The height is the height from your eye-
level, so you must find how far from the ground that is, and add it on.

Here are some suggestions for objects that you and your friends can calculate
the heights of. You should think of others.
1   The main school building.
2   The church tower or steeple.
3   The high-rise flats.
4   The tallest tree in the park.
5   Your bedroom window.
6   A double-decker bus.

10. **Gradients of lines**

On graph paper, draw the x-axis from 0 to 8 and the y-axis from 0 to 10, using a scale of 2 cm to 1 unit on both axes. Draw the graphs of these lines, showing as much of each line as fits on the paper.

$y = \frac{1}{4}x$, $y = \frac{1}{3}x$, $y = \frac{1}{2}x$, $y = x$, $y = 2x$, $y = 3x$, $y = 4x$

Measure the angle between each line and the x-axis and show these results in a table.
What is the connection between the equations and the angles ?

11. **Tangents in a circle**

You know that the other use of the word tangent in mathematics is for a line which touches a circle.

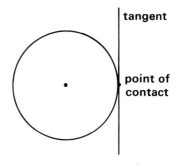

tangent

point of contact

We want to investigate lengths using a circle of unit radius, but a circle with radius 1 cm is rather small so we will let the unit be 5 cm. Draw a circle of radius 1 unit (5 cm), with centre O, and draw a horizontal line to cut the circumference at X. At X draw a line at right angles to OX. This line is a tangent to the circle.

Draw a line through O making an angle of 10° with OX, cutting the tangent at A. Measure the length of AX in cm, and divide this by 5 since 5 cm = 1 unit. Repeat with angles of 20°, 30°, . . . up to 60° or 70° if the line meets the tangent on your paper.

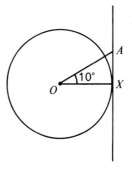

Make a table to show the angles and the distances AX (in units, not cm), and comment on any connection between them.
Why do you think the word **tangent** was chosen for the trigonometrical ratio ?

PUZZLE

35.   Which looks higher, a peak 9000 m high 30 km away, or one 1800 m high 6 km away ?

8 Thinking about indices and

Indices

Powers of numbers are written using indices, e.g. $5^3 = 5 \times 5 \times 5$ (3 is the index)

Ancient systems

The Ancient Egyptian systems of weights and measures used powers of 2 (as did the British system).
The Ancient Babylonian system of weights used powers of 3.

Using your calculator

Begin with any number x greater than 1 and press $\boxed{\sqrt{}}$ repeatedly.
What happens ?
You are finding the value of $(((x^{\frac{1}{2}})^{\frac{1}{2}})^{\frac{1}{2}}) \ldots$
Does it make any difference if you begin with a positive number y less than 1 ?

What is the value of $\sqrt[6]{7} \times \sqrt[3]{7} \times \sqrt{7}$?

This is the same as $7^{\frac{1}{6}} \times 7^{\frac{1}{3}} \times 7^{\frac{1}{2}}$.
You can find the answer using your calculator and you can check that it is correct by using the rules of indices. Which method do you prefer to use ?

Prefixes and their meanings

mega	1 000 000	10^6	deci	0.1	10^{-1}
kilo	1 000	10^3	centi	0.01	10^{-2}
hecto	100	10^2	milli	0.001	10^{-3}
deca	10	10^1	micro	0.000001	10^{-6}

tandard form

Standard form

Large numbers or small numbers can be expressed in standard form.
This is in the form $a \times 10^n$, where a is a number between 1 and 10 and n is a positive or negative whole number.

The Rheinfall

The rapids of the Rhine on the northern boundary of Switzerland are a very impressive sight. The volume of water flowing over the falls is about 6.0×10^7 m³ per day, rising to about 9.5×10^7 m³ in the summer months when the river is swollen by melting snow.

Ancestors

You have 2 parents, 4 grandparents, 8 great-grandparents. How many ancestors do you have altogether in the last 10 generations, assuming that they are all different people ?

How many would there be in the last 40 generations ?

8 Indices and Standard Form

Indices

x^2 means x squared, i.e. $x \times x$
x^3 means x cubed, i.e. $x \times x \times x$
x^4 means x to the 4th power, i.e. $x \times x \times x \times x$
and so on.

Here are the rules for using index numbers.

$$a^m \times a^n = a^{m+n}$$
$$a^m \div a^n = a^{m-n}$$
$$(a^m)^n = a^{mn}$$

We assume that m and n are positive whole numbers, and in the second rule, a is not 0 and m is greater than n.

Examples

$$7^2 = 7 \times 7 = 49$$
$$1^3 = 1 \times 1 \times 1 = 1$$
$$10^6 = 10 \times 10 \times 10 \times 10 \times 10 \times 10 = 1\,000\,000 \quad \text{(one million)}$$
$$5^3 \times 5^4 = 5^{3+4} = 5^7$$
$$6^5 \div 6^2 = 6^{5-2} = 6^3$$
$$(3^4)^2 = 3^{4 \times 2} = 3^8$$

Up to now we have not given any meaning to numbers with indices which are not positive whole numbers.
However, these numbers do exist and they obey the same rules.

$$5^{\frac{1}{2}} \times 5^{\frac{1}{2}} = 5^{\frac{1}{2}+\frac{1}{2}} = 5^1 = 5 \qquad \text{(Read } 5^{\frac{1}{2}} \text{ as 5 to the half.)}$$

But we know that

$$\sqrt{5} \times \sqrt{5} = 5$$

so $5^{\frac{1}{2}}$ means $\sqrt{5}$ (the square root of 5)

Similarly, $9^{\frac{1}{2}} = \sqrt{9} = 3$

$$10^{\frac{1}{2}} = \sqrt{10} \ (=3.16 \text{ to 2 dec pl.})$$

Also $\left(7^{\frac{1}{3}}\right)^3 = 7^{\frac{1}{3} \times 3} = 7^1 = 7$ (Read $7^{\frac{1}{3}}$ as 7 to the one-third.)

But we know that

$$(\sqrt[3]{7})^3 = 7$$

so $7^{\frac{1}{3}}$ means $\sqrt[3]{7}$ (the cube root of 7)

Similarly, $8^{\frac{1}{3}} = \sqrt[3]{8} = 2$

$10^{\frac{1}{3}} = \sqrt[3]{10}$ (= 2.15 to 2 dec pl.)

You are unlikely to need other roots, but the rules are similar.

$2^{\frac{1}{4}}$ means $\sqrt[4]{2}$ (the 4th root of 2)

$81^{\frac{1}{4}}$ means $\sqrt[4]{81} = 3$ (since $3^4 = 81$)

$x^{\frac{1}{2}} = \sqrt{x}$, the square root of x

$x^{\frac{1}{3}} = \sqrt[3]{x}$, the cube root of x

$x^{\frac{1}{4}} = \sqrt[4]{x}$, the 4th root of x

$x^{\frac{1}{n}} = \sqrt[n]{x}$, the nth root of x

Using your calculator

x^2 There will be a key labelled x^2 so you can find 15^2 by pressing 15 $\boxed{x^2}$ and you will get 225.

x^3 There may be a key labelled x^3.
         If not, you can use the y^x key (or it may be labelled x^y).
         Press *number* $\boxed{y^x}$ 3 $\boxed{=}$
         The 3 is because you want x^3.
         A quicker way to try is to press *number* $\boxed{\times}$ $\boxed{x^2}$ $\boxed{=}$
         This may give the correct answer. Can you say why this works ?

x^4 Since x^4 is $(x^2)^2$, the quickest way to find x^4 is to
         press *number* $\boxed{x^2}$ $\boxed{x^2}$

         Alternatively, using the y^x key, press *number* $\boxed{y^x}$ 4 $\boxed{=}$

You can find higher powers using the y^x key.
e.g. For 2^6, press 2 $\boxed{y^x}$ 6 $\boxed{=}$

$x^{\frac{1}{2}}$ or $\sqrt{x}$ There will be a square root key labelled $\sqrt{}$ so you can find $81^{\frac{1}{2}}$ by pressing
81 $\boxed{\sqrt{}}$ and you will get 9.

$x^{\frac{1}{3}}$ or $\sqrt[3]{x}$ There may be a cube root key labelled $\sqrt[3]{}$, so you can find $64^{\frac{1}{3}}$ by pressing
64 $\boxed{\sqrt[3]{}}$

If there is no cube root key, use the inverse key to y^x, which is $\sqrt[x]{y}$ (or it
may be labelled $y^{\frac{1}{x}}$).
For $64^{\frac{1}{3}}$ press 64 $\boxed{\sqrt[x]{y}}$ 3 $\boxed{=}$
The 3 is because you want the **cube** root.

Exercise 8.1

1.   Simplify these expressions, giving your answers in index form.

   1 $5^2 \times 5^2$ **5** $9^5 \div 9$ **8** $6^{\frac{1}{3}} \times 6^{\frac{1}{3}} \times 6^{\frac{1}{3}}$
   2 $7^6 \div 7^3$ **6** $10^{\frac{1}{2}} \times 10^{\frac{1}{2}}$ **9** $2^{10} \div 2^7$
   3 $6^3 \times 6$ **7** $(4^4)^3$ **10** $3^{\frac{1}{4}} \times 3^{\frac{1}{4}}$
   4 $(8^3)^5$

2.   Express these numbers using index notation.

   1   5 squared   **4**   7 to the 4th power
   2   6 cubed   **5**   the cube root of 5
   3   the square root of 3

3.   Find the exact value of these numbers, using your calculator if necessary.

   1 2^6 **5** 7^3 **8** $1^{\frac{1}{3}}$
   2 8^2 **6** $121^{\frac{1}{2}}$ **9** $0.25^{\frac{1}{2}}$
   3 $16^{\frac{1}{2}}$ **7** 3^5 **10** $216^{\frac{1}{3}}$
   4 $1000^{\frac{1}{3}}$

4.   Use your calculator to find the values of these numbers, giving them correct to
      3 significant figures.

1 12^3

2 2.52^2 **5** $100^{\frac{1}{3}}$ **8** 0.7^6

                                              6 $200^{\frac{1}{2}}$ **9** $0.05^{\frac{1}{3}}$

3 $1.83^{\frac{1}{2}}$ **10** 1.1^5

4 51^4 **7** $2^{\frac{1}{3}}$

Powers of 10

$10^6 = 10 \times 10 \times 10 \times 10 \times 10 \times 10 = 1\,000\,000$
$10^5 = 10 \times 10 \times 10 \times 10 \times 10 \qquad = \quad 100\,000$
$10^4 = 10 \times 10 \times 10 \times 10 \qquad\qquad = \quad\ \ 10\,000$
$10^3 = 10 \times 10 \times 10 \qquad\qquad\qquad = \quad\ \ \ \ 1\,000$
$10^2 = 10 \times 10 \qquad\qquad\qquad\qquad = \quad\ \ \ \ \ \ 100$
$10^1 = 10 \qquad\qquad\qquad\qquad\qquad\ = \quad\ \ \ \ \ \ \ \ 10$

Calculating with large numbers, using powers of 10

Using your calculator, multiply two large numbers.

e.g. $7\,000\,000 \times 500\,000$
The answer is $3\,500\,000\,000\,000$
The calculator will give the answer as 3.5   12 as it cannot fit all 13 figures on.
This is how the calculator displays 3.5×10^{12}, and you can check that this answer is
correct.
3.5×10^{12} is an example of a number expressed in **standard index form**. This is
often referred to as **standard form**.
The first part of the number is between 1 and 10, and the second part of the number is
a power of 10.

You can express any number in standard form.

Examples

6579 = 6.579 × 1000 = 6.579 × 10^3
71 800 000 = 7.18 × 10 000 000 = 7.18 × 10^7
20 = 2 × 10 = 2 × 10^1

220.56 = 2.2056 × 100 = 2.2056 × 10^2

Can you see any connection between the number of figures before the decimal point in the original number, and the index of 10 ?

Your calculator will turn numbers into standard form. (Calculators do not all work in the same way so you may have to investigate to see how yours will do this.)

To turn 840 000 into standard form.
Press 840 000 $=$ $F \leftrightarrow E$ and it will show 8.4   05 which means 8.4 × 10^5.

Press $F \leftrightarrow E$ again and it will return to showing 840 000.

To enter a number which is already given in standard form, use the EXP key.

To enter 8.4 × 10^5 press 8.4 EXP 5 $=$ and it will work it out to 840 000.

You can get back to 8.4   05 by pressing $F \leftrightarrow E$

You can also find the value of 8.4 × 10^5 by pressing 8.4 $\times$ 10 y^x 5 $=$

If a number is too big for the calculator to display all the figures it cannot change it out of standard form.

Examples

Use your calculator to find the values of:
(2.46 × 10^7) × (1.23 × 10^2),
(2.46 × 10^7) ÷ (1.23 × 10^2),
(2.46 × 10^7)^2,
$\sqrt{2.401 × 10^7}$.

For (2.46 × 10^7) × (1.23 × 10^2) press

2.46 EXP 7 $\times$ 1.23 EXP 2 $=$ and the calculator will show 3 025 800 000.

If you press $F \leftrightarrow E$ this will change to 3.0258   09, which means 3.0258 × 10^9.

For (2.46 × 10^7) ÷ (1.23 × 10^2) press

2.46 EXP 7 $\div$ 1.23 EXP 2 $=$ and the calculator will show 200 000.

If you press $\boxed{F \leftrightarrow E}$ this will change to 2.   05 which means 2×10^5.

For $(2.46 \times 10^7)^2$ press 2.46 $\boxed{\text{EXP}}$ 7 $\boxed{x^2}$ and the calculator will show 6.0516   14

This means 6.0516×10^{14}, which is 605 160 000 000 000.
This number is too big to be shown on the calculator as an ordinary number.

For $\sqrt{2.401 \times 10^7}$ press 2.401 $\boxed{\text{EXP}}$ 7 $\boxed{\sqrt{}}$ and the calculator will show 4900.

If you press $\boxed{F \leftrightarrow E}$ this will change to 4.9   03 which means 4.9×10^3.

Exercise 8.2

1.   Express these numbers in standard index form. Try to do them first without using
     your calculator, then do them again with your calculator to check the answers.

1	207	**5**	60 400	**8**	15.1
2	5178	**6**	5 000 000	**9**	256 000
3	91.06	**7**	23 790	**10**	1 700 000 000
4	8500				

2.   These numbers are given in standard form. Write them as ordinary numbers. Try to
     do them first without using your calculator, then do them again with your
     calculator to check the answers.

1	1.62×10^2	**5**	1.005×10^4	**8**	8×10^4
2	4×10^4	**6**	7.6×10^3	**9**	6.2315×10^7
3	5.7×10^6	**7**	1.1×10^6	**10**	9.99×10^5
4	8.03×10^2				

3.   Use your calculator to work out these calculations.
     Express the answers in standard form.

1	$(5.6 \times 10^3) \times (2.3 \times 10^5)$	**6**	$\sqrt{9.61 \times 10^6}$
2	$(8.2 \times 10^4) \times (1.5 \times 10^6)$	**7**	$(2.75 \times 10^9) \div (1.1 \times 10^4)$
3	$(6.8 \times 10^5) \div (1.7 \times 10)$	**8**	$(1.6 \times 10^3)^2$
4	$(5.5 \times 10^4)^2$	**9**	$(2.59 \times 10^6) \div (7.4 \times 10^2)$
5	$(9.3 \times 10^2) \times (6.1 \times 10^7)$	**10**	$\sqrt{5.476 \times 10^9}$

Calculating with small numbers, using powers of 10

We continue the pattern of powers of 10 downwards. After 10^1 the numbers in the first column are 10^0, 10^{-1}, 10^{-2}, 10^{-3}, ... (read as 10 to the nought, 10 to the minus one, 10 to the minus two, etc.)
Notice that each number in the other column is the number above divided by 10.
So continuing the pattern the next few rows are 1, 0.1, 0.01, 0.001, ...

Here is the complete table

$$10^6 \ = \ 1\,000\,000$$
$$10^5 \ = \ 100\,000$$
$$10^4 \ = \ 10\,000$$
$$10^3 \ = \ 1\,000$$
$$10^2 \ = \ 100$$
$$10^1 \ = \ 10$$
$$10^0 \ = \ 1$$
$$10^{-1} = \ 0.1 \qquad \text{or} \qquad \tfrac{1}{10}$$
$$10^{-2} = \ 0.01 \qquad \text{or} \qquad \tfrac{1}{100}$$
$$10^{-3} = \ 0.001 \qquad \text{or} \qquad \tfrac{1}{1000}$$
$$10^{-4} = \ 0.0001 \quad \text{or} \qquad \tfrac{1}{10000}$$
$$\ldots$$

This gives a meaning to 10^0 $(=1)$ and 10 with negative indices.
e.g. $10^{-1} = \tfrac{1}{10} = 0.1$, $10^{-2} = \tfrac{1}{100} = 0.01$, and so on.

$$10^0 = 1$$
$$10^{-n} = \frac{1}{10^n}$$

Using your calculator, multiply two very small numbers.

e.g. 0.0000006×0.00004
The answer is 0.000000000024
The calculator will give this answer as 2.4 -11 as it cannot fit all 12 figures on.
This is how the calculator displays 2.4×10^{-11}, and you can check that this answer is correct.

2.4×10^{-11} is an example of a small number in standard index form. The first part of the number is between 1 and 10 and the second part of the number is a power of 10.

Examples

Here are some small numbers expressed in standard form.

$0.6423 = 6.423 \times \frac{1}{10} = 6.423 \times 10^{-1}$

$0.00912 = 9.12 \times \frac{1}{1000} = 9.12 \times 10^{-3}$

$0.00001 = 1 \times \frac{1}{100000} = 1 \times 10^{-5}$

Can you see any connection between the number of 0's after the decimal point in the number, and the index of 10 ?

Your calculator will turn small numbers into standard form.
Press 0.0047 $=$ $\boxed{F \leftrightarrow E}$ and it will show 4.7   −03 which means 4.7×10^{-3}.

To enter a number which is already given in standard form use the $\boxed{EXP}$ key.

To enter 4.7×10^{-3} press 4.7 $\boxed{EXP}$ 3 $\boxed{^+/_-}$ $\boxed{=}$ and it will work it out to 0.0047.

You can get back to 4.7 −03 by pressing $\boxed{F \leftrightarrow E}$.

You can also find the value of 4.7×10^{-3} by pressing
4.7 $\boxed{\times}$ 10 $\boxed{y^x}$ 3 $\boxed{^+/_-}$ $\boxed{=}$

If a number is too small for the calculator to display it normally it cannot change it out of standard form.

For numbers already between 1 and 10, there is usually no need to express them in standard form, but if this is needed then the power of 10 is 10^0, (since $10^0 = 1$).
e.g. $8.3 = 8.3 \times 10^0$. A calculator would show 8.3   00

Examples

Use your calculator to find the values of:
$(1.35 \times 10^{-3}) \times (9.8 \times 10^{-2})$,
$(3.92 \times 10^{-5}) \div (9.8 \times 10^{-3})$,
$(1.3 \times 10^{-3})^2$,
$\sqrt{4.9 \times 10^{-7}}$.

For $(1.35 \times 10^{-3}) \times (9.8 \times 10^{-2})$ press

1.35 $\boxed{EXP}$ 3 $\boxed{^+/_-}$ $\boxed{\times}$ 9.8 $\boxed{EXP}$ 2 $\boxed{^+/_-}$ $\boxed{=}$ and the calculator will show 0.0001323

If you press $\boxed{F \leftrightarrow E}$ this will change to 1.323   −04 which means 1.323×10^{-4}.

For $(3.92 \times 10^{-5}) \div (9.8 \times 10^{-3})$ press

3.92 $\boxed{EXP}$ 5 $\boxed{^+/_-}$ $\boxed{\div}$ 9.8 $\boxed{EXP}$ 3 $\boxed{^+/_-}$ $\boxed{=}$ and the calculator will show 0.004

If you press $\boxed{F \leftrightarrow E}$ this will change to 4.   −03 which means 4×10^{-3}.

For $(1.3 \times 10^{-3})^2$ press 1.3 $\boxed{\text{EXP}}$ 3 $\boxed{^+/_-}$ $\boxed{x^2}$ and the calculator will show 0.00000169

If you press $\boxed{\text{F} \leftrightarrow \text{E}}$ this will change to 1.69 −06 which means 1.69×10^{-6}.

For $\sqrt{4.9 \times 10^{-7}}$ press 4.9 $\boxed{\text{EXP}}$ 7 $\boxed{^+/_-}$ $\boxed{\sqrt{}}$ and the calculator will show 0.0007

If you press $\boxed{\text{F} \leftrightarrow \text{E}}$ this will change to 7. −04 which means 7×10^{-4}.

Exercise 8.3

1. Express these numbers in standard index form. Try to do them first without using your calculator, then do them again with your calculator to check the answers.

1	0.056	**5**	0.000238	**8**	0.09307
2	0.00028	**6**	0.0062	**9**	0.00002
3	0.000009	**7**	0.00000041	**10**	0.103
4	0.157				

2. These numbers are given in standard form. Write them as ordinary numbers. Try to do them first without using your calculator, then do them again with your calculator to check the answers.

1	4.1×10^{-1}	**5**	2.981×10^{-4}	**8**	6.1×10^{-1}
2	5.23×10^{-5}	**6**	7.6×10^{-2}	**9**	2.7×10^{-4}
3	8.6×10^{-2}	**7**	3×10^{-3}	**10**	9.99×10^0
4	1.04×10^{-1}				

3. Use your calculator to work out these calculations. Give the answers in standard form.

1	$(3.2 \times 10^{-2}) \times (1.9 \times 10^{-1})$	**8**	$1.73 \times 10^{-4} \times (2 \times 10^8)$
2	$(2.73 \times 10^{-1}) \div (4.2 \times 10^{-2})$	**9**	$(7 \times 10^5) \div (3.5 \times 10^{-1})$
3	$(4.87 \times 10^{-3}) \times 2.6 \times 10^{-2}$	**10**	$\sqrt{2.89 \times 10^{-4}}$
4	$(7.3 \times 10^{-3})^2$		
5	$(1.32 \times 10^{-4}) \div (4 \times 10^3)$	**11**	$(5.42 \times 10^{-3}) + (2.3 \times 10^{-4})$
6	$(8.5 \times 10^5) \times (1.3 \times 10^{-3})$	**12**	$(8.79 \times 10^{-1}) - (3.9 \times 10^{-2})$
7	$\sqrt{6.4 \times 10^{-5}}$		

Exercise 8.4   Applications and Activities

1.   Find the value of *n* in these equations.

1	$11^n = 121$	**6**	$6^n \div 6 = 36$
2	$2^n = 64$	**7**	$49^n = 7$
3	$3^n = 81$	**8**	$8^n = 2$
4	$4^n = \dfrac{4^3 \times 4^4}{4^2}$	**9**	$9^2 \times 9^n = 243$
5	$5^n = \sqrt{5}$	**10**	$10^n = \frac{1}{100}$

2.   Express the numbers in these statements as ordinary numbers.

  1   The world's horse population is
        estimated to be 7.5×10^7.
  2   The UK dog population is estimated to
        be 6.6×10^6, and the cat population
        6.5×10^6.
  3   In the UK there is an estimated number
        of 1.3×10^8 chickens.
  4   In the UK there are 2.1×10^4 species of
        insects.
  5   In the UK there is an estimated
        population of over 5×10^{14} spiders.

3.   Express the quantities in these statements in standard form.

  1   The mass of a cubic centimetre of hydrogen is 0.000899 g.
  2   The lowest temperature ever attained is 0.000000002 K.
  3   The wavelength of red light is 0.0000007 m.
  4   The lightest metal is lithium, of which a cubic centimetre weighs 0.5334 g.
  5   The thickness of an atom is about 0.0000000001 m.

4.   A swimming pool is 50 m long and 12 m wide and the depth is 2.5 m.
     Find how many litres of water are required to fill the pool, giving the answer in
     standard form.

5. The mass of the Earth is 5.98×10^{21} tonnes. Mercury's mass is 0.056 of the Earth's mass.
   Find Mercury's mass, giving your answer in standard form, correct to 2 significant figures.

6. A population of bacteria, used in an experiment, doubles in number every hour. At noon on the first day the population is approximately 100.
   What will the population be at 3 pm ?
   Express in index form a formula for n, the number of bacteria t hours after noon.

   By putting $t = \frac{1}{2}$ in the formula, find the approximate number of bacteria after $\frac{1}{2}$ hour.
   If the experiment could be continued, approximately how many bacteria would there be at noon on the next day. Give the answer in standard form, correct to 2 significant figures.

7. For any radio wave, the frequency, f hertz, and the wavelength, w metres, are connected by the formula $fw = 3 \times 10^8$. A radio station is broadcasting on a frequency of 9.6×10^7 hertz. Find the wavelength, in metres, correct to 2 significant figures.

   The number 3×10^8 is the speed of radio waves in m/s. How long does it take a broadcast to travel 45 km ? Give the answer in seconds, in standard form.

Broadcasting House, London

8. A packet of 500 sheets of paper is 4.8 cm thick. Write down, in standard form, the thickness, in mm, of one sheet.

9. The speed of light is 3×10^8 m/s. It takes 4.38 years for light to reach Earth from the nearest visible star, Alpha Centauri. How far away is that star ? Give the answer in km, in standard form, correct to 2 significant figures.
   Assume that a year has $365\frac{1}{4}$ days.

10. A litre tin of paint is said to be sufficient to cover an area of $18 \, m^2$. Find the thickness of a coat of this paint. Give the answer in mm, in standard form, correct to 2 significant figures.

11.   If £100 is invested at R% interest per year, and the interest is paid annually and added to the money in the account, then after n years, the amount £A in the account is given by the formula $A = 100 (1 + \frac{R}{100})^n$.

   If £100 was invested at 12% interest per year, and the interest was added to the money in the account, what would be the total amount of money after 20 years, to the nearest £ ?

   If the investment could be left for 100 years altogether, what would it amount to then ? Give this result in standard form to 3 significant figures.

   You could do a further investigation of the amounts received when different rates of interest are used.

12.   A drop of oil $0.5 \, mm^3$ in volume is observed to cover an area of $6000 \, cm^2$ when put on the surface of some water. If the oil is evenly spread, find the thickness of the oil layer, in cm, giving the answer in standard form to 2 significant figures.

PUZZLES

36.   Here are the prices on the breakfast menu at the work's canteen. Can you decode them ? The prices are in pence, with each letter representing a different figure.

	price
Egg and bacon	AB
Egg and sausage	CD
Egg	BA
Bacon	CA
Egg, bacon and sausage	DC

   I decide to have just a sausage this morning. What will I pay for it ?

37.   Andrew, Bernard, Clive, and their wives, Dulcie, Edna and Fiona, went shopping, with plenty of money. Each paid as many £'s per article as they bought articles, and each man spent £63 more than his wife. Andrew spent £143 more than Dulcie, and Edna spent £897 more than Bernard.
   Who was married to whom ?

38.   Two gardeners are planting seedlings in a triangular patch so that the 40 rows will contain 1, 2, 3, . . . 38, 39, 40 plants. One begins planting at the end of the longest row, the other one begins at the point of the triangle. If they continue straight along the rows and plant at the same rate, in which row will they meet ?

9 Thinking about probability

The beginning

In the 17th Century there was a French gambler called the Chevalier de Méré.
He won wagers by betting even money that he would score at least one six in 4 throws of a single die.

After reading this chapter you will be able to calculate the probability of winning, which is $1 - (\frac{5}{6})^4$.
Use your calculator to find the value of this expression.
Since the probability is just greater than 0.5, de Méré would win, in the long run.

He decided to change the wager, and he betted even money that he would score at least one double six in 24 throws of two dice.
Unfortunately, in the long run, he began to lose his money.

The outcome of this was that he asked advice from the great French mathematician, Blaise Pascal.
Pascal corresponded with another great mathematician, Pierre de Fermat, and between them they developed the Theory of Probabilities.

Can you calculate the probability of the second wager winning ?
When de Méré was told that this probability was less than 0.5, he said that arithmetic was nothing but a swindle.

Blaise Pascal, 1623–1662

tombola stall at a fete

A modern gambling machine

Uses of probability

When you insure against some unfortunate happening, you are betting the insurance company that it will happen, and the insurance company is charging a price based on the probability that it will not happen.

Tim has got a new bicycle for Christmas. His father insured it as an extension to the house contents insurance he pays. The extra premium costs £10 per year. The policy covers the loss of the bicycle by fire or theft from the home. Tim is also covered for legal liability, so that if he is involved in causing accidental damage to someone else's property, the insurance company will pay for the damage.

Elaine's hobby is riding, and she has bought a horse. She has insured it, and the premium costs £200 per year. The policy includes cover for the loss of the horse by theft, or by accidental death, vet's fees, and the owner's legal liability to other people.

Probability of Independent Events

Independent Events

When a coin is tossed twice in succession, or two coins are tossed, the second result does not depend on whether the first result was heads or tails.

When a die is tossed twice in succession, or two dice are tossed, the second result does not depend on the number shown by the first result.

If there are coloured beads in a bag, and one is picked out and its colour noted, and then it is replaced and the beads mixed up, the colour of the next bead picked out does not depend on the colour of the first one.

Such events, where the outcome of the second event does not depend on the outcome of the first event, are called **independent events**.

We can show the combined outcomes of both events in a list, a table or a tree-diagram.

Table of results of the combined outcomes of two events.

Example

1   The outcomes when two dice are thrown.

These are independent events.

Table

		1st die					
		1	2	3	4	5	6
	1	1,1	2,1	3,1	4,1	5,1	6,1
2nd	2	1,2	2,2	3,2	4,2	5,2	6,2
die	3	1,3	2,3	3,3	4,3	5,3	6,3
	4	1,4	2,4	3,4	4,4	5,4	6,4
	5	1,5	2,5	3,5	4,5	5,5	6,5
	6	1,6	2,6	3,6	4,6	5,6	6,6

The 36 outcomes are equally likely.

What is the probability of scoring a 6 on both dice ?

Probability $= \dfrac{s}{n}$

where n is the total number of equally likely outcomes,
    and s is the number of successful outcomes.

Probability $= \frac{1}{36}$

You can compare this result with the probability of the separate events.

P(1st die shows a six) $= \frac{1}{6}$

P(2nd die shows a six) $= \frac{1}{6}$

These are independent events. The combined outcome is that the 1st number is a six and the 2nd number is a six.

Can you suggest a rule for finding the probability of a combined outcome from the separate probabilities of the two events ?

What is the probability that the 1st die shows a number less than 3 and the 2nd die shows a number greater than 3 ?

From the table, the number of successful outcomes = 6.

Probability $= \dfrac{s}{n} = \frac{6}{36} = \frac{1}{6}$

Here are the probabilities of the separate events.

P(1st die shows less than 3) $= \frac{2}{6} = \frac{1}{3}$

P(2nd die shows greater than 3) $= \frac{3}{6} = \frac{1}{2}$

Does your rule for the probability of the combined outcome work in this example ?

The AND rule

If there are two independent events A and B, then the probability of both A and B occurring = the probability of A occurring × the probability of B occurring.

i.e. P(A and B) = P(A) × P(B)

If there are 3 independent events A, B and C, then
$$P(A \text{ and } B \text{ and } C) = P(A) \times P(B) \times P(C)$$
The rule is similar if there are more than 3 events.

Examples

2   A coin and a die are tossed together. What is the probability of them showing a tail and a one ?

P(tail) $= \frac{1}{2}$
P(one) $= \frac{1}{6}$

P(tail and one) = P(tail) × P(one)
$$= \tfrac{1}{2} \times \tfrac{1}{6} = \tfrac{1}{12}$$

3 A playing card is drawn from a pack of 52 cards and after replacing it and shuffling the pack, a second card is drawn.
What is the probability that both cards drawn are aces ?
What is the probability that the 1st card is a heart and the 2nd card is not a heart ?

These events are independent because the 1st card is replaced before the 2nd card is drawn.

$$P(\text{1st card an ace}) = \tfrac{1}{13}$$
$$P(\text{2nd card an ace}) = \tfrac{1}{13}$$

$$P(\text{both cards are aces}) = P(\text{1st an ace and 2nd an ace}) = \tfrac{1}{13} \times \tfrac{1}{13} = \tfrac{1}{169}$$

$$P(\text{1st card a heart}) = \tfrac{1}{4}$$
$$P(\text{2nd card not a heart}) = \tfrac{3}{4}$$

$$P(\text{1st card a heart and 2nd not a heart}) = \tfrac{1}{4} \times \tfrac{3}{4} = \tfrac{3}{16}$$

4 A seed manufacturer guarantees that 90% of a particular type of flower seed will germinate.
If 5 seeds of this type are sown, what is the probability that they will all germinate ?
What is the probability that none of them will germinate ?

P(one seed germinates) = 90% = 0.9
P(all seeds germinate) = P(1st, 2nd, 3rd, 4th and 5th seeds germinate)
$$= 0.9 \times 0.9 \times 0.9 \times 0.9 \times 0.9$$
$$= 0.59049$$
$$= 0.59, \text{ to 2 dec pl.}$$

P(one seed does not germinate) = 0.1
P(no seeds germinate) = P(1st, 2nd, 3rd, 4th and 5th do not germinate)
$$= 0.1 \times 0.1 \times 0.1 \times 0.1 \times 0.1$$
$$= 0.00001$$

(These answers assume that the results are independent and that the conditions are satisfactory. If the seeds were not planted in the right soil, not kept at a suitable temperature or not watered properly, it is much more probable that none of the seeds would germinate.)

Two events are less likely to happen than one of the events

When finding the probability of two or more independent events, the probabilities of the separate events are **multiplied**.
Since these probabilities are numbers less than 1, the result is smaller than any of the separate probabilities.

e.g. The probability of scoring a 6 on both of 2 dice is smaller than the probability of scoring a six on 1 die.

The probability of scoring a number less than 3 on one die and a number greater than 3 on another die is smaller than either separate probability.

The probability of 5 seeds with a 90% germination rate all germinating is less than the probability that one seed will germinate.

The probability that no seeds germinate is less than the probability that one seed will not germinate.

Of course, if one of two probabilities is 1 (certain to happen) then the probability of the 2 events happening = the probability of the other event happening.
If one of the probabilities is 0 (certain not to happen) then the probability of the combined event happening = 0.

Exercise 9.1

1. In a fairground game, a pointer is spun. Assuming that it is equally likely to come to rest in any sector, what is the probability of winning 5 times in 5 spins ?

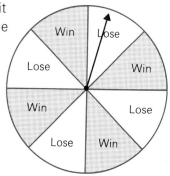

2. With a particular type of drawing-pin, if one is dropped onto a table, the probability that it will land point upwards ⊥ is approximately 0.7.

    If 3 drawing-pins are dropped, what is the probability that they will all land point upwards ?
    What is the probability that they will all land on their sides, like this ⬯ ?

3. The wrappers of a chocolate bar sometimes include a token. The tokens are included on $\frac{1}{8}$ of the bars. If Jenny buys 3 bars of this chocolate,
    1   what is the probability that she gets a token on all 3 bars,
    2   what is the probability that she does not get a token on the 1st 2 bars, but gets one on the 3rd bar ?

4. Packets of tea each contain 1 picture card, which belongs to a set of 50.
Hanif wants just card number 27 to complete his set.
What is the probability that he gets this card in the first packet of tea that he opens ?
What is the probability that he does not get the card in the first packet he opens, but gets it in the second packet ?
(Assume that there are equal numbers of each card and they are put into the packets at random.)

5. Before the start of a cricket match, the captains toss a coin to decide who has the choice of whether to bat or to field first.
What is the probability, in 3 matches, of our captain
   1 winning the toss every time,
   2 losing the toss every time,
   3 losing the toss in the 1st 2 matches and winning the toss in the 3rd match ?

6. In a computer game the probability of scoring a hit is $\frac{3}{8}$.
What is the probability that the 1st player misses and the 2nd player scores a hit ?

7. When this spinner is spun, it is equally likely to come to rest on any of its five edges, and the number on that edge is the score.
   1 If the spinner is spun twice, what is the probability of getting an odd number on the 1st spin followed by an even number on the 2nd spin ?
   2 What is the probability of getting a 1 four times in succession in 4 spins ?

8. A card is drawn from a full pack of 52 cards and a second card is drawn from another full pack.
What is the probability that
   1 the 1st card is a diamond and the 2nd card is a spade or a club,
   2 the 1st card is a picture card (Jack, Queen or King) and the 2nd card is an Ace ?

9. A computer is producing a set of random numbers from 1 to 10.
If it prints 4 numbers, what is the probability that
   1 all the numbers are less than 5,
   2 all the numbers are greater than 5,
   3 the 1st 3 numbers are even and the last number is odd ?

10. It is estimated that the probability that Susie will win in the breast stroke swimming event is $\frac{1}{5}$, and that she will win in the free-style race is $\frac{1}{4}$.
   1 What is the probability that Susie wins in both events ?
   2 What is the probability that she wins the breast stroke race but does not win the free-style race ?

The OR rule

Remember the OR rule for mutually exclusive events, i.e. events when one or other can happen, but not both.

$$P(A \text{ or } B) = P(A) + P(B)$$
$$P(A \text{ or } B \text{ or } C) = P(A) + P(B) + P(C)$$

Tree-diagrams

When there are two or more independent events, we can show the combined results on a tree-diagram.

Example 1

The outcomes and the probabilities when 2 coins are tossed.

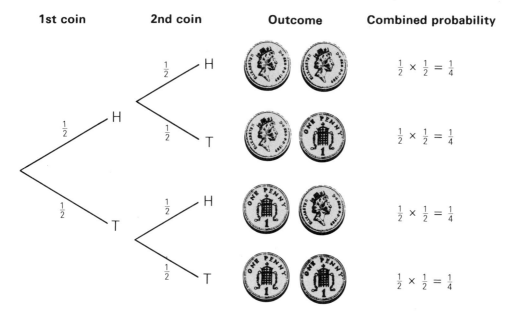

We can also show the outcomes and the probabilities in a table.

		1st coin	
		H $(\frac{1}{2})$	T $(\frac{1}{2})$
2nd coin	H $(\frac{1}{2})$	HH $\frac{1}{2} \times \frac{1}{2}$	TH $\frac{1}{2} \times \frac{1}{2}$
	T $(\frac{1}{2})$	HT $\frac{1}{2} \times \frac{1}{2}$	TT $\frac{1}{2} \times \frac{1}{2}$

We can also show the outcomes in a list.

HH
HT   Since these are equally likely outcomes,
TH   the probability of each outcome is $\frac{1}{4}$.
TT

The probability of 2 heads $= \frac{1}{4}$

The probability of 1 head and 1 tail $=$ P(head then tail **or** tail then head)

$$= P(HT) + P(TH)$$
$$= \tfrac{1}{4} + \tfrac{1}{4} = \tfrac{1}{2}$$

The probability of 2 tails $= \frac{1}{4}$

Note that the total of the probabilities is 1, because it is certain that one of these outcomes will happen.

We can extend the tree-diagram to show the results of tossing 3 coins.

1st coin	2nd coin	3rd coin	Outcome	Probability
		$\frac{1}{2}$ H	HHH	$\frac{1}{2} \times \frac{1}{2} \times \frac{1}{2} = \frac{1}{8}$
	$\frac{1}{2}$ H	$\frac{1}{2}$ T	HHT	$\frac{1}{8}$
		$\frac{1}{2}$ H	HTH	$\frac{1}{8}$
$\frac{1}{2}$ H	$\frac{1}{2}$ T	$\frac{1}{2}$ T	HTT	$\frac{1}{8}$
		$\frac{1}{2}$ H	THH	$\frac{1}{8}$
$\frac{1}{2}$ T	$\frac{1}{2}$ H	$\frac{1}{2}$ T	THT	$\frac{1}{8}$
		$\frac{1}{2}$ H	TTH	$\frac{1}{8}$
	$\frac{1}{2}$ T	$\frac{1}{2}$ T	TTT	$\frac{1}{8}$

Since there are 3 events, we cannot show the outcomes in a table, but we can show them in a list.

HHH
HHT
HTH
THH
HTT
THT
TTH
TTT

$P(3 \text{ heads}) = \frac{1}{8}$

$P(2 \text{ heads and } 1 \text{ tail}) = \frac{1}{8} + \frac{1}{8} + \frac{1}{8} = \frac{3}{8}$

$P(1 \text{ head and } 2 \text{ tails}) = \frac{3}{8}$

$P(3 \text{ tails}) = \frac{1}{8}$

(The probability of 2 heads and 1 tail involves the 3 possible orders, either HHT, HTH or THH, each with probability $\frac{1}{8}$. These are mutually exclusive events and their probabilities are added.)

Example 2

Emily goes to school by bus or car, or she walks. The probability of going by bus is $\frac{1}{2}$, of going by car is $\frac{1}{3}$, and of walking is $\frac{1}{6}$.

When she comes home from school, she either walks, with probability $\frac{1}{2}$, or goes by bus, with probability $\frac{2}{5}$, or occasionally gets a lift home in a friend's car, with probability $\frac{1}{10}$. This is regardless of which way she travelled to school in the morning.

Here is a tree-diagram showing the combined outcomes.
W = walk, B = by bus, C = car.

Going	Coming	Outcome	Probability
	W	WW	$\frac{1}{6} \times \frac{1}{2} = \frac{1}{12}$
	B	WB	$\frac{1}{6} \times \frac{2}{5} = \frac{1}{15}$
W	C	WC	$\frac{1}{6} \times \frac{1}{10} = \frac{1}{60}$
	W	BW	$\frac{1}{2} \times \frac{1}{2} = \frac{1}{4}$
B	B	BB	$\frac{1}{2} \times \frac{2}{5} = \frac{1}{5}$
	C	BC	$\frac{1}{2} \times \frac{1}{10} = \frac{1}{20}$
	W	CW	$\frac{1}{3} \times \frac{1}{2} = \frac{1}{6}$
C	B	CB	$\frac{1}{3} \times \frac{2}{5} = \frac{2}{15}$
	C	CC	$\frac{1}{3} \times \frac{1}{10} = \frac{1}{30}$

Write all the results as fractions with denominator 60 to check that the total probability is 1.

We can also show the outcomes and the probabilities in a table.

			Going			
		W $(\frac{1}{6})$		B $(\frac{1}{2})$		C $(\frac{1}{3})$
Coming home	W $(\frac{1}{2})$	WW $\frac{1}{6} \times \frac{1}{2}$	BW $\frac{1}{2} \times \frac{1}{2}$	CW $\frac{1}{3} \times \frac{1}{2}$
	B $(\frac{2}{5})$	WB $\frac{1}{6} \times \frac{2}{5}$	BB $\frac{1}{2} \times \frac{2}{5}$	CB $\frac{1}{3} \times \frac{2}{5}$
	C $(\frac{1}{10})$	WC $\frac{1}{6} \times \frac{1}{10}$	BC $\frac{1}{2} \times \frac{1}{10}$	CC $\frac{1}{3} \times \frac{1}{10}$

What is the probability of Emily walking either to or from school, or both ways ?

Look at all the results in the diagram or table which include W. These are mutually exclusive events and must be added

$$P(\text{walk at least one way}) = P(WW) + P(WB) + P(WC) + P(BW) + P(CW)$$
$$= \frac{1}{12} + \frac{1}{15} + \frac{1}{60} + \frac{1}{4} + \frac{1}{6}$$
$$= \frac{5 + 4 + 1 + 15 + 10}{60}$$
$$= \frac{35}{60} = \frac{7}{12}$$

What is the probability of Emily using transport both ways ?
The events are BB, BC, CB, CC. These are mutually exclusive events and must be added.

$$P(\text{using transport both ways}) = \frac{1}{5} + \frac{1}{20} + \frac{2}{15} + \frac{1}{30}$$
$$= \frac{12 + 3 + 8 + 2}{60}$$
$$= \frac{25}{60} = \frac{5}{12}$$

You might have noticed that the last two answers add up to 1.
Either Emily walks at least one way **or** she uses transport both ways.
So you could find the 2nd answer by subtraction.

$$P(\text{using transport both ways}) = 1 - P(\text{walks at least one way})$$
$$= 1 - \frac{7}{12} = \frac{5}{12}$$

Exercise 9.2

1. On the way to work Miss Desai passes through 2 sets of traffic lights. The probability that the 1st set of lights will be showing green is $\frac{2}{3}$, and the probability that the 2nd set of lights will be showing green is $\frac{3}{5}$. These sets of lights work independently of each other.
    Copy and complete the tree-diagram or the table showing the combined probabilities.
    G = green, N = not green.

    What is the probability that
    1   both sets of lights will be showing green,
    2   Miss Desai will have to stop at at least one of the sets of lights,
    3   she will have to stop at both sets of lights ?

1st set	**2nd set**	**Outcome**	**Probability**
	$\frac{3}{5}$ G	GG	$\frac{2}{3} \times \frac{3}{5} =$
$\frac{2}{3}$ G	$\frac{2}{5}$ N		
$\frac{1}{3}$ N	$\frac{3}{5}$ G		
	$\frac{2}{5}$ N		

		1st set	
		G $\left(\frac{2}{3}\right)$	N $\left(\frac{1}{3}\right)$
2nd set	G $\left(\frac{3}{5}\right)$	GG $\frac{2}{3} \times \frac{3}{5}$	NG
	N $\left(\frac{2}{5}\right)$	GN	NN

2. Kay plays a game where she can win, draw or lose.
    The probability of her winning is $\frac{4}{7}$, the probability of her drawing is $\frac{2}{7}$. What is the probability of her losing ?

    Show the results of 2 games on a tree diagram or in a table.
    1   What is the probability that Kay loses both games ?
    2   What is the probability that she wins at least one of the games ?

3.   Alan, Bob and Craig are the only competitors in a 100 m race and also in the high jump. The result of the high jump will not be affected by their performances in the race.

Here are the probabilities of each boy winning.

Competitors	Alan	Bob	Craig
100 m race	$\frac{1}{3}$	$\frac{1}{6}$	$\frac{1}{2}$
High jump	$\frac{1}{8}$	$\frac{1}{2}$	$\frac{3}{8}$

Show in a table or tree-diagram the combined outcomes of winners in the race followed by the high jump.

What is the probability that
1   Alan will win both events,
2   Alan will not win in either event,
3   the same boy will win in both events ?

4.   A bag contains 8 marbles of which 5 are red, 2 are blue and 1 is green. A marble is taken out, and then replaced before the next marble is taken out.

Show the results of 2 drawings on a list, a table or tree-diagram, using R = red, B = blue, G = green.
Find the probability that
1   both marbles drawn out are red,
2   one marble is red and the other is blue,
3   both marbles are the same colour.

5.   Anna, Beth and Claire are playing a game with a die and have reached the point where each one has to throw a 1 to win the game. It is Anna's turn. What is the probability that Anna gets a 1 and wins ?
Beth goes 2nd. What is the probability that Anna does not get a 1 and then Beth gets a 1 and wins ?
Claire goes 3rd. What is the probability that Anna and Beth do not get 1's and then Claire does, and wins ?
What is the probability that no-one gets a 1, so that the game continues for another round ?

Exercise 9.3   Applications and Activities

1. A certain competition sometimes held at charity fairs is to win a car. You have to throw 7 dice and get 7 sixes.
    What is the probability of winning ?
    Give the answer correct to 3 significant figures. Also write it in standard form.

2. **Monopoly**

    This is a very well-known game, and if you have never played it, we suggest that you borrow the game and try it out, with friends.
    It should give you good practice in mental arithmetic, in learning about wise or unwise use of money (although not real money), and since two dice are used, a knowledge of the probabilities of the various totals is very useful.
    How many people playing Monopoly are aware that they are 6 times more likely to throw a total of 7 than a total of 2 ?

    1   If you throw doubles (the same number on both dice) three times in succession you 'Go to Jail'. What is the probability of throwing doubles with 2 dice ? What is the probability of throwing doubles 3 times in succession ?

    2   If you are in Jail, you can have 3 tries to get out without payment by throwing doubles.
    What is the probability of **not** throwing doubles on the 1st try ?
    What is the probability of not throwing doubles on all 3 tries ? This is the probability of having to pay to get out of Jail.

    3   Nina is on Bond Street and she has to throw 2 dice.
    What is the chance of her landing on Liverpool Street Station ?
    What is the chance of her landing on Park Lane ?
    What is the chance of her landing on the Super Tax square ?
    What is the chance of her landing on Mayfair ?

    If she lands on Park Lane or Mayfair she will have to pay so much that she will have to retire from the game.
    What is her chance of landing on Park Lane or Mayfair on that turn ?
    What is the chance of her not landing on Park Lane or Mayfair on that turn ?

3. At a fair a rectangular board, measuring 2.7 m by 2 m, has 250 cards pinned to it.
    Each card is rectangular, measuring 9 cm by 6 cm, and the cards do not overlap.
    Bill throws darts at random, towards the board.
    Assuming that all points on the board are equally likely to be hit, in a throw that
    hits the board show that the probability that a card is hit is $\frac{1}{4}$.

    Find the probability that in Bill's 3 throws, which all hit the board,
    1   a card will be hit each time,
    2   none of the 3 throws hits a card.

4. **The number of heads when several coins are tossed**

    Here are bar-line graphs of the probabilities of different numbers of heads when
    coins are tossed.

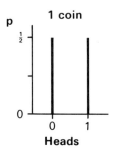 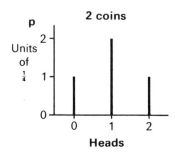

    Find the theoretical probabilities of the different numbers of heads when 3 coins
    are tossed, and draw a bar-line graph, using a scale on the vertical axis with
    units of $\frac{1}{8}$.

    Repeat this when 4 coins are tossed using units of $\frac{1}{16}$, and with 5 coins using
    units of $\frac{1}{32}$.

    Compare the bar-line graphs and comment on them.

    You can collect some experimental results, by tossing coins, or using results of
    previous tosses, or using simulated results from a computer or random number
    tables, (odd numbers could be heads and even numbers tails).
    You can compare your experimental results with the theoretical ones.

    You can continue this work by taking 6, 7, 8, 9 coins.
    When 10 coins are tossed, here are the theoretical probabilities of 0 to 10 heads
    respectively, all given as numerators of fractions which have a denominator
    of 2^{10}.
    1, 10, 45, 120, 210, 252, 210, 120, 45, 10, 1.

    Draw the bar-line graph showing these probabilities and compare it with the
    other graphs.

5.   **Insurance**

There are many risks that you can insure against. For example, every car owner must have third party insurance, and many owners choose to pay more to have comprehensive insurance.

If you book a holiday abroad with a travel firm, you will probably take out insurance against unforseen problems, the main one being a serious accident or illness for which you will need medical treatment which is expensive.

Insurance companies collect money (premiums) from many people. Then they can use this money to pay out compensation to the few people who make a claim.
In order to fix premiums fairly, the companies need to be able to estimate the probability of anyone making a claim.

A few years ago there was a very severe storm in the South of England. The probability of such a severe storm was thought to be very small. However, it happened, and there were many claims to the insurance companies for damage caused to buildings and cars by the force of the wind, and by falling trees, etc.

Find out all you can about insurance. First, ask at home to see if the family is insured for any risks, and get details of what is covered and what the premiums are.
Has your family had to make any claims recently ?

Then look at newspapers and magazines and find articles or advertisements mentioning insurance, and make a collection of cuttings.

Find out about life assurance.

Find out about insuring a car or motor cycle. What is meant by third-party insurance, and comprehensive insurance? What is a 'no claim' bonus ?

Make a list of all the different types of insurance and write a few details about each one.

If you knew a newly married couple, just moving into a new house, and with a new car, what types of insurance would you advise them to have ?

PUZZLE

39.   In this sum, each figure is represented by a different letter.
Given that V = 4 and S = 8, find which figures the other letters represent.

```
    M A T H S
        A T
+   L E V E L
    ─────────
    E I G H T
```

10 Thinking about graphs of functions

Using graphs

A graph is drawn for a purpose.
It can show the relationship between two variables.
It can be used to read information from it. This may be information about the values used in drawing the graph, or by using the line or curve of the graph, estimations of other values.

Springs

The connection between the extension and the elastic energy of a spring is

$E = \dfrac{\lambda x^2}{2l}$, where E is the energy, x is

the extension, λ is the elastic constant for the spring and l is the unstretched length of the spring.

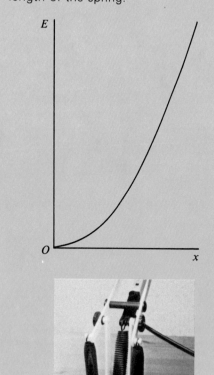

Spheres

The connection between the radius and volume of a sphere is $V = \frac{4}{3}\pi r^3$.

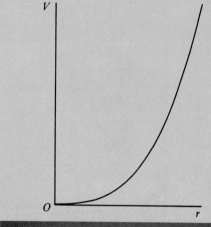

Curves and their equations

Here are some equations which are represented by interesting curves.

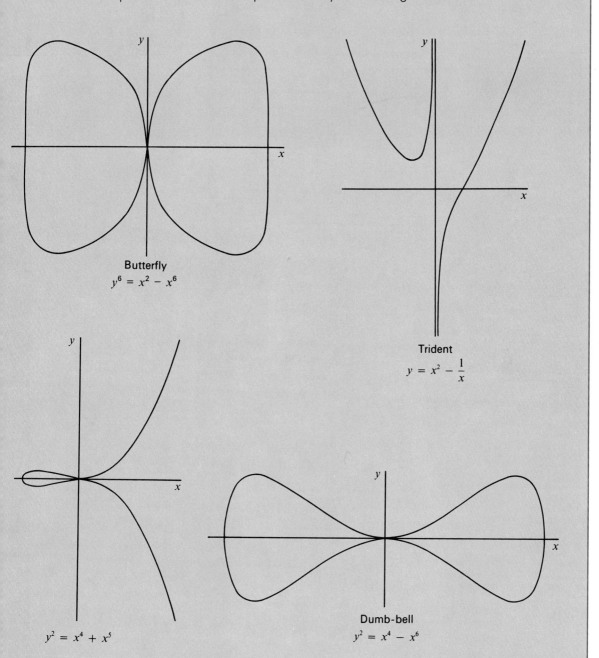

Butterfly
$$y^6 = x^2 - x^6$$

Trident
$$y = x^2 - \frac{1}{x}$$

$$y^2 = x^4 + x^5$$

Dumb-bell
$$y^2 = x^4 - x^6$$

10 Graphs of functions

Quadratic functions

Example

The simplest quadratic function is $y = x^2$
Here is a table of values for x from -8 to 8

x	-8	-7	-6	-5	-4	-3	-2	-1	0	1	2	3	4	5	6	7	8
y	64	49	36	25	16	9	4	1	0	1	4	9	16	25	36	49	64

Notice that $(-8)^2 = (-8) \times (-8) = +64$, and that x^2 is never negative.

To draw a graph of the function

To draw the x-axis from -8 to 8, taking a scale of 1 cm to 1 unit, means putting the y-axis down the centre of the page.
To draw the y-axis from 0 to 70, taking a scale of 2 cm to 10 units, means putting the x-axis at the bottom of the page.

Plot the points $(-8, 64)$, $(-7, 49)$, etc.
Notice that the points do not lie on a straight line. They lie on a curve.

You can plot extra points to help you.
There is a big gap between $(-8, 64)$ and $(-7, 49)$ so you can find the value of y when $x = -7.5$.
When $x = -7.5$, $y = 56.25$, so plot $(-7.5, 56.25)$, and a corresponding point when $x = 7.5$.

Draw the curve, in pencil, freehand. It is easier to draw if you turn your graph paper round. It is not stuck to your desk! Arrange it so that you are drawing from the inside of the curve. Your curves will improve as you get more practice. They should look smooth without sharp changes of direction, or bumps. (Look along the curve at eye-level. If you were riding along it on a toboggan, would it be a smooth ride ?)

If you look at your curve upside down, the shape is the same as that made if you throw a cricket ball at an angle into the air.
This curve is called a **parabola**.

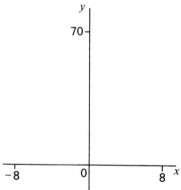

All quadratic functions, i.e. functions whose highest power of x is x^2, have graphs of this shape.
The point where the graph turns round is called a maximum point or a minimum point.

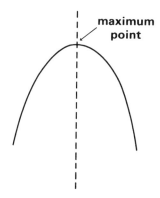

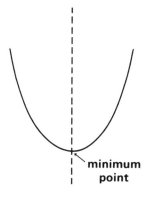

There is a line of symmetry passing through this point.
(Sometimes the values of x that you use may mean that the turning point is not shown on your curve.)

Exercise 10.1

1. Copy and complete this table of values for the function
   $y = x^2 - 4x$.

x	-2	-1	0	1	2	3	4	5	6
x^2 $-4x$	4 8								
y	12								

Draw axes with x from -2 to 6, using a scale of 2 cm to 1 unit, and y from -4 to 12, using a scale of 1 cm to 1 unit.
Plot the points given by the table.
2 extra points you can plot are $(-1\frac{1}{2}, 8\frac{1}{4})$ and $(5\frac{1}{2}, 8\frac{1}{4})$.
Draw the graph.

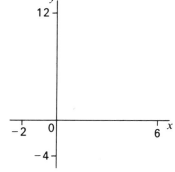

What are the coordinates of the minimum point on the curve ?
What are the values of x at the points where the curve crosses the x-axis ?

2. Copy and complete this table of values for the function
    $y = x^2 - 5x + 2$.

x	-1	0	1	2	3	4	5	6
x^2 $-5x$ $+2$	1 5 2	0 0 2						
y	8	2						

Draw axes with x from -1 to 6, using a scale of 2 cm to 1 unit, and y from -6 to 8, using a scale of 1 cm to 1 unit.
Plot the points given by the table.
Draw the graph.

What is the equation of the line which is an axis of symmetry of the curve ?
The curve cuts the x-axis at 2 points. State the values of x at these points, correct to 1 decimal place.

3. Copy and complete this table of values for the function
    $y = 10 - x^2$.

x	-4	-3	-2	-1	0	1	2	3	4
10 $-x^2$	10 -16	10 -9	10						
y	-6	1							

Draw axes with x from -4 to 4, using a scale of 2 cm to 1 unit, and y from -6 to 10, using a scale of 1 cm to 1 unit.
Plot the points given by the table.
Draw the graph.

What are the coordinates of the maximum point on the curve ?
State the values of x at the points where the curve cuts the x-axis, correct to 1 decimal place.

4. Copy and complete this table of values for the function
   $y = (2x - 1)(x + 2)$

x	-4	-3	-2	-1	0	1	2	3
$2x - 1$	-9							
$x + 2$	-2							
y	18							

(y is found by multiplying the last 2 numbers.)

Draw axes with x from -4 to 3, using a scale of 2 cm to 1 unit, and y from -5 to 25, using a scale of 2 cm to 5 units (so that 2 small squares represent 1 unit).
Plot the points given by the table.
Draw the graph.

5. Copy and complete this table of values for the function
   $y = 7 + 2x - x^2$.

x	-3	-2	-1	0	1	2	3	4	5
$-x^2$	-9								
$+2x$	-6								
7	7								
y	-8								

Draw axes with x from -3 to 5, using a scale of 2 cm to 1 unit, and y from -8 to 8, using a scale of 1 cm to 1 unit.
Plot the points given by the table.
Draw the graph.

What are the coordinates of the maximum point on the curve ?

Other simple functions

Cubic functions

Example

The simplest cubic function is $y = x^3$.
Here is a table of values for x from -4 to 4.

x	-4	-3	-2	-1	0	1	2	3	4
y	-64	-27	-8	-1	0	1	8	27	64

Notice that $(-4)^3 = (-4) \times (-4) \times (-4) = -64$

To draw the graph of the function, draw axes with x from -4 to 4, using a scale of
2 cm to 1 unit, and y from -70 to 70, using
a scale of 1 cm to 10 units.

Plot the points given by the table.

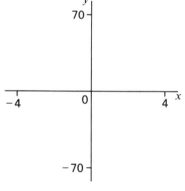

There is a big gap between the first two
points, and the last two points, so find the
value of 3.5^3 on your calculator and plot
points for $x = -3.5$ and $x = 3.5$.

Join the points with a smooth curve.
It is a curve which curves one way and then
changes to curve the other way at the
origin, which is a point of symmetry.

Sketch graph

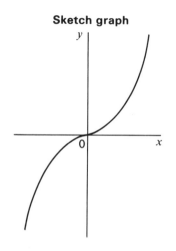

You can use your graph to find cubes and
cube roots of numbers. For 2.8^3 find the
value of y at the point on the curve where
$x = 2.8$. For $\sqrt[3]{30}$ find the value of x at the
point on the curve where $y = 30$.

The function $y = \dfrac{1}{x}$ when $x > 0$

This is an interesting curve.
To see its properties, we have chosen special values of x in the table of values.

x	$\frac{1}{6}$	$\frac{1}{5}$	$\frac{1}{4}$	$\frac{1}{3}$	$\frac{1}{2}$	1	2	3	4	5	6
y	6	5	4	3	2	1	$\frac{1}{2}$	$\frac{1}{3}$	$\frac{1}{4}$	$\frac{1}{5}$	$\frac{1}{6}$

e.g. When $x = \frac{1}{6}$, $y = 1 \div \frac{1}{6} = 1 \times 6 = 6$

Draw the x and y axes from 0 to 6, taking a scale of 2 cm to 1 unit.
Plot the points given by the table.
To plot $(\frac{1}{6}, 6)$, this is approximately $(0.17, 6)$.
Each small square on each axis represents
0.1 so 0.17 is between the 1st and 2nd
small squares, 0.1 and 0.2, and is nearer
to 0.2.

Join the points with a smooth curve.

The curve has an axis of symmetry.
What is its equation ?

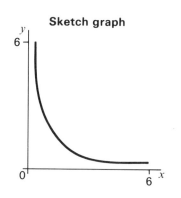

Sketch graph

Exercise 10.2

1. Copy and complete this table of values for the function
    $y = x^3 - 9x$.

x	-4	-3	-2	-1	0	1	2	3	4
x^3	-64								
$-9x$	36								
y	-28								

Draw axes with x from -4 to 4, using a scale of 2 cm to 1 unit, and y from -30
to 30, using a scale of 2 cm to 10 units.
Plot the points given by the table and also the points $(-3.5, -11.4)$, $(-0.5, 4.4)$,
$(0.5, -4.4)$ and $(3.5, 11.4)$.
Draw the graph.
Comment on its shape.

2. Copy and complete this table of values for the function

    $y = \dfrac{48}{x}$.

x	1	1.5	2	3	4	5	6	8	9.6	12	16	24	32	48
y	48	32												

    Draw x and y axes from 0 to 50, using a scale of 2 cm to 10 units.
    Plot the points given by your table.
    Draw the graph.

3. **The graph of $y = 2^x$**

    Copy and complete the table of values for the graph of $y = 2^x$.

x	1	2	3	4	5	6
y	2					64

    You will notice that this is a doubling pattern for the y-values. By continuing the
    patterns for x and y backwards we can find some more values for the table.

x	-2	-1	0	1	2	3	4	5	6
y	$\frac{1}{4}$	$\frac{1}{2}$	1	2					64

    Draw the x-axis from -2 to 6, taking a scale of 2 cm to 1 unit, and the y-axis
    from 0 to 70, taking a scale of 2 cm to 10 units.
    Plot the points given by the table and also the point (5.5, 45.3), which was
    found using a calculator.
    Draw the graph.

Exercise 10.3   Applications and Activities

1. The maximum volume, $y \, \text{cm}^3$, of a cone of slant height $x \, \text{cm}$ is given by the

    equation $y = \dfrac{2\pi x^3}{9\sqrt{3}}$.   This is approximately $y = 0.4x^3$.

    Make a table of values and draw the graph of $y = 0.4x^3$ for $x = 0$ to 6.

    If a cone has slant height 5.5 cm, use your graph to find the maximum volume it
    can have.

2. Boyle's Law for gases states that Pressure × Volume is constant.
    If the pressure is y units and the volume is x units, then $xy = k$, where k is a constant number.

    i.e. $y = \dfrac{k}{x}$

    In a particular situation, the volume of a gas was 30 units when the pressure was 2 units.
    In the equation, find the value of k.

    With this value of k, make a table of values for y when x = 10, 20, 30, 40, 50, 60, 80.

    Plot the graph of $y = \dfrac{k}{x}$, for values of x from 10 to 80.

    (Draw the x-axis from 0 to 80 and the y-axis from 0 to 6.)

    Use your graph to find the pressure when the volume is 75 units.

3. In a certain machine the amount of friction, y units, is connected to the angular speed, x revolutions per second, by the equation $y = 12 - 5x + x^2$.

    Work out a table of values and draw the graph of this function for x = 0 to 6.

    Find the speed for which the friction is least, and the amount of friction when the machine is running at this speed.

4. **The graph of $y = \dfrac{1}{x}$**

    The graph has been drawn for positive values of x, page 175, but there can also be negative values of x. However, x cannot be 0 (since we cannot divide by 0), thus the curve does not cross the y-axis, and it is in two parts.

    Draw x and y axes from -6 to 6, taking a scale of 1 cm to 1 unit.
    Plot the points given by the table on page 175, and draw the part of the curve where x is positive.

    Now find all the corresponding values where x is negative and plot them on the graph.
    e.g. When $x = -\frac{1}{6}$, $y = -6$; when $x = -1$, $y = -1$.
    Draw the part of the curve where x is negative.

    The complete curve is called a **rectangular hyperbola**. It has 2 axes of symmetry. What are their equations ?

5. A large metal box, without a lid, is to be made to have a volume of $13.5\,\text{m}^3$.
    If it has a square base with sides x m long, what is its height, in terms of x ?

    Find an expression for the total area $y\,\text{m}^2$ of the base and the 4 sides and show that

    $$y = x^2 + \frac{54}{x}.$$

    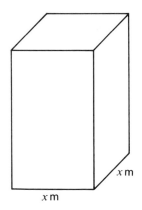

    Copy and complete this table of values for $y = x^2 + \frac{54}{x}$.

x	1	2	3	4	5	6
x^2	1	4				
$\dfrac{54}{x}$	54	27				
y	55	31				

    Draw the x-axis from 0 to 6 and the y-axis from 0 to 60.
    Plot the points and draw the graph for $x = 1$ to 6.
    For what value of x is y least ?

    What measurements should the box have, in order to use the least area of sheet metal ?

6. **Using a graphics calculator or a computer**

    If you have such a calculator, or can borrow one, then you can use it to draw the graphs used in this chapter, as well as others.
    Some of the functions can be plotted very quickly.
    (Your calculator may not work in the same way as this one, but try
    graph $\boxed{x^2}$ $\boxed{\text{EXE}}$ to get the graph of $y = x^2$.)

    However, it takes time to learn which keys to press to plot other graphs, so you will need to look at the manual and practise this.

If you have a computer, you can plot
graphs on the screen. You may do this
using a BASIC program, or you may use a
graph plotting program.

PUZZLES

40.   There is a chess board whose squares are 4 cm
      wide, and a disc with diameter 32 cm, the
      same measurement as the width of the board.
      If the disc is placed centrally on the board,
      how many squares will it completely cover ?

41.   Without using a calculator, can you find which is greater, $9 \times \sqrt{3}$ or $7 \times \sqrt{5}$?

42.   Two vertical poles stand on horizontal
      ground. The top of each is connected
      to the foot of the other by straight
      wires which meet at a point A.
      How high is A above the ground ?

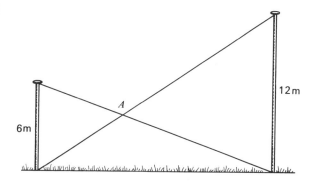

43.   200 soldiers stand in a rectangular array of 10 rows and 20 columns. The shortest man in
      each <u>row</u> is told to step out of place, and Stephen is the tallest of these men. After the
      men have returned to their original places, the tallest man in each <u>column</u> is told to step
      out. Thomas is the shortest of these men.
      Who is the taller, Stephen or Thomas ?

Miscellaneous Section B

Aural Practice

These aural exercises, B1 and B2, should be read to you, probably by your teacher or a friend, and you should write down the answers only, doing any working out in your head. You should do the 15 questions within 10 minutes.

Exercise B1

1. What decimal is equivalent to the fraction $\frac{3}{4}$?

2. What is the value of xy if $x = -6$ and $y = -7$?

3. If a woman earns £56 for working 8 hours, what should she earn for working 20 hours ?

4. Express as simply as possible $3a^2 \times 2a$.

5. The attendance at a match was 43 thousand. Write down this number in standard form.

6. Transform the formula $A = lb$, to write it in terms of b.

7. If $4x - 3$ is less than 17, what can you say about x ?

8. The base of a triangle is 10 cm and its height is 12 cm. What is its area ?

9. Two independent events can happen with probabilities of $\frac{1}{4}$ and $\frac{1}{3}$ respectively. What is the probability of both events happening ?

10. How many vertices (corners) has a cube ?

11. What is the value of $x^{\frac{1}{2}}$ when $x = 25$?

12. To make a pattern smaller, a length of 32 cm has to be decreased in the ratio 7 : 8. What is the reduced length ?

13. After 9 innings a cricketer has scored a total of 340 runs. How many runs must he score in his 10th innings to have an average, over the 10 innings, of 40 runs per innings ?

14.   Express as simply as possible, $y^5 \div y^2$.

15.   Two triangles are similar with lengths in the ratio 5 : 7. The perimeter of the larger triangle is 35 cm. What is the perimeter of the smaller one ?

Exercise B2

1.   Marion gets to the bus stop at 3.55 pm and the next bus is due at 4.20 pm. How many minutes should she have to wait ?

2.   If $x = -3$, what is the value of $x^2 + x$?

3.   5 lengths are measured. 4 of them are 1.5 m and one is 4 m. What is the average of the 5 lengths ?

4.   Express as simply as possible, $a \times a^2 \times a^3$.

5.   If an isosceles triangle has two angles of 35°, what size is the third angle ?

6.   Oliver spent $\frac{1}{2}$ of his money in one shop and $\frac{1}{8}$ of it in another. What fraction had he left ?

7.   If a 500 gram bottle of disinfectant costs £1.20, what should a 750 gram bottle cost, at the same rate ?

8.   If $\frac{1}{4}x$ is greater than 12, what can you say about x ?

9.   The capacity of a tank, in standard form, is 3.7×10^4 litres. Write this amount in litres, using an ordinary number.

10.   Write in factor form the expression $x^2 - 2x$.

11.   £16 is divided into 3 shares in the proportion 1 : 3 : 4. What is the smallest share ?

12.   What is the value of $8^{\frac{1}{3}}$?

13.   The probability of scoring a six on a certain biased die is $\frac{2}{5}$. What is the probability of scoring two sixes in two throws ?

14.   What is the value of y, if $y = mx + c$ and $x = 3$, $m = 2$ and $c = -6$?

15.   Two rectangles are similar and their lengths are in the ratio 3 : 5. The length of the smaller rectangle is 6.3 cm. What is the length of the other one ?

Exercise B3   Revision

1.   Mrs Robins and Mrs Yates both do a similar part-time job. Mrs Robins works for 12 hours a week and earns £45. How much should Mrs Yates earn, if she works for 16 hours per week ?

2.   The total surface area of this hemisphere is $S\,\mathrm{cm}^2$, where $S = 3\pi r^2$.
     Write this formula in terms of r.

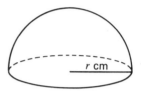

3.   A game-warden at the top of a tower 65 m high sees an elephant at an angle of depression of 12°. If the ground at the base of the tower is horizontal, how far away from the base is the elephant ?

4.   Find the values of these expressions when $x = -3$.

     1 $(x - 2)(x + 4)$

     2 $\dfrac{3x - 1}{2x + 5}$

     3 $5x^3 - 2x^2$

5.   Explain why triangles ABC, DEC are similar.
     If AE is a straight line, explain why BCD is also a straight line.
     If $\angle A = 127°$, what is the size of $\angle D$?

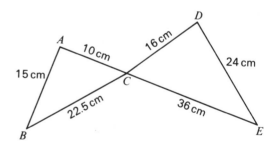

6. x and y are connected by the equation $y = \frac{4}{9}(x - 10)$.
     Find the value of x when $y = 2\frac{2}{3}$.

7.   Mr Collins won some money in a competition. He gave $\frac{1}{5}$ of it to his daughter and $\frac{1}{4}$ of the remainder to his son.
     He gave £160 to his wife and he kept £200 for himself.
     How much did he win ?

8. Water is taken out of a reservoir at the
    rate of 7 l/s.
    How much water is taken out in 1 day
    (24 hours) ?
    Give the answer in standard form, correct
    to 2 significant figures.

9. Simplify these fractions.

    1 $\dfrac{x}{4} + \dfrac{7x}{20} - \dfrac{2x}{5}$

    2 $\dfrac{3a^3}{4bc} \times \dfrac{28c^2}{15ab}$

    3 $\dfrac{27d^3}{4e} \div \dfrac{9d}{8e^2}$

10. What is the gradient of the line PQ ?

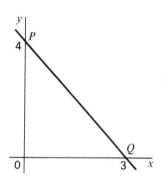

11. Give the range of values of x if:

    1 $x^2 \leqslant 49$

    2 $x^2 - 8 \geqslant 1$

    3 $2x^2 - 15 > 17$ and $0 < x < 6$.

12. In one bag there are 5 discs numbered from 6 to 10, and in a second bag there
    are 4 discs numbered from 11 to 14.
    Make a table to show the possible totals if one disc is drawn at random from
    each bag.
    What is the probability that:

    1 the total is an even number,

    2 the total is a prime number,

    3 the total is a multiple of 3 ?

    4 If after drawing the two discs, they are replaced before another drawing
        is made, what is the probability that in 2 successive drawings of two discs
        the total 24 is obtained twice ?

13. **1** Simplify $(6^3)^2 \times (6^2)^4$, leaving the answer in index form.

2 Simplify $\left(5^{\frac{1}{3}}\right)^6$, and state its value.

3 Find the value of $\left(\frac{2}{3}\right)^3 \times \left(\frac{3}{4}\right)^2$

14. If 3 cups of coffee and a cake cost £1.90 and 2 cups of coffee and 3 cakes cost £2.20, what is the price of a cup of coffee ?

15. Expand $(x + 2y)^2$.
Use the result to find the value of $6.54^2 \ + \ 4 \times 6.54 \times 1.73 \ + \ 4 \times 1.73^2$.

16. This list shows the number of people employed in a hospital.

Ancillary staff	360
Professional and technical	270
Administration and clerical	270
Nursing	1020
Medical, including consultants	192
Works and maintenance	48
	2160

A local hospital

Draw a pie chart showing this information.

17. The formula for the total surface area of a cone
is $S = \pi r^2 + \pi rl$

Factorise the right-hand side of this formula.
Without using your calculator, find the total
surface area when $r = 10\frac{1}{2}$ cm and $l = 19\frac{1}{2}$ cm.
Take π as $\frac{22}{7}$.

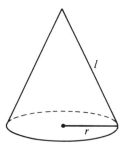

18. Express the amounts in these statements in standard form.

1 The world's smallest spider measures 0.00043 m in length.
2 The pressure of the quietest sound which can be heard is about 0.00002 Pa.
3 A virus measures about 0.0000003 m in length.

19. *ABCD* is a rectangle whose diagonals
     cut at *X*.
     PXQ is any line cutting *AB* at *P* and
     CD at *Q*.
     If *AB* = 12 cm, *BC* = 16 cm,
     1 find the lengths of *AC* and *AX*,
     2 find the range of possible
            lengths of the line *PQ*.

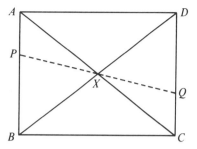

20. Copy and complete the table of values for the function
     $y = (3 + x)(2 - x)$.

x	-4	-3	-2	-1	0	1	2	3
$3 + x$ $2 - x$	-1 6							
y	-6							

Draw axes with *x* from -4 to 3, using a scale of 2 cm to 1 unit, and *y* from -6
to 8, using a scale of 1 cm to 1 unit.
Plot the points given by the table.
Draw the graph of the function.
What is the maximum value of *y* on the graph ?

Exercise B4   Activities

1. **The graph of $y = \tan x°$**

    Draw the *x*-axis from 0 to 90 taking a scale of 2 cm to 10 units. (Use the paper
    sideways if necessary.)
    Draw the *y*-axis from 0 to 8 taking a scale of 2 cm to 1 unit.
    Use your calculator to find the values of *y*, and plot the points, for *x* = 0, 5, 10,
    15, . . . to 70, and then for *x* = 71, 72, 73, . . . , until *y* is too big to plot.
    Join the points with a smooth curve.
    Explain what happens to the graph as *x* gets near to 90.

2. **A survey of pets**

Design a questionnaire and make a survey of your friends and relatives to find out the sort of pets people have.

If you are interested in keeping dogs as pets you can also find out about the different breeds of dogs that people keep, and you can do similar surveys for other types of pet.

You can find out the various reasons why people keep pets, and reasons why other people don't have pets.

You could ask people what sort of pet they would like to own.

You can work out the average number of pets per family. What kind of average will you use ?

Then ask people about the costs of keeping their various pets.
Here are some of the costs to consider:
>   Somewhere for the pet to live—hutch, cage, fish tank, stable.
>   Weekly food bill, including different sorts of food for a healthy diet.
>   Costs of cleaning out—cat litter, sawdust for cage, straw for stable.
>   Necessary vet's bills, for inoculations, etc.
>   Unexpected vet's bills, an average cost of treatment for illnesses.
>   Insurance, and any other costs.

Next, you could ask about the amount of time people spend each week on looking after their pets. This will vary from the time spent looking after a goldfish, which needs very little attention, to a dog or pony, which needs regular exercise.

Organise the data you collect and display it on a poster about pets. Include on your poster suitable statistical diagrams or graphs, and add some pictures or photographs as well.

Are there any problems caused by pets ? You could find out about these, and add details to your poster.

Do you think that it is a good idea for a family to have a pet ?

3. **The 3 discs problem**

    There are 3 discs in a bag. One is red on both sides, one is blue on both sides
    and the third one is red on one side and blue on the other.
    One disc is removed from the bag at random, and placed flat on the table so that
    only one side is visible.
    Predict these probabilities:
    If the top side is red, what is the probability that the other side is red ?
    If the top side is blue, what is the probability that the other side is blue ?

    Before checking these theoretically, try it out experimentally.
    You can make 3 identical discs and colour them as stated.
    Carry out the experiment 100 or 200 times and see if your results match the
    predictions you have made for the probabilities.

    To find the theoretical probabilities, label the three red sides R1, R2, R3 and the
    three blue sides B1, B2, B3.
    Make a list of **all** the outcomes, showing which side is on top and which is
    underneath in each case. Since these outcomes are equally likely, you can work
    out the probabilities.
    Do these theoretical results match your predictions ?
    Do the theoretical results match the experimental results ?

4. **Units in formulae**

    To find a length, such as a perimeter, you use **length** units such as cm, m or km.
    Any formula to find a length only involves units of length, and **has** to involve
    units of length.

    Examples are
    $P = 2(l + b)$
    l and b are length units, so $l + b$ is a length unit.

    $C = 2\pi r$
    r is a length unit. π is simply a number.

To find an area you use area units such as cm^2, m^2, km^2.
Any formula to find an area involves units of length × units of length.

Examples are
$A = lb$
l and b are length units, lb is an area unit.

$A = \pi r^2$
r is a length unit so r^2 is an area unit.

$S = 2lb + 2lh + 2bh$
l, b, h are length units so lb, lh, bh are all area units and so is $2lb + 2lh + 2bh$.

To find a volume you use volume units such as cm^3, m^3.
Any formula to find a volume involves
units of length × units of length × units of length,
or units of area × units of length.

Examples are
$V = lbh$,
$V =$ area of base × height,
$V = \frac{4}{3}\pi r^3$
r is a length unit so r^3 is a volume unit.

Formulae which involve combinations of these units such as $2\pi r + \pi r^2$, $lbh + 5r$,
are not giving either lengths, areas or volumes.
$2\pi r$ is a length formula because it involves r, in length units.
πr^2 is an area formula because it involves r^2, in area units.
$2\pi r + \pi r^2$ does not represent length or area.

lbh is a volume formula because it involves l, b, h, all lengths.
$5r$ is a length formula because it involves r, in length units.
$lbh + 5r$ does not represent volume or length.

A formula which involves area units ÷ length units will give a length.

e.g. Height of triangle $= \dfrac{2 \times \text{area}}{\text{base}}$

A formula which involves $\sqrt{\text{area units}}$ will give a length.

e.g. Radius of circle $= \sqrt{\dfrac{A}{\pi}}$

A formula which involves volume units ÷ area units will give a length.

e.g. Height $= \dfrac{\text{volume of cylinder}}{\text{area of base}}$

A formula which involves $\sqrt[3]{\text{volume units}}$ will give a length.

e.g. Radius of sphere $= \sqrt[3]{\dfrac{3V}{4\pi}}$

A formula which involves volume units ÷ length units will give an area.

e.g. Area of cross-section $= \dfrac{\text{volume}}{\text{height}}$

For these formulae, decide if X represents a length, area or volume.
a, l, b, h, r are all lengths. A is an area and V is a volume.

1 $X = 2\pi r^3$

2 $X = \dfrac{lb}{\pi h}$

3 $X = 4\pi r^2$

4 $X = l + h$

5 $X = lb + \pi r^2$

6 $X = \frac{1}{2}lr$

7 $X = 5lbh$

8 $X = \pi ab$

9 $X = \dfrac{l^3}{\pi r h}$

10 $X = \dfrac{l^2 b}{a}$

11 $X = \dfrac{A}{b}$

12 $X = \dfrac{V}{a}$

13 $X = \dfrac{V}{A}$

14 $X = \sqrt{4A}$

15 $X = \sqrt[3]{2V}$

The same idea can be used to check the units used in other formulae, such as for speed and density.

Speed $= \dfrac{\text{distance}}{\text{time}}$, so speed units are $\dfrac{\text{distance units}}{\text{time units}}$.

Density $= \dfrac{\text{mass}}{\text{volume}}$, so density units are $\dfrac{\text{mass units}}{\text{volume units}}$.

16 If distance is in km and time in hours, in what units is the speed ?

17 If mass is in grams and volume in cm^3, in what units is the density ?

18 If speed is in m/s, what are the units for distance, and for time ?

19 If density is in g/cm^3, what are the units for mass, and for volume ?

5. **Powers and prime numbers**

You are going to investigate numbers of the form $a^p - a$, where p is a prime number and a is any positive whole number which is not equal to p or a multiple of p.

Copy and complete this table, putting in the main part of the table the values of $a^p - a$ for the different values of a and p.   E.g. when $a = 3$ and $p = 2$ you want the value of $3^2 - 3$.

(The values where crosses are shown are not wanted because a is equal to p or is a multiple of p.)

Do not fill in the spaces where the result is too large to be shown **exactly** on your calculator. Approximate values, which will be shown in standard form, are no use for this investigation.

Values of $a^p - a$

	$p =$ 2	3	5	7	11	13	17	19
$a = 2$	X							
3		X						
4	X							
5			X					
6	X	X						
7				X				
8	X							
9		X						
10	X		X					
11					X			
12	X	X						

When you have filled in as many numbers as possible, check which of them divide exactly by their value of p.

e.g. For the numbers in the 1st column, where $p = 2$, check whether they divide by 2. (If they do not, cross them out.)

For the numbers in the 2nd column, where $p = 3$, check whether they divide by 3. (If they do not, cross them out.)

Continue for the other columns.

What do you notice ?

We will discuss this activity again later. Keep your table to refer to.

6. **Throwing dice**

Here are the bar-line graphs of the probabilities of each total when 1 die, and 2 dice, are thrown.

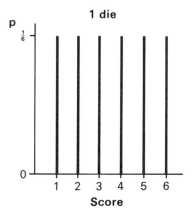

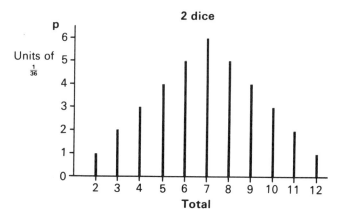

When 3 dice are thrown, you cannot find the probability of each total from a table, and a tree-diagram would be too complicated.
The best way is to see how many ways there are of getting each total in turn.

e.g. For a total of 9

1 and 2 and 6,	in	6 ways.	(Why are there 6 ways ?)
1 and 3 and 5,	in	6 ways.	
1 and 4 and 4,	in	3 ways.	(Why are there 3 ways ?)
2 and 2 and 5,	in	3 ways.	
2 and 3 and 4,	in	6 ways.	
Total		24 ways	

There are 6^3 (=216) combinations altogether, so
P(a total of 9) $= \frac{24}{216}$ $(=\frac{1}{9})$

Perhaps a group of you could work out the number of ways for each total from 3 to 18.
Check that they add up to 216.
Then calculate the probabilities.

Draw a bar-line graph of the probabilities using units of $\frac{1}{216}$ on the vertical axis.
Compare it with the other graphs and comment about them.

You could do a practical experiment by throwing dice, or using results of previous throws, or by using simulated results from a computer.
You can find experimental results for throwing 1 die, then for 2 dice by taking the results in pairs, and finally for 3 dice by taking the results in 3's.
You can work out the experimental probabilities by using the relative frequencies.
Compare your experimental results with the theoretical ones.

7. **Following the Highway Code**

Shortest stopping distances—in feet

mph	Thinking distance	Braking distance	Overall stopping distance
20	20	20	40
30	30	45	75
40	40	80	120
50	50	125	175
60	60	180	240
70	70	245	315

The details above are given in the Highway Code, which gives rules for safety on the roads.

If cars drive too close, then if the one in front has to stop suddenly, the car following may either run into it, or swerve and cause a different accident. Therefore the gap between cars should not be less than the overall stopping distance shown.

Draw a graph to show these figures, which are the shortest distances for a dry road, a car with good brakes and tyres, and an alert driver.

Put speed in mph on the x-axis, up to 70 mph, which is the maximum speed allowed in Britain.

Put distances in feet on the y-axis, up to 350 feet.

1   Plot the points showing the thinking distances, and join them with a straight line, which passes through the origin.

2   Plot the points showing the braking distances. Join them with a smooth curve which passes through the origin, and let it also pass through the point (10, 5).

3   Plot the points showing the overall stopping distances, and join them with a smooth curve.

4   If a driver is driving a car along a motorway at 65 mph, use your graph to find the shortest overall stopping distance.

5 If a driver is driving a car along a road in town at 25 mph, what is the shortest overall stopping distance in good conditions ? On wet or icy road the gap left between vehicles should be at least doubled. If the road is icy, what is the least gap the driver should leave between his car and the vehicle in front ?

6 The curve you have drawn for the braking distance suggests that it is the graph of a quadratic function.
Copy and complete this table, where b ft is the braking distance.

speed x mph	20	30	40	50	60	70
x^2	400					
distance b ft	20					

From the table, find the equation for b in terms of x.

If the thinking distance is t feet, what is the equation for t in terms of x ?

If the overall stopping distance is y feet, what is the equation for y in terms of b and t ?

What is the equation for y in terms of x ?

Use your equation to find the answers to **4** and the first part of **5**, to check the answers you got from the graph.

8. **A snowflake curve**

Make this drawing on a sheet of plain paper.

Stage 1:
Begin by drawing an equilateral triangle of side 16.2 cm.

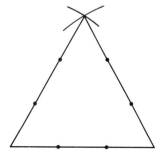

Stage 2:

Divide each side of the outline of the figure into 3 equal parts.
Draw an equilateral triangle on the centre part of each side, on the outside of the figure.
How many sides has the outlined figure now ?

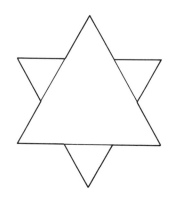

If the original triangle had perimeter of length p cm, how long are the sides of the outlined figure now ?
What is the perimeter of the figure, in terms of p ?

Stage 3:

Repeat stage 2.

Stage 4:

Repeat stage 2 again.

Stage 5:

If you can manage to draw the small triangles you can repeat stage 2 once again.

Colour the snowflake to hide the inside lines.

State the number of sides at each stage, as a sequence of numbers. How many sides would there be at the nth stage ?
State the perimeter of the figure at each stage, as a sequence of numbers in terms of p. What would be the perimeter at the nth stage ?
Find the perimeter if you could continue making the curve for 20 stages, in terms of p, and by putting $p = 48.6$, find the actual length.

You can investigate the sequence of the additional area to the figure at each stage, in terms of A, the original area. You can see from the diagram how each smaller triangle compares in area to the triangle it is on the side of.

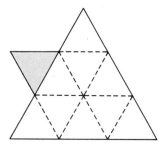

You can also draw an anti-snowflake curve. You draw the triangles on the inside of the figure, and then the centre parts of the sides which you have used are rubbed out. The area shrinks. When you have got as far as you can, colour the inside region.
Investigate the perimeter of the curve and the area inside it, at each stage.

9. **The third stellation of the icosahedron**

Here are the instructions for making this interesting solid figure.
Use thin cardboard.
First, here is the model, together with curves on the outside edges.

To make a pyramid

Draw a circle of radius 5 cm. Mark a point
on the circle and starting from that point
use your compasses, with radius 5 cm, to
mark off 5 other points on the circle.
Join the points as shown. Score along all
the straight lines. Cut out the circle.
Cut along the thick lines. (One of the small
circular segments is cut off.)
Bend all the lines, bending away from the
side you have scored on.

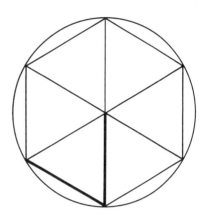

Glue together the two triangles next to the cut line, one over the other so that
you get a 5-sided pyramid whose bottom edges are curved and slightly bent. The
side of the cardboard showing the drawing is on the outside so that the inside is
the clean side.

When you have made 12 pyramids, glue 2 of the pyramids together, just joining
them along one of their small curved pieces. (From now on, you only glue along
the small curved pieces. You do not glue any more triangles.)
When the glue is dry, glue a third pyramid to the first two using curved pieces
next to the one already used. (Now the points of the pyramids will be inside the
model and the clean sides will be on the outside.)
Then glue a fourth pyramid to two of the first three, again using curved pieces
next to one already used. Build up the rest of the model in the same way.

When you have finished making your model you can decide whether to paint it,
and if so, what colour scheme to use.

Notice how the model is composed of intersecting planes.

If you want to make the correct model without the curved parts showing, score
the lines which are the sides of the hexagon on the other side, then they will
bend the other way and you will use the circular segments as tabs, glueing them
on the inside of the model. (In fact, you need not make them curved, if you prefer
straight tabs.) You will only use half of the tabs, cutting the others off when you
find out which ones are not needed.

11 Thinking about trigonometry

Sine and cosine ratios

In this chapter, two more trigonometrical functions are used.

$$\sin \theta = \frac{\text{opp}}{\text{hyp}} \qquad \cos \theta = \frac{\text{adj}}{\text{hyp}}$$

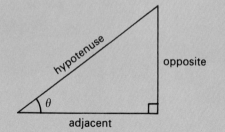

Using the cosine ratio

The walls of a chalet are 8 m apart.
If the roof slopes at 24° to the horizontal, how long are the sloping roof panels ?

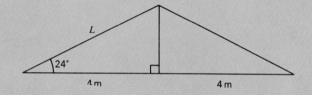

You can find the answer on your calculator by finding
(4 ÷ cos 24°).

Angle of elevation

To fire a projectile a distance *d* metres, when the speed of projection is *u* m/s, means

that the angle of elevation of the gun barrel should be $\frac{1}{2}\theta$, where $\sin \theta = \dfrac{dg}{u^2}$.

(*g* m/s^2 is the acceleration due to gravity and is approximately 9.8 m/s^2).

To fire a cannon-ball a distance of 120 m, if the speed of projection was 35 m/s, at what angle should the gun be elevated ?

The same distance will be reached if the angle is $90° - \frac{1}{2}\theta$. What is the second possible angle of elevation ?

Cannon of 1628, with method of obtaining elevation.

Using the sine ratio

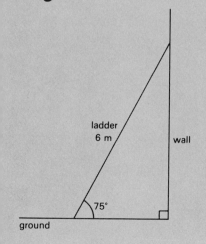

For safety, the angle θ between a ladder and the horizontal ground should be about 75°. If a ladder is 6 m long, what will be the height the ladder will reach up the vertical wall, if it is inclined at this angle ?

11 Trigonometry (2)

In Chapter 7 you used the tangent ratio to calculate an unknown side or an unknown angle in a right-angled triangle.

There are two other ratios which can be used. Both involve the hypotenuse.

$$\sin \theta = \frac{\text{opposite}}{\text{hypotenuse}}$$

$$\cos \theta = \frac{\text{adjacent}}{\text{hypotenuse}}$$

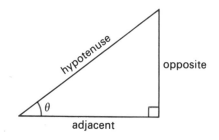

sin is short for sine, and is pronounced like sign.
cos is short for cosine, and is pronounced like coz.

These functions are shown in tables, and are stored in your scientific calculator.

For sin 28°, press 28 $\boxed{\sin}$ and you will get 0.469 . . .

(Make sure your calculator is working in degrees.)

For cos 32°, press 32 $\boxed{\cos}$ and you will get 0.848 . . .

Using the sine or cosine ratio to find a side

These ratios are used when you know the length of the hypotenuse.

Example

1   If you are using $\angle A$, then BC
    is the side opposite $\angle A$, and to
    find BC you will use the sine ratio.

$$\sin A = \frac{\text{opp}}{\text{hyp}}$$

$$\sin 36° = \frac{x}{7}$$

$$x = 7 \times \sin 36°$$
$$(= 7 \times 0.5877 \ldots)$$
$$= 4.114$$
$$BC = 4.1 \text{ cm, to the nearest mm.}$$
$$(BC = 4.11 \text{ cm, to 3 sig fig.})$$

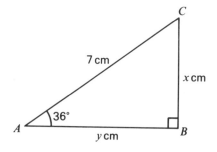

You will use your calculator to find $7 \times \sin 36°$.
Press 7 $\boxed{\times}$ 36 $\boxed{\sin}$ $\boxed{=}$ and you will get 4.114. . .

AB is the side adjacent to $\angle A$, so to find AB you will use the cosine ratio.

$$\cos A = \frac{\text{adj}}{\text{hyp}}$$

$$\cos 36° = \frac{y}{7}$$

$$y = 7 \times \cos 36°$$
$$(= 7 \times 0.8090 \ldots)$$
$$= 5.663$$
$$AB = 5.7 \, \text{cm, to the nearest mm.}$$
$$(AB = 5.66 \, \text{cm, to 3 sig fig.})$$

On your calculator press 7 $\boxed{\times}$ 36 $\boxed{\cos}$ $\boxed{=}$

You can check that the answers seem reasonable. Both AB and BC must be less than 7 cm, and since $\angle A$ is less than $\angle C$, BC will be smaller than AB.

Since $\angle A = 36°$, $\angle C = 90° - 36° = 54°$. You could have used $\angle C$ instead of $\angle A$. Then you would have had $x = 7 \times \cos 54°$ and $y = 7 \times \sin 54°$. You can check that these would give the same answers.

Using the sine or cosine ratio to find an angle

You must know the lengths of the hypotenuse and one other side.

Examples

2   To find $\angle A$

$$\sin A = \frac{\text{opp}}{\text{hyp}}$$

$$= \frac{7}{12} \, (= 0.5833 \ldots)$$

$$\angle A = 35.7°$$

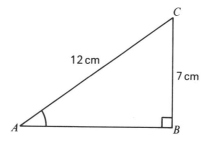

You will use your calculator to find the angle.
To get the inverse of the sine function press $\boxed{F}$ then $\boxed{\sin}$.

Press 7 $\boxed{\div}$ 12 $\boxed{=}$ $\boxed{\text{inverse sin}}$ and you will get 35.68 . . .

To 1 decimal place $\angle A = 35.7°$
(Also $\angle C = 90° - \angle A = 90° - 35.7° = 54.3°$.)

3 To find $\angle A$

$$\cos A = \frac{\text{adj}}{\text{hyp}}$$

$$= \frac{9}{13} \ (= 0.6923 \ldots)$$

$$\angle A = 46.2°$$

(and $\angle B = 90° - \angle A = 90° - 46.2° = 43.8°$)

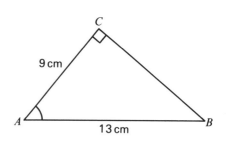

Exercise 11.1

1. Use your calculator to find the value of sin A, correct to 3 decimal places, if $\angle A$
    equals
    1 17°   **2** 69°   **3** $32\frac{1}{2}°$ **4** 81°   **5** 4°

2. Use your calculator to find the value of cos B, correct to 3 decimal places, if $\angle B$
    equals
    1 8°   **2** 85°   **3** 39°   **4** $66\frac{1}{2}°$ **5** 21°

3. Use your calculator to find the size of $\angle C$, in degrees correct to 1 decimal place,
    if sin C equals

    1 0.9   **2** 0.632   **3** 0.387   **4** $\dfrac{5}{9}$ **5** $\dfrac{4.5}{6.2}$

4. Use your calculator to find the size of $\angle C$, in degrees correct to 1 decimal place,
    if cos C equals

    1 0.8   **2** 0.419   **3** 0.205   **4** $\dfrac{11}{12}$ **5** $\dfrac{1.1}{3.8}$

5. Find the stated sides in these right-angled triangles. Give the answers in cm, to 3 significant figures.

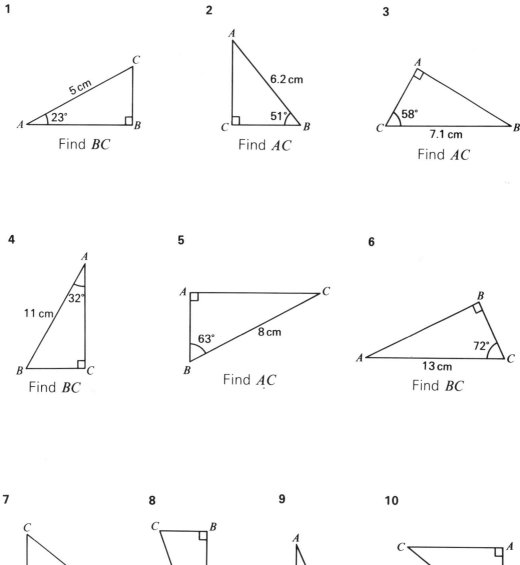

1

5 cm, 23°, Find BC

2

6.2 cm, 51°, Find AC

3

58°, 7.1 cm, Find AC

4

11 cm, 32°, Find BC

5

63°, 8 cm, Find AC

6

72°, 13 cm, Find BC

7

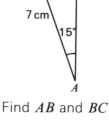

9.4 cm, 38°, Find AB and AC

8

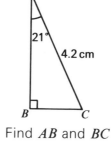

7 cm, 15°, Find AB and BC

9

21°, 4.2 cm, Find AB and BC

10

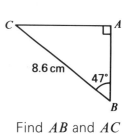

8.6 cm, 47°, Find AB and AC

6. Find the marked angle in these right-angled triangles, and then by subtraction find the 3rd angle of the triangle. Give the answers in degrees, correct to 1 decimal place.

1

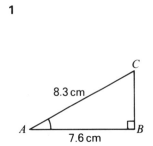

2

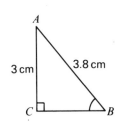

3

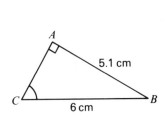

4

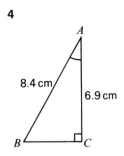

5

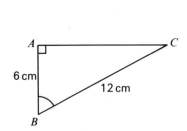

6

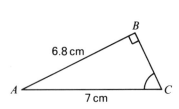

7

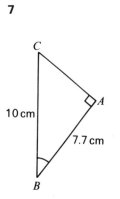

8

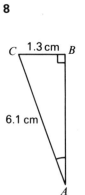

9

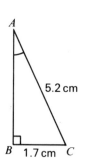

10

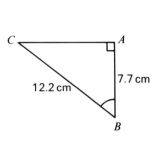

To find the hypotenuse

Example

To find AB

$$\sin A = \frac{\text{opp}}{\text{hyp}}$$

$$\sin 18° = \frac{5}{x}$$

$$x \times \sin 18° = 5$$

$$x = \frac{5}{\sin 18°}$$

$$= 16.180 \dots$$

$$AB = 16.2 \text{ cm, to 3 sig fig.}$$

On your calculator, press 5 $\boxed{\div}$ 18 $\boxed{\sin}$ $\boxed{=}$

If you had known the length of AC instead of AB you would have used the cosine ratio, or alternatively used $\angle B$ which is 72°.

Now that you have learnt how to use the sine and cosine ratios, don't forget that you have also learnt how to use the tangent ratio. This is used whenever the hypotenuse is not involved in the question.

Here are the 3 ratios.

$$\sin \theta = \frac{\text{opp}}{\text{hyp}} \qquad \cos \theta = \frac{\text{adj}}{\text{hyp}} \qquad \tan \theta = \frac{\text{opp}}{\text{adj}}$$

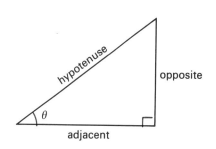

Exercise 11.2

1. Use the sine or cosine ratio to find the length of the hypotenuse in these right-angled triangles. Give the answers in cm, to 3 significant figures.

1

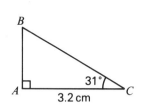

2

3

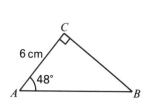

4

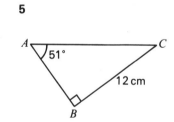

5

6

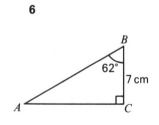

7

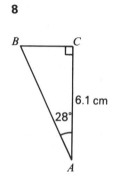

8

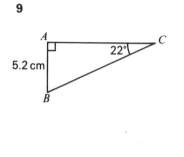

9

10

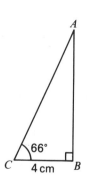

2. Use the sine, cosine or tangent ratio as appropriate, to find the stated side in
    these right-angled triangles. Give the answers in cm, to 3 significant figures.

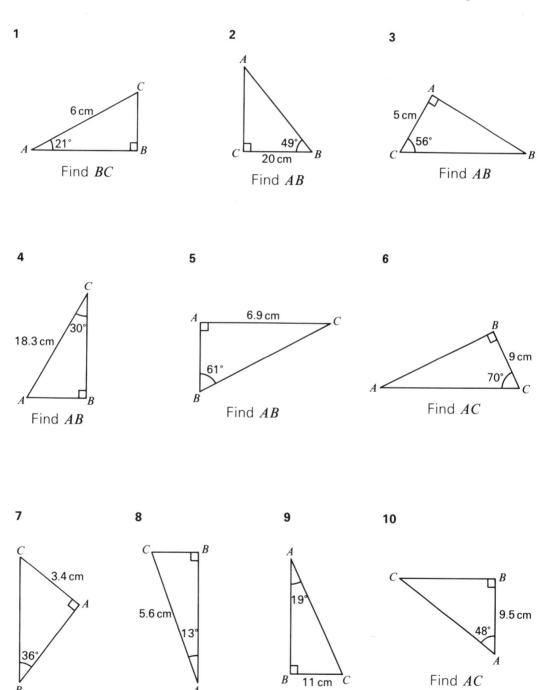

1

6 cm

21°

Find *BC*

2

49°
20 cm

Find *AB*

3

5 cm

56°

Find *AB*

4

30°
18.3 cm

Find *AB*

5

6.9 cm

61°

Find *AB*

6

9 cm

70°

Find *AC*

7

3.4 cm

36°

Find *AB*

8

5.6 cm

13°

Find *BC*

9

19°

11 cm

Find *AC*

10

9.5 cm

48°

Find *AC*

3.   Use the sine, cosine or tangent ratio as appropriate, to find the marked angle in these triangles. Then by subtraction find the 3rd angle of the triangle. Give the answers in degrees, correct to 1 decimal place.

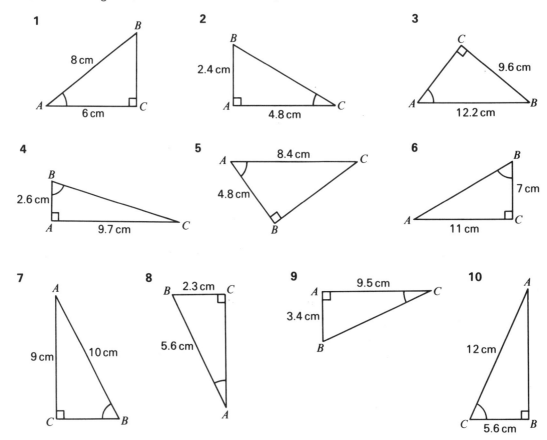

Exercise 11.3   Applications and Activities

1.   A ladder 7 m long leans against the side of a wall, and makes an angle of 63° with the horizontal ground. How high up the wall is the top of the ladder ?

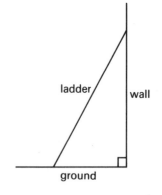

2. A mine shaft is entered at ground level, at *A*, and descends along an even slope to a point *B*, which is 200 m from *A*. If *B* is 30 m below ground level, what is the angle of slope which *AB* makes with the horizontal ground ?

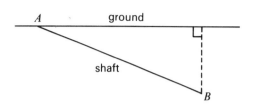

3. A ship sails 10 km on a bearing of 025° and then 8 km on a bearing of 038°. How far North is it from its starting point ?

4. A skier is climbing up a slope at an angle of 12° with the horizontal. After he has gone a distance of 250 m, how much higher up the slope is he, measured vertically, than when he started ?

5. A pendulum 1.8 m long swings through an angle of 10° on either side of the vertical. How high does the tip of the pendulum rise above the lowest point of its swing ?

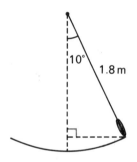

6. A kite is flying at a height of 100 m above the ground at the end of a string which makes an angle of 28° with the vertical. What is the length of the string ?

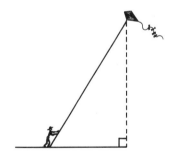

7. A hot-air balloon rises vertically from a point *B*. An observer at *A*, 150 m from *B* on level ground, sees the balloon at an angle of elevation of 24°. How high is the balloon ? When the balloon rises to twice that height, what will the angle of elevation be then, from *A* ?

8. A ladder **AB** is leant against a wall and
    just clears the top of a fence **CD** which
    is 2 m tall. The distance **AC** = 1.6 m.

    1 What is the size of ∠**A** ?
    2 If the ladder is 6 m long, how high
          up the wall does it reach ?

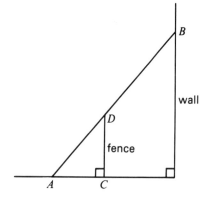

9. A ramp is to be made to ascend a height
    of 2 m, at a slope of 18° with the
    horizontal. How long will the ramp be,
    to the nearest 0.1 m ?

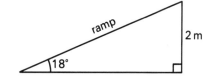

10. A rope 10 m long from the top of a vertical
    pole to a point on the ground, makes an angle of 23°
    with the pole.
    How high is the pole ?

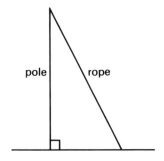

11. A ship leaves a port **P** and travels for 2 hours at a speed of 20 km/h on a
    bearing of 312°, to a point **Q**.
    1 How far North of **P** is it then ?
    2 How far West of **P** is it then ?

    For the next 3 hours it travels due West at the same speed to a point **R**.
    3 Find the size of ∠**QRP**.
    4 If the ship then goes directly from **R** to **P**, what is the bearing on which it
          must travel ?

12.   **Isosceles triangles and regular polygons**

An isosceles triangle can be made into
2 congruent right-angled triangles by
drawing the line of symmetry.
In the diagram, where $AB = AC$ and
$\angle B = \angle C$, the line AM is the line of
symmetry.
AM bisects $\angle BAC$, and AM bisects BC, so
$\angle BAM = \frac{1}{2}\angle BAC$ and $BM = \frac{1}{2}BC$.

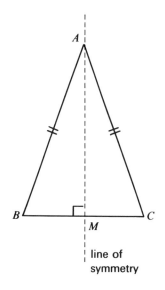

line of
symmetry

Use the line of symmetry in these questions.

1

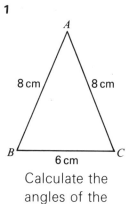

Calculate the
angles of the
triangle.

2

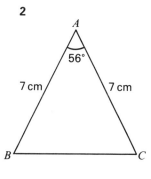

Calculate the
length of BC.

3

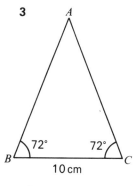

Calculate the
length of AB.

Regular polygons

e.g. A regular polygon $ABCDE$ is to
be inscribed in a circle centre O
of radius 6 cm. Find the length
of the sides of the polygon.

What is the size of $\angle AOB$?
What is the size of $\angle AOM$?
Use $\triangle AOM$ to calculate the
length of AM and hence the
length of AB.

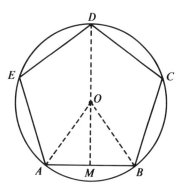

A similar method can be used in any regular polygon.

13. **Special ratios**

Half of a square

Use Pythagoras' theorem to calculate the length of AC, leaving it in square root form.

Write down as fractions the values of tan 45°, sin 45°, cos 45°.

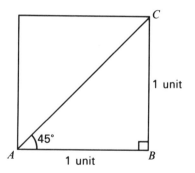

Half of an equilateral triangle

What is the length of EG ?
Use Pythagoras' theorem to calculate the length of DG, leaving it in square root form.

Write down as fractions the values of tan 60°, sin 60°, cos 60°.

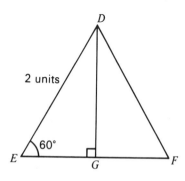

Which angle is 30° ?
Write down as fractions the values of tan 30°, sin 30°, cos 30°.

You can work out the decimal equivalents of these fractions with your calculator and check that they are correct.

14. **Graphs of $y = \sin x°$ and $y = \cos x°$**

For the graph of $y = \sin x°$, draw the x-axis from 0 to 90 taking a scale of 2 cm to 10 units (using the graph paper sideways if necessary). Draw the y-axis from 0 to 1 taking a scale of 1 cm to 0.1 unit.
Use your calculator to find values of y and plot the points for $x = 0, 5, 10, 15, \ldots$ to 90.
Join the points with a smooth curve.
Draw the graph of $y = \cos x°$, either on the same axes, or on a separate graph with the same scales.
Compare the two graphs and comment about them.

PUZZLES

44.   Hanif and Iqbal have 5 20p coins and 5 5p
       coins to share out. They place these in a
       circle, and Hanif begins counting coins round
       the circle, taking the 8th coin. Then Iqbal
       continues from the next coin in the circle and
       he takes the 8th coin. This is followed by
       Hanif again, then Iqbal again, and so on, until
       all the coins are taken.
       When the sharing was completed, Iqbal was
       rather annoyed because he got all the 5p
       coins and Hanif had all the 20p coins.
       With which coin did Hanif start the counting,
       and did he go clockwise or anticlockwise ?

45.   Copy the diagram on squared paper and
       fill in the answers to the clues on your
       copy.

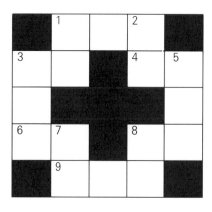

Across

1   A square number.
3   The square root of **5** down.
4   A multiple of the sum of the
       digits of **6** across.
6   The sum of the digits of **5** down,
       reversed.
8   The product of the digits of **1** across.
9   A cube number.

Down

1   The product of the digits of **3** down.
2   A multiple of **7** down.
3   A multiple of **8** across.
5   A palindromic number.
7   The square root of **1** across.
8   The cube root of **9** across multiplied by the sum of the digits of **4** across,
       reversed.

12 Thinking about cumulative frequenc

What is the meaning of the word 'cumulative' ?
Another word with a related meaning is 'accumulate'.

Cumulus clouds

Rounded masses heaped onto a horizontal base.

An accumulator bet

An accumulator bet is one where the winnings of each race are staked on the next race, for several races.

Discarded light bulbs

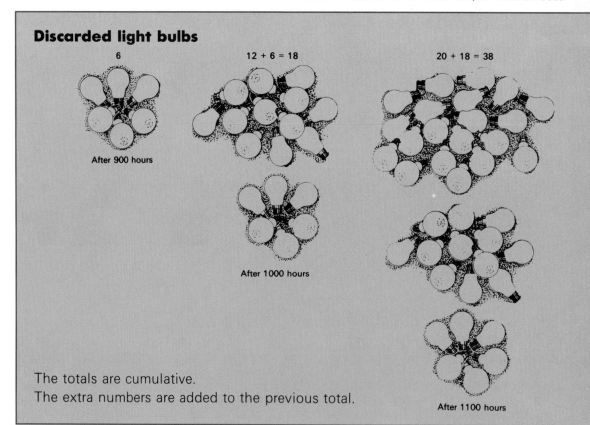

6

12 + 6 = 18

20 + 18 = 38

After 900 hours

After 1000 hours

After 1100 hours

The totals are cumulative.
The extra numbers are added to the previous total.

The median

The halfway value in a distribution.

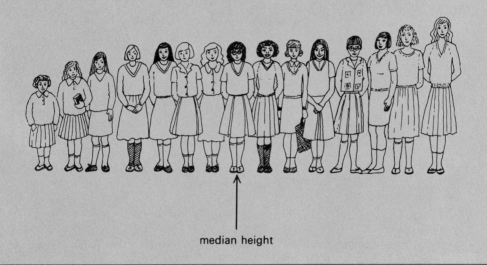

median height

The quartiles and the interquartile range

The quartiles are the quarter-way values in a distribution.

The interquartile range is the range of the middle half of the values, those between the lower quartile and the upper quartile.

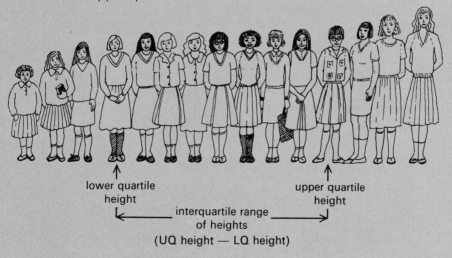

lower quartile
height

upper quartile
height

interquartile range
of heights
(UQ height — LQ height)

12 Cumulative Frequency

If we have a frequency table of grouped data we can use it to make a **cumulative frequency table**.

Examples

1 The frequency table shows the distribution of the lifetimes of a sample of 200 electric light bulbs.

Lifetime in hours	Number of bulbs
800 to under 900	6
900 to under 1000	12
1000 to under 1100	20
1100 to under 1200	36
1200 to under 1300	71
1300 to under 1400	34
1400 to under 1500	14
1500 to under 1600	7
	200

There are no bulbs with lifetimes less than 800 hours.
There are 6 bulbs with lifetimes less than 900 hours.
There are 18 bulbs altogether with lifetimes less than 1000 hours (6 + 12).
There are 38 bulbs altogether with lifetimes less than 1100 hours (18 + 20), and so on.

If we set this information down in a table it is a cumulative frequency table.

Lifetimes (Hours)	Cumulative frequency
less than 800	0
less than 900	6
less than 1000	18
less than 1100	38
less than 1200	74
less than 1300	145
less than 1400	179
less than 1500	193
less than 1600	200

The first row is not essential, but it forms a useful beginning to the table, and gives a starting point on the graph we are going to draw.

The last row's cumulative frequency is 200 because there were 200 bulbs altogether in the frequency table. If you do not get the same total you have made a mistake somewhere.

The wording in the frequency table was 800 to **under** 900.

That is why the wording in the cumulative frequency table is **less than** 800, etc. Sometimes the grouping is different.

2   The frequency table shows the examination marks of 160 students, and the cumulative frequency table is constructed from it.

Frequency table

Mark	Number of students
1–10	2
11–20	9
21–30	21
31–40	27
41–50	40
51–60	33
61–70	13
71–80	8
81–90	4
91–100	3
	160

Cumulative frequency table

Mark	cum. freq.
0	0
10 or less	2
20 or less	11
30 or less	32
40 or less	59
50 or less	99
60 or less	132
70 or less	145
80 or less	153
90 or less	157
100 or less	160

Exercise 12.1

Make cumulative frequency tables of the data given in these frequency distributions.
(In the first two questions you are shown how the table begins.)
The symbol < has been used for 'less than'.
These tables will be used again in the next exercise.

1.   The heights of 150 girls.

Height in cm	f
135 to <140	4
140 to <145	9
145 to <150	17
150 to <155	38
155 to <160	50
160 to <165	23
165 to <170	6
170 to <175	3
	150

Cumulative frequency table

Height in cm	cumulative frequency
<135	0
<140	4
<145	13
. . .	. .

2.   The lengths of 300 leaves from a certain type of plant were recorded, each to the nearest mm.

Length (mm)	f
45–49	7
50–54	43
55–59	73
60–64	62
65–69	55
70–74	43
75–79	17
	300

Cumulative frequency table

Length in mm	cumulative frequency
<44.5	0
<49.5	7
<54.5	50
. . .	. .

Note that, because the measurements are to the nearest mm, the boundaries are 44.5, 49.5, 54.5, etc.

3.   The weights of 400 men.

Weight in kg	f
60 to <6?	4
63 to <66	15
66 to <69	62
69 to <72	83
72 to <75	95
75 to <78	65
78 to <81	48
81 to <84	22
84 to <87	5
87 to <90	1
	400

4.   The examination marks of 100 students.

Mark	1–10	11–20	21–30	31–40	41–50	51–60	61–70	71–80	81–90	91–100	Total
f	5	9	10	12	15	16	12	11	6	4	100

5.   The weights of 250 parcels.

Weight (kg)	1 to <2	2 to <3	3 to <4	4 to <5	5 to <6	6 to <7
f	25	43	65	51	48	18

A cumulative frequency curve

When you have made a cumulative frequency table, the data can be plotted on a graph called a cumulative frequency curve.

Example 1, continued.

Using the data of example 1, page 214, lifetimes are labelled on the horizontal axis, from 800 to 1600 hours.
Cumulative frequency is labelled on the vertical axis, from 0 to 200.
(The cumulative frequency is **always** labelled on the vertical axis.)

The 1st point is plotted at (800, 0).
The 2nd point is plotted at (900, 6).
The 3rd point is plotted at (1000, 18),
and so on, ending with the point (1600, 200).

Make your own copy of the graph and plot the points.
(On the horizontal axis use a scale of 2 cm to 100 hours, on the vertical axis use 2 cm to 20.)
Join the points with a smooth curve, drawn freehand.
The curve is often a sort of S-shaped curve, as in this example, although not always. It is sometimes called an **ogive** (pronounced oh-jive) as this is an architectural term for this shape of curve.

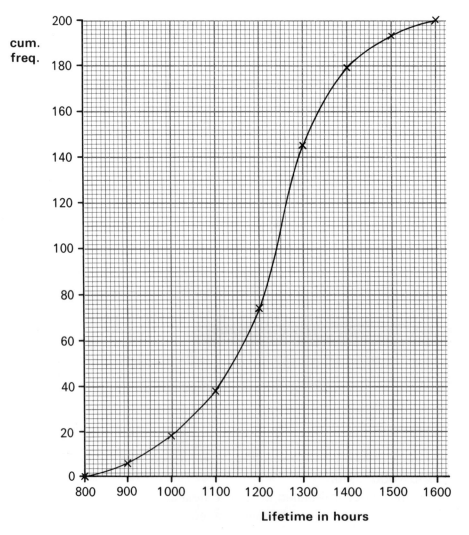

Cumulative frequency graph of lifetimes of bulbs

Note. In this chapter we are joining the points by a smooth curve. You may find questions elsewhere where you are asked to draw a **cumulative frequency polygon**. In that case, you use your ruler and join each point to the next one with a straight line, so that the graph is a series of straight lines.

Cumulative frequency polygon

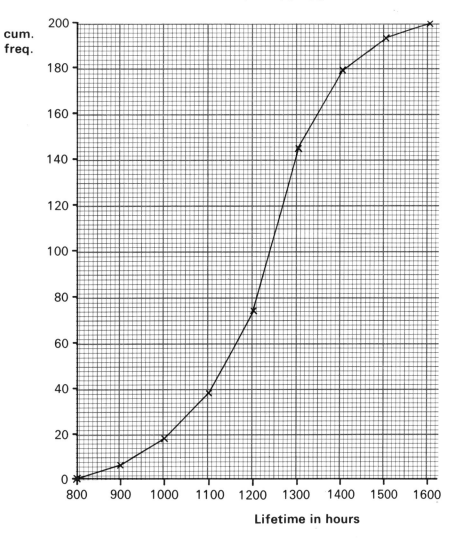

Exercise 12.2

The graphs drawn here will be used again in the next exercise.

1. Using the cumulative frequency table you have made in question 1, Exercise 12.1, draw the cumulative frequency curve.
    Label the horizontal axis, for height in cm, from 135 to 175, taking a scale of 2 cm to 5 units, and label the vertical axis for cumulative frequency, from 0 to 150 taking a scale of 2 cm to 20 units.
    Plot the points and join them with a smooth curve.
    Give the graph a heading, e.g. Cumulative frequency graph of girls' heights.

2. Using the cumulative frequency table you have made in question 2, Exercise 12.1, draw the cumulative frequency curve.
    You should label the horizontal axis, for lengths in mm, from 40 to 80, using 2 cm to 5 units, and then plot the points at 44.5, 49.5, etc.
    On the vertical axis a suitable scale might be 2 cm to 40 units or to 50 units. Do not use 2 cm to 30 units.

3 to 5.   Using the cumulative frequency tables you have made in Exercise 12.1, questions 3, 4 and 5, draw the cumulative frequency curves.
    In question 3 label the horizontal axis from 60 to 90 using a scale of 2 cm to 5 units. On the vertical axis use 2 cm to 40 units or 50 units.

6. Using the cumulative frequency table of example **2**, page 215, draw the cumulative frequency curve.
    If necessary to get a larger scale on the horizontal axis, you may prefer to use the graph paper sideways.

Using the cumulative frequency curve

To find the median of the distribution

You will remember that the median is the halfway value.

If there are 200 light bulbs, as in example **1**, pages 214 and 217, the median is the lifetime halfway between the 100th and 101st bulbs.

We find this value from the cumulative frequency curve by drawing a median line at $\frac{1}{2}$ of 200 (=100).

We do not draw the line at $100\frac{1}{2}$. This is because the measurements are continuous and the line at 100 gives the correct value. This is a bit complicated to explain, so do not worry about understanding exactly why we do this.

Even if the data is not continuous, as, for example, with examination marks, there is so little difference between lines at 100 and $100\frac{1}{2}$ that you can still draw the line at 100.

Spread or Dispersion

Up to now the measure of spread we have used is the **range**.

   Range = highest value − lowest value

When the data are grouped, we do not know the exact highest and lowest values, but we can find the greatest possible value of the range.

In example **1**, the greatest possible value of the range = (1600 − 800) hours

                                    = 800 hours

A much more useful measure of spread is the **interquartile range**.

Just as you can find the median (halfway value), you can find quarter-way values. These are called **quartiles**.

If there are 200 items, the lower quartile is at $\frac{1}{4}$ of 200, i.e. 50, and the upper quartile is at $\frac{3}{4}$ of 200, i.e. 150.

The interquartile range = value of upper quartile − value of lower quartile

The interquartile range is the range of the middle half of the data, and it is a much more reliable measure of spread than the range, because it is not using the very low or the very high values, which can affect the range.

Example 1, continued from page 219.

Use your graph to find the median, the quartiles and the interquartile range.

Sketch graphs

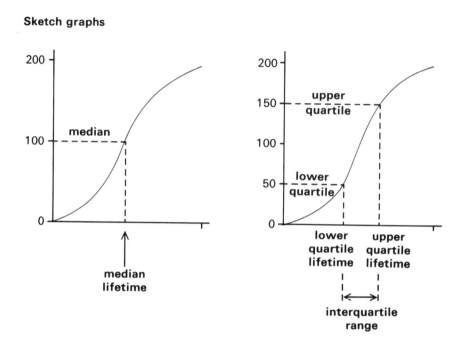

To find the median
Draw a line horizontally from 100 on the cumulative frequency axis, to meet the curve, and then a line vertically downwards to find the reading on the horizontal axis. On our graph the reading is 1240 hours.

To find the lower quartile
Draw a line horizontally from 50 on the cumulative frequency axis, to meet the curve, and then a line vertically downwards to find the reading on the horizontal axis. On our graph the lower quartile is 1140 hours.

To find the upper quartile, draw a line from 150 and find the reading. On our graph the upper quartile is 1310 hours.

The interquartile range = upper quartile − lower quartile
$$= (1310 - 1140) \text{ hours} = 170 \text{ hours}$$

(Your readings may not be exactly the same as ours.)

Exercise 12.3

1. Use the cumulative frequency graph you have drawn for question 1, Exercise 12.2.
    Draw lines at cumulative frequencies 75, 37.5 and 112.5 to find the median
    height, the lower quartile height and the upper quartile height. Find the
    interquartile range.

Questions 2 to 6.

Using the cumulative frequency graphs you have drawn in Exercise 12.2,
questions 2 to 6, find the median value and the lower and upper quartile values.
Find the interquartile range.

Exercise 12.4   Applications and Activities

1. A machine is manufacturing metal bars which should be 50 cm long.
    The 200 bars in a batch are measured and the results are shown in the frequency
    distribution table.

Length in cm	f
49.7	14
49.8	25
49.9	30
50.0	62
50.1	45
50.2	18
50.3	5
50.4	1
	200

Make a cumulative frequency table of the data.
Since the lengths have been measured to the
nearest 0.1 cm, the table will begin like this:
Less than 49.65,   0
Less than 49.75,   14
Less than 49.85,   39

Draw a cumulative frequency graph. (Label the
horizontal axis from 49.6 to 50.5, using a scale
of 1 cm to 0.1 unit, and plot the points at 49.65,
49.75, etc.)

Use the graph to find the median length of bar, the quartile lengths and the
interquartile range.
If all rods greater than 50.2 cm have to be filed down, use your graph to estimate
how many rods must be filed.

2.   The table shows the marks obtained by 120 candidates in an examination.

Mark	freq.
1 –10	6
11–20	10
21–30	12
31–40	14
41–50	17
51–60	19
61–70	16
71–80	14
81–90	8
91–100	4
	120

Make a cumulative frequency table of the data.

Draw a cumulative frequency graph.

Use the graph to find the median mark, the quartile marks and the interquartile range.

Use the graph to estimate how many candidates scored a mark of over 75.

3.   The table shows the distribution of ages of children in a Youth Organisation, in a certain region.
(Ages in completed years, frequencies to the nearest ten.)

Age (years)	freq.
5	200
6	350
7	920
8	1170
9	1050
10	850
11	630
12	460
13	250
14	120
	6000

Make a cumulative frequency table of the data.
The table will begin like this:
less than 5,   0
less than 6, 200
less than 7, 550
. . .

Draw a cumulative frequency graph.

Use the graph to find the median age, the quartile ages and the interquartile range.

Use the graph to find what percentage of the membership is over $12\frac{1}{2}$ years old.

4.   A survey of 200 cars in 1991 gave the following distribution of ages.

Age (years)	f
0 to <2	31
2 to <4	35
4 to <6	39
6 to <8	44
8 to <10	24
10 to <12	22
12 to <14	5
	200

Make a cumulative frequency table of the data.

Draw a cumulative frequency graph.

Use the graph to find the median age, the quartile ages and the interquartile range.

Cars over 3 years old have to have an MOT test. Use your graph to estimate how many of these cars have to be tested.

5.   You may have done some investigations in previous years for which you made frequency distributions, drew histograms and found the means. You can use the data to construct cumulative frequency graphs and find medians and interquartile ranges.

You can compare the mean and median of a distribution and decide which would be the better average to quote.

In some cases, you may decide to do an up-to-date survey and compare it with the previous one.

You can think of ideas for new surveys. You can look at the distribution of examination marks in different subjects, heights or weights of people, and various measurements involving lengths, times, etc.

PUZZLE

46.   Alice, Beryl, Carol, Diane and Ellen are talking about the result of a recent test.

Alice said: 'Carol was two places higher than Beryl.'
Beryl said: 'I was third.'
Carol said: 'Diane was last.'
Diane said: 'Beryl was fourth.'
Ellen said: 'Carol was three places higher than Alice.'

Only the person who had come bottom of the list had made a true statement, the other statements were all untrue. What was the correct order ?

13 Thinking about sketch graphs

A sketch graph shows the general connection between two variables.
It often shows variation over a period of time, with time on the horizontal axis. Scales need not be shown.

Sales in the UK of LP's and compact discs, in recent years

Comment about the trends shown by the graph.

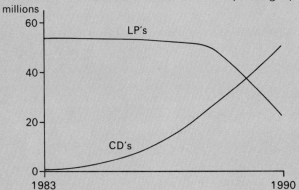

Sales of Christmas trees

Here is how a sketch graph, showing the number of trees sold over the twelve months, might look.

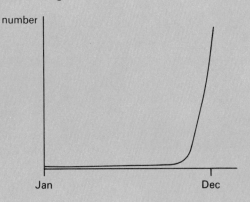

Rainfall graphs

These graphs show the average rainfall for each of the twelve months of the year, from January to December.

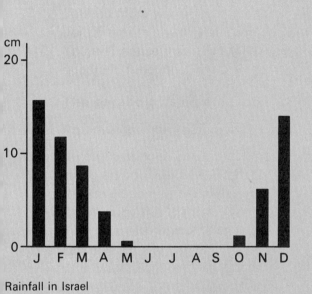

Rainfall in Israel

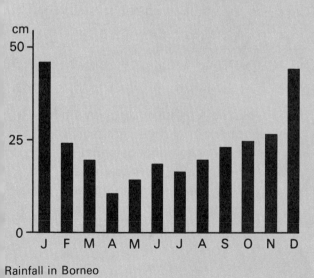

Rainfall in Borneo

Compare the two graphs and comment about them.

13 Sketch Graphs

These can show the general relationship between two variables, without showing exact details.

Often, one of the variables is time, and that usually goes on the horizontal axis.

Examples

Distance-time graphs

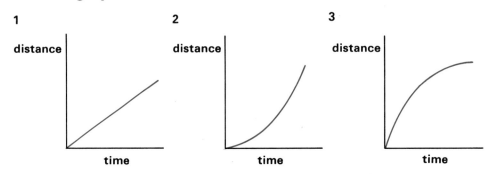

1   shows an object moving with a steady speed.
2   shows an object moving with an increasing speed (i.e. it is accelerating).
3   shows an object moving with a decreasing speed (i.e. it is slowing down).

Profits of a firm

4   shows that there is a steady increase in profits.
5   shows that there is a steady decrease in profits.
6   shows that for the first few months of the year, profits increased, but the rate of increase slowed down and profits reached a maximum, and then slowly fell. (If these profits were plotted every month, then the graph would not be a curve, because the readings are not continuous. It would be a line-graph (time-series graph), with points joined by a series of straight lines. However, in a sketch graph which shows the general relationship, it is reasonable to draw a curve.)

Other graphs

7   **8**

A wave graph   A cooling graph

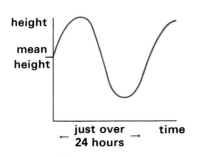

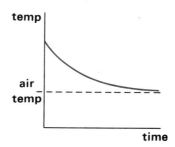

7 e.g. the height of the tide in a harbour.
8 The hot liquid cools quickly at first, then more slowly as it gets nearer to air temperature.

Graphs of functions

Direct proportion

When two quantities x, y are in direct proportion then the connection between them is $y = kx$, where k is a constant number, and the graph is a straight line passing through the origin.

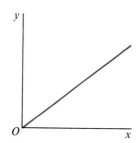

Examples

Time and distance, when the speed is steady.
Conversion graphs for foreign currency, British and metric units, etc. (The graph of temperature conversion from °C to °F is a straight line but it does not go through the origin.)

Inverse proportion

When two quantities x, y are in inverse proportion then the connection between them is $y = \dfrac{k}{x}$, and the graph looks like this.

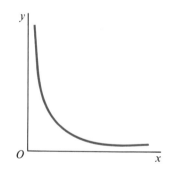

Examples

Length and breadth of a rectangle when the area is constant.
Pressure and volume of a gas when temperature is constant.

Quadratic functions

1

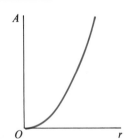

2

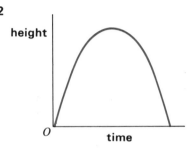

1 The connection between radius and area of a circle is $A = \pi r^2$, so the graph is the same shape as $y = \pi x^2$.
2 The height of a cricket ball at different times after it is thrown into the air obeys a quadratic equation law and looks like this.

Exercise 13.1

1. Draw sketch graphs to show the general relationships between these variables. It may help you to make a table of values first, in some cases.
    If the relationship is represented by a straight line, draw it using a ruler, not freehand.

    1 The connection between the number of hours worked and wage received if the rate is £5 per hour.

Hours	0	1	2	3
Wage (£)				

2   The connection between °C and °F.

°C	0	100
°F		

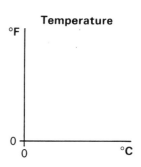

3   The connection between the length of an edge, in cm, and the volume, in cm³, of a cube.

Edge (cm)	0	1	2	3
Vol (cm³)				

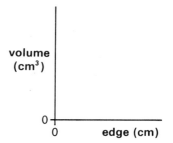

4   The quantity of water left in a tank if there is 100ℓ in it at first, and it is running out steadily at the rate of 20ℓ per hour.

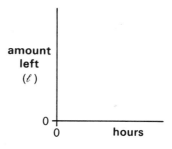

5   The height h metres above ground level reached by a stone after various times t seconds, when it is dropped off the edge of a cliff 180 m high.
(The equation connecting h and t is $h = 180 - 5t^2$)

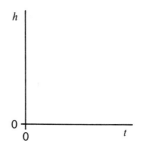

2. These sketch graphs show the sales of a new weekly magazine over several weeks.
    Identify which sketch matches each of these statements.

    1 We are pleased to say that the sales are rising steadily.
    2 The number of copies sold is increasing each week, and at an increasing rate.
    3 For the first few weeks the sales increased gradually until they reached a satisfactory level, and since then we have kept the sales at that level.
    4 For the first few weeks the sales increased but, unfortunately, they are beginning to fall now.

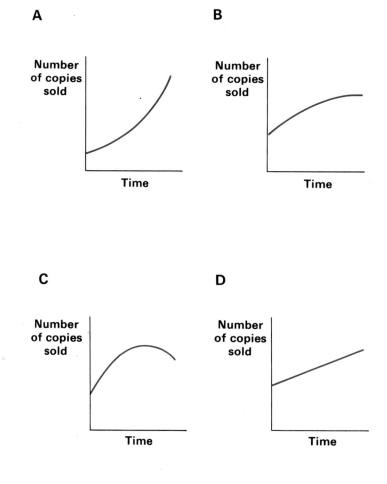

    5 Draw a sketch graph to match this description:
    After a promising beginning, the weekly sales began to drop gradually, for a few weeks, until last week when there was a slight rise in the number of copies sold.

3.   These sketch graphs show these relationships. Identify which is which.

   1   The length of a side, x cm, and the perimeter, y cm, of an equilateral triangle.
   2   To do a fixed job of work, the number of men employed, x, and the time the job will take, y days.
   3   The time, x seconds, and the distance travelled, y m, for a train which is slowing down and eventually stops.
   4   The number of bacteria, y, in a culture at various times, x hours, when the population doubles every hour.

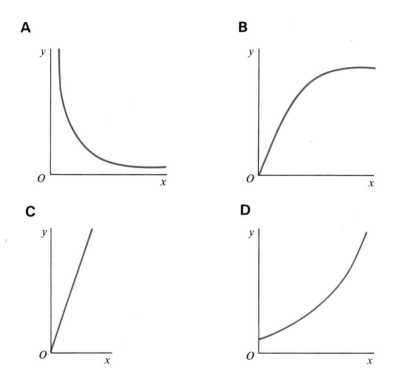

4.   **Speed-time graphs**

   (Do not confuse these with distance-time graphs.)

   Draw sketch graphs to show the relationship between time and speed under these conditions.

   1   The speed is kept constant, at 20 m/s.
   2   The speed increases at a steady rate, from 10 m/s to 30 m/s over 5 seconds.
   3   The speed decreases at a steady rate, from 30 m/s to rest in 5 seconds.

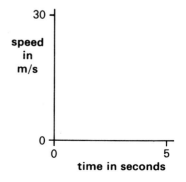

Exercise 13.2   Applications and Activities

1. Matthew rows a boat at a steady speed
    from a boathouse at A to a jetty at B, and
    then after a short rest he rows back to A.
    One direction is with the current, the other
    with the current against him.
    Which is which ?

    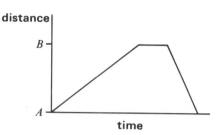

2. Here are descriptions of the attendances at a 12-week season of a seaside
    summer show.
    Draw sketch graphs showing the attendances over the 12 weeks.

    1   We have had full houses every evening for the whole season.
    2   The season started badly and for the first 3 weeks we had very poor
         audiences. Then the numbers rose steadily week by week, and for the last
         6 weeks we have had full houses.
    3   When we opened, we had half-full houses in the first week, and we did not
         do as well as that in the second week. We were back to half-full houses for
         the next 3 weeks, and then our numbers rose, and recently we have had full,
         or nearly full, houses.
    4   The first 8 weeks were very good, with full houses. After that the attendances
         started falling slightly, until by the last week the theatre was only half-full.

3. The sketch graph shows the petrol in the tank of a car on one day.
    Describe the activities of the motorist, using the information given by the graph.

    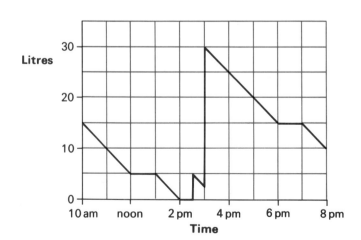

4. **Inflation**

The graph shows the way prices rose or fell in the years 1900 to 1970.
(The scale of the graph is an unusual one. This is because prices are shown by an index, which in 1900 was given as 100. When the index was 200, prices had doubled, and when the index was 400, prices had doubled again. So the scale between 400 and 200 is made equal to the scale between 200 and 100.)
Describe what happened to prices in the years 1914–1920.
Why do you think this was ?
Describe what happened to prices in the years 1920–1935.
Why do you think this was ?
When the index was 500, the prices were 5 times as high as in 1900. When, approximately, was this ?
If you can obtain recent figures for the retail price index, you could draw a graph showing how prices have changed recently.
You could also find out more about inflation. How does present-day inflation in Britain compare with that in other countries ?

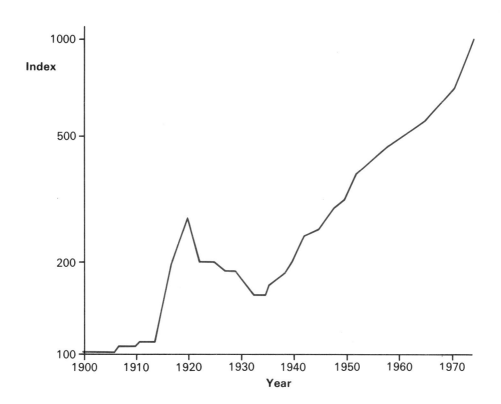

5. The graphs show the maximum temperatures, January to December, for 4 places.
    They are London; Timbuktu in Mali, Africa; Sydney, Australia and Reykjavik,
    Iceland.
    Say which graph is which.

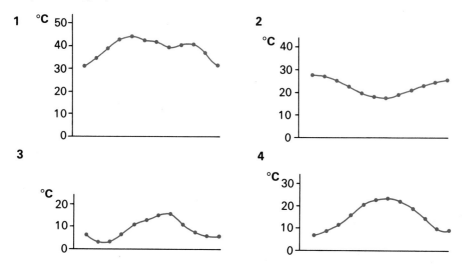

6. The graph shows the number of births in Britain in recent years.
    During which period of several years did the birth-rate fall ?
    (Perhaps you can find out the reason for this.)
    How have the changes in the birth-rate affected schools in recent years ?
    In many industries and professions, employers expect to recruit and train school
    leavers and other young people as replacements for older people who leave on
    retirement or for other reasons.
    What effect will the past changes in the birth-rate have on the numbers of young
    people available for such work in the next few years ?

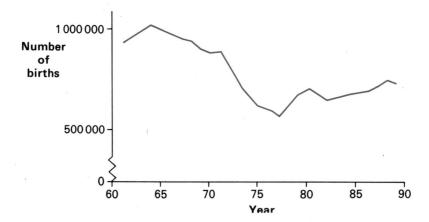

7. A train travels normally for 1 hour, then it has to stop for unforseen problems for $\frac{1}{2}$ hour. Afterwards it can only proceed at $\frac{1}{4}$ of its previous speed and it takes another hour to complete its journey.
    Sketch a distance-time graph of the journey.

8. **Distance-time graphs in sporting events**

    Try sketching the graphs showing the connection between distance and time in various events.
    For example, in a short race the competitor will start from rest, build up speed very quickly to a maximum, and try to maintain that speed for the rest of the race. What happens after passing the finishing line ?
    What happens in a longer race ?

    In a fell race, the competitors run up and down a steep hillside. As they get near the top, they go slower and slower. Having reached the top, they come downhill at speed.

    There are several events which might have interesting graphs. What about a hurdles race, a long jump or a javelin event ?
    The graph of a competitor in a darts match is an unusual one to draw.

    You could also show graphs of the connection between time and the height of competitors from ground level. Examples you could consider are hurdles races, high jump, ski-jumping, horse jumping, diving, etc.

14 Thinking about vectors

A vector is a quantity which has a direction as well as a size.
Examples of vectors are distances, velocities and forces.

Using vectors

The movement from the windmill to the Church is described as $\begin{pmatrix} 2 \\ -1 \end{pmatrix}$.

This means 2 steps in the x-direction and 1 step downwards in the y-direction.

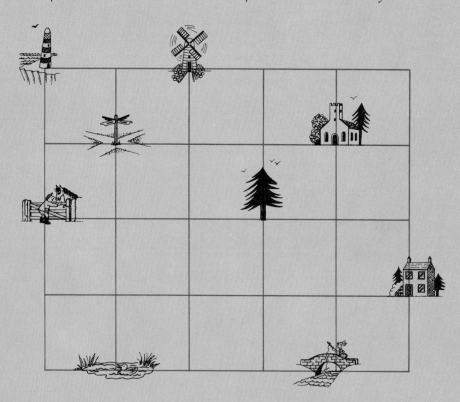

Describe these movements in the same way.
From the tree to the lighthouse.
From the house to the pond.
From the pond to the bridge.
From the gate to the Church.

Which movements from the crossroads can be described as $\begin{pmatrix} -1 \\ -1 \end{pmatrix}$, $\begin{pmatrix} 0 \\ -3 \end{pmatrix}$, $\begin{pmatrix} 4 \\ -2 \end{pmatrix}$?

Translation

Translation is a movement where every part of the object is moved in the same direction for the same distance.

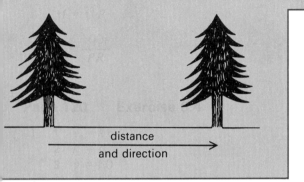

distance
and direction

Moves in chess

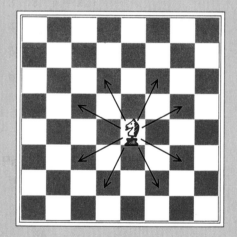

The knight has an odd move and this can be described by the vectors $\begin{pmatrix} 1 \\ 2 \end{pmatrix}$,

$\begin{pmatrix} 1 \\ -2 \end{pmatrix}$, $\begin{pmatrix} -1 \\ 2 \end{pmatrix}$, $\begin{pmatrix} -1 \\ -2 \end{pmatrix}$ and four others.
What are these others ?
Can you describe the moves of other chess pieces, using vectors ?

Look for translations on wallpaper patterns

14 Vectors

A vector quantity has a size and a direction.

We can represent vectors by lines drawn on squared paper or graph paper.

Example

The line AB can represent the vector of a displacement from A to B.
This displacement is 3 units in the x-direction and 2 units in the y-direction.

The vector can be represented by $\begin{pmatrix} 3 \\ 2 \end{pmatrix}$ or (3, 2).

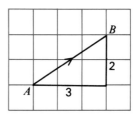

(We will use $\begin{pmatrix} 3 \\ 2 \end{pmatrix}$ in this chapter.)

The displacement in the x-direction is always written first.

If a vector is represented by a line AB this vector is written as $\overrightarrow{AB}$, $\overline{AB}$ or **AB**.

$\overrightarrow{AB}$ means the line in the direction from A to B.

$$\overrightarrow{AB} = \begin{pmatrix} 3 \\ 2 \end{pmatrix}$$

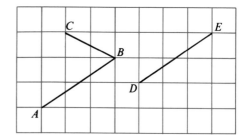

$\overrightarrow{BA}$ means the line in the direction from B to A.

$$\overrightarrow{BA} = \begin{pmatrix} -3 \\ -2 \end{pmatrix}$$

Any other line parallel to AB and with the same length also represents the vector $\begin{pmatrix} 3 \\ 2 \end{pmatrix}$

e.g. $\overrightarrow{DE}$ also represents the vector $\begin{pmatrix} 3 \\ 2 \end{pmatrix}$

$\overrightarrow{BC}$ represents the vector $\begin{pmatrix} -2 \\ 1 \end{pmatrix}$, and $\overrightarrow{CB}$ represents $\begin{pmatrix} 2 \\ -1 \end{pmatrix}$.

If A and C were joined with a straight line, what vector would $\overrightarrow{AC}$ represent ?
What vector would $\overrightarrow{CA}$ represent ?

Which two points could be joined with a line to represent the vector $\begin{pmatrix} 6 \\ 0 \end{pmatrix}$?

Vectors can also be represented by small letters in heavy type, such as **a**, **b**, **c**. This is how they would be shown in printed books.
In handwritten work the letters are underlined instead, as a, b, c, etc.

Exercise 14.1

Describe the vectors represented by the lines $\overrightarrow{AB}$, $\overrightarrow{BC}$ and $\overrightarrow{AC}$ in these diagrams.

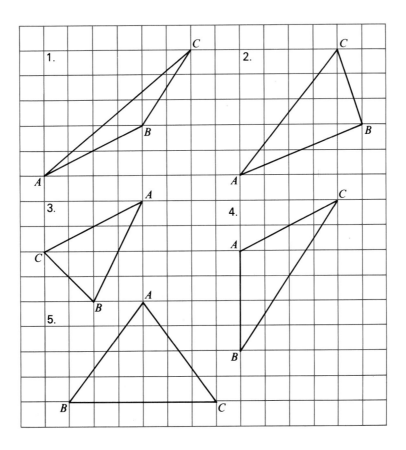

Questions 6 to 9.

On graph paper or squared paper, draw lines to represent these vectors $\overrightarrow{PQ}$ and $\overrightarrow{QR}$. Join PR and describe the vector $\overrightarrow{PR}$.

6. $\overrightarrow{PQ} = \begin{pmatrix} 1 \\ 4 \end{pmatrix}$, $\overrightarrow{QR} = \begin{pmatrix} 4 \\ -5 \end{pmatrix}$ 7. $\overrightarrow{PQ} = \begin{pmatrix} 0 \\ 4 \end{pmatrix}$, $\overrightarrow{QR} = \begin{pmatrix} 5 \\ -4 \end{pmatrix}$

8. $\overrightarrow{PQ} = \begin{pmatrix} 3 \\ -3 \end{pmatrix}$, $\overrightarrow{QR} = \begin{pmatrix} 4 \\ 0 \end{pmatrix}$ 9. $\overrightarrow{PQ} = \begin{pmatrix} -2 \\ -5 \end{pmatrix}$, $\overrightarrow{QR} = \begin{pmatrix} -3 \\ 3 \end{pmatrix}$

10. On graph paper or squared paper, draw x and y axes labelled from 0 to 8, and plot the points A (2, 4), B (8, 1), C (8, 7), D (6, 8).
Join AB, BC, CD, DA.
Write down the vectors $\overrightarrow{AB}$, $\overrightarrow{BC}$, $\overrightarrow{DC}$, $\overrightarrow{AD}$.

Position vectors

If the coordinates of A are (3, 5) then

$\overrightarrow{OA} = \begin{pmatrix} 3 \\ 5 \end{pmatrix}$, where O is the origin.

$\begin{pmatrix} 3 \\ 5 \end{pmatrix}$ is said to be the position vector of A.

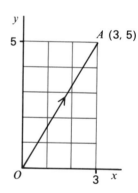

Translation

The dotted outlines show the translation of the triangles when every point has been moved an equal distance in the same direction.

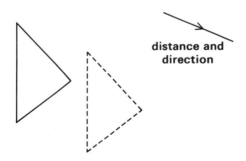

distance and direction

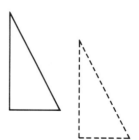

We can represent a translation by a vector.

Example

1 A (1, 1) is translated into A' (8, 2),
B (2, 5) is translated into B' (9, 6),
C (5, 3) is translated into C' (12, 4).

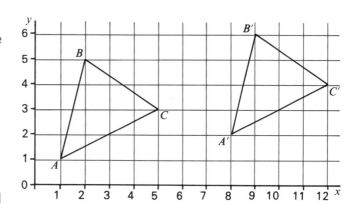

The translation is 7 units in the
x-direction and 1 unit in the
y-direction, and it can be
represented by the vector $\begin{pmatrix} 7 \\ 1 \end{pmatrix}$.

Every point on the line AB is
translated into a point on the
line $A'B'$.
Every point on BC is translated
into a point on $B'C'$.
Every point on AC is translated into a point on $A'C'$.
Every point on $\triangle ABC$ is translated into a point on $\triangle A'B'C'$.

Multiplication of a vector by a number

Examples

2   If $\overrightarrow{AB} = \begin{pmatrix} 1 \\ -2 \end{pmatrix}$, then

$$3\overrightarrow{AB} = 3 \times \begin{pmatrix} 1 \\ -2 \end{pmatrix} = \begin{pmatrix} 3 \\ -6 \end{pmatrix}$$

This is shown on the diagram, where $\overrightarrow{CD}$
represents $3\overrightarrow{AB}$.

Note that the lines are parallel, and that CD
is 3 times as long as AB.

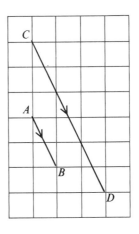

If a vector is multiplied by a negative number, the new vector is still parallel to the
original vector but its direction is reversed.

3   If $\overrightarrow{AB} = \begin{pmatrix} 1 \\ -2 \end{pmatrix}$, then

$$\overrightarrow{EF} = -2\overrightarrow{AB} = -2 \times \begin{pmatrix} 1 \\ -2 \end{pmatrix} = \begin{pmatrix} -2 \\ 4 \end{pmatrix}.$$

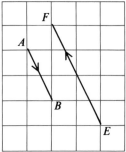

Exercise 14.2

1.   Draw x and y axes from -8 to 8 and plot the points with these position vectors,
     described from the origin O.

     A has position vector $\begin{pmatrix} 2 \\ 0 \end{pmatrix}$, B has a position vector $\begin{pmatrix} 3 \\ 5 \end{pmatrix}$, C has position vector $\begin{pmatrix} -4 \\ 2 \end{pmatrix}$,

     D has position vector $\begin{pmatrix} -8 \\ -8 \end{pmatrix}$, E has position vector $\begin{pmatrix} 6 \\ -2 \end{pmatrix}$, F has position vector $\begin{pmatrix} 8 \\ 8 \end{pmatrix}$.

     Join these lines and state their vectors:
     AB, BC, CD, DA, DE, EF.
     Which of these lines are parallel ?
     Which line has a vector equal to $2\overrightarrow{AB}$?
     Which line has a vector equal to $-\frac{1}{2}\overrightarrow{DE}$?

2.   Copy the diagram on squared paper and translate the figure *ABCDEFG* using the

     vector $\begin{pmatrix} -7 \\ -4 \end{pmatrix}$, drawing the figure in its new position on your diagram.

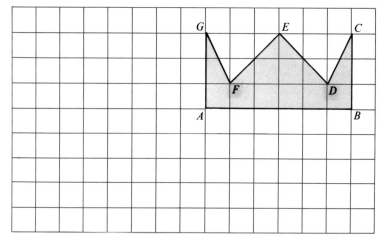

3. Name the vector which translates
   ΔABC into ΔDEF.
   Name the vector which translates
   ΔDEF into ΔABC.

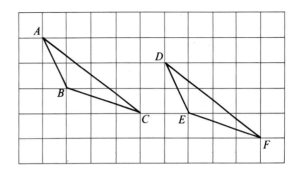

4. **1** Describe the vectors **a, b, c, d, e, f, g, h, j, k, m, n**.
    2 Which 2 vectors are equal ?
    3 Which vector is equal to 2**b** ?
    4 Which vector is equal to −**d** ?
    5 Which vector is equal to $\frac{1}{3}$**e** ?

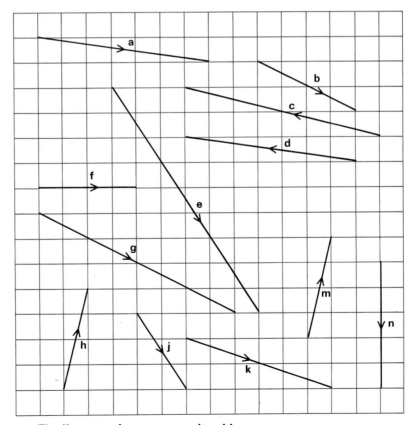

The lines are drawn on a unit grid.

5.   Draw the x-axis from -5 to 5 and the y-axis from 0 to 4.
     Mark the points with these position vectors:

     $A, \begin{pmatrix} -2 \\ 1 \end{pmatrix};$ $B, \begin{pmatrix} -5 \\ 2 \end{pmatrix};$ $C, \begin{pmatrix} 5 \\ 0 \end{pmatrix}.$

     Join AB and state the vector $\overrightarrow{AB}$.
     From C draw a line CD such that $\overrightarrow{CD} = 3\overrightarrow{AB}$.
     State the position vector of D.

6.   Draw x and y axes from -4 to 4.
     Mark the points with these position vectors:

     $P, \begin{pmatrix} -3 \\ -1 \end{pmatrix};$ $Q, \begin{pmatrix} -4 \\ 4 \end{pmatrix};$ $R, \begin{pmatrix} 1 \\ 3 \end{pmatrix}.$

     Join PQ and state the vector $\overrightarrow{PQ}$.
     From R draw a line RS such that $\overrightarrow{RS} = -\overrightarrow{PQ}$.
     State the position vector of S.

     Join QR and PS.
     What sort of figure is $PQRS$?

7.   Draw the x-axis from -6 to 8 and the y-axis from -3 to 4.
     Draw the triangle ABC where A, B, C have position vectors

     $A, \begin{pmatrix} -6 \\ 1 \end{pmatrix};$ $B, \begin{pmatrix} -4 \\ 4 \end{pmatrix};$ $C, \begin{pmatrix} -2 \\ -1 \end{pmatrix}.$

     Translate the triangle using a vector $\mathbf{a} = \begin{pmatrix} 9 \\ -2 \end{pmatrix}$, to form a new triangle DEF.

     State the position vectors of D, E and F.

Exercise 14.3   Applications and Activities

1.   Draw axes with x from -2 to 6 and y from -4 to 6.

     Draw the lines AB and AC where A is the point $(-2, -4)$, $\overrightarrow{AB} = \begin{pmatrix} 4 \\ 5 \end{pmatrix}$ and

     $\overrightarrow{AC} = \begin{pmatrix} 6 \\ 2 \end{pmatrix}.$

     Plot point D such that $\overrightarrow{BD} = \frac{1}{2}\overrightarrow{AC}$.

     Plot point E such that $\overrightarrow{BE} = \overrightarrow{AB}$.
     State the coordinates of D and E.
     State the vectors $\overrightarrow{CD}$ and $\overrightarrow{DE}$.
     What can you say about the points C, D and E ?

2. For each part, draw the x-axis from 0 to 12 and the y-axis from 0 to 10.

1 Draw the lines AB and BC where A is the point (0, 1) and $\overrightarrow{AB} = \begin{pmatrix} 2 \\ 6 \end{pmatrix}$,

$\overrightarrow{BC} = \begin{pmatrix} 10 \\ 2 \end{pmatrix}$.

Find a point D such that $ABCD$ is a parallelogram.
Draw AD and CD.
State the vectors $\overrightarrow{AD}$, $\overrightarrow{DC}$.
Join the diagonals of the parallelogram and let them cross each other at E.
State the vectors $\overrightarrow{AE}$, $\overrightarrow{EC}$ and $\overrightarrow{BE}$, $\overrightarrow{ED}$.
What do these show about the diagonals of the figure ?

2 On a separate diagram, repeat part **1** with A as (1, 7), $\overrightarrow{AB} = \begin{pmatrix} -1 \\ -3 \end{pmatrix}$,

$\overrightarrow{BC} = \begin{pmatrix} 9 \\ -3 \end{pmatrix}$.

What sort of parallelogram is $ABCD$?

3 On a separate diagram, repeat part **1** with A as (4, 9), $\overrightarrow{AB} = \begin{pmatrix} 8 \\ 1 \end{pmatrix}$,

$\overrightarrow{BC} = \begin{pmatrix} -4 \\ -7 \end{pmatrix}$.

What sort of parallelogram is $ABCD$?

4 On a separate diagram, repeat part **1** with A as (6, 1), $\overrightarrow{AB} = \begin{pmatrix} -5 \\ 3 \end{pmatrix}$,

$\overrightarrow{BC} = \begin{pmatrix} 3 \\ 5 \end{pmatrix}$.

What sort of parallelogram is $ABCD$?

3. Draw x and y axes from -6 to 7.
Plot the points A (2, 1), B (1, 6), C (7, 3) and draw triangle ABC.

Translate $\triangle ABC$ to $\triangle DEF$ by moving each point by the vector $\begin{pmatrix} -7 \\ -2 \end{pmatrix}$.

State the coordinates of D, E, F.

Then translate $\triangle DEF$ to $\triangle GHJ$ by moving each point by the vector $\begin{pmatrix} 5 \\ -4 \end{pmatrix}$.

State the coordinates of G, H, J.
What single translation would translate $\triangle ABC$ into $\triangle GHJ$?

15 Thinking about making and

Proof

In a Court of Law, the idea of
proof is very important.
Evidence is given and the jury
decide whether the case has been
proved, or not.

A mathematical proof is similar.
Certain facts which are already
known to be true can be used to
give reasons for further statements
to be true.

The Old Bailey, London
(The Central Criminal Court)

Equal areas

In around 460 BC, Hippocrates
showed that the sum of the areas of
the two black curved portions is
equal to the area of the triangle.
Can you prove this ?

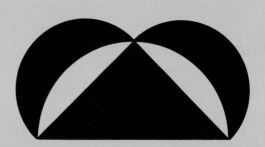

Let the shorter sides of the triangle
have length $2x$.
What is the length of the
hypotenuse, in terms of x ?
Find the area of (semicircle $A + C$) +
(semicircle $B + D$), in terms of x.
Find the area of semicircle $C + D + E$,
in terms of x.
What does this prove about (area
A + area B) ?
Is the result still true if the triangle is
not isosceles ?

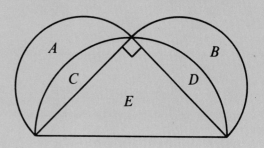

roving statements

Euclid

He lived about 300 BC, and taught at Alexandria. His 13 books, called The Elements, collected up all known facts about Geometry. He began with some assumptions, e.g. that only one straight line can be drawn between two points; and went on to prove other geometrical results. When the printing press was invented, The Elements were among the first books to be printed. Until about a century ago, the study of geometry meant the study of Euclid's writings. Much of the geometry you learn in school is taken from The Elements.

An example of a geometrical proof

To prove: If two sides of a triangle are unequal, the greater side has the greater angle opposite to it.

Given: $\triangle ABC$ with $AC > AB$
To prove: $\angle ABC > \angle ACB$
Proof: From AC cut off a part AX
                equal to AB. Join BX.
                Since $AB = AX$,
                $\angle ABX = \angle AXB$
                But exterior angle $AXB >$
                interior opposite angle XCB.
                So $\angle ABX > \angle XCB$
                But $\angle ABC > \angle ABX$
                So $\angle ABC > \angle XCB$ or $\angle ACB$

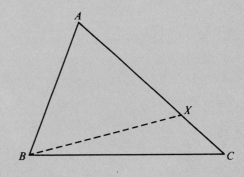

The converse of this theorem is:
If two angles of a triangle are unequal, the greater angle has the greater side opposite to it.
Can you prove this result by showing that the side opposite the greater angle cannot be less than or equal to the side opposite the other angle ?

To disprove a statement

Einstein once said, 'No amount of experimentation can ever prove me right but a single experiment might prove me wrong'.

15 Making and Proving Statements

In Mathematics, we learn a great many facts about numbers and shapes.

Here are some statements. Copy and complete them.

1 If ABC is a triangle, then $\angle A + \angle B + \angle C = \ldots$

2 If $ABCD$ is a quadrilateral, then $\angle A + \angle B + \angle C + \angle D = \ldots$

3 If in $\triangle ABC$, $\angle C = 90°$, then $AB^2 = \ldots$

4 If 2 fair coins are tossed, then the probability of getting 2 heads is $\ldots$

5 If 2 dice are thrown, then the probability of getting a double (the same number on each) is $\ldots$

6 If there are 9 red beads and 11 similar blue beads in a bag and you pick a bead out at random, then you are more likely to get a $\ldots$ bead.

7 If you add any two odd numbers then the result will be an $\ldots$ number.

8 If you multiply any two odd numbers then the result will be an $\ldots$ number.

9 If a number is a square number then its unit digit can be one of these numbers $\ldots$ and cannot be one of these numbers $\ldots$

10 $(a + b)^2 = a^2 + \ldots$

We would not just accept these statements without being sure that they are correct.

In many cases we can **prove** that they are correct. This means that we can show that a statement is certain to be correct, based on reasoning using mathematical facts which are known to be true.

Examples

1 If ABC is a triangle, then $\angle A + \angle B + \angle C = 180°$

You can show that this statement is likely to be true, by drawing several triangles of different shapes and measuring the angles. (There may be slight errors of 1° or 2° due to measuring to the nearest degree.)

But that is not a **proof**.

Here is one way to prove it.
We assume these facts are true, to use in the proof:
adjacent angles on a straight line add up to 180°,
corresponding angles made with parallel lines are equal,
alternate angles made with parallel lines are equal.

To prove   In a $\triangle ABC$, $\angle A + \angle B + \angle C = 180°$

Produce (extend) BC to a point D.
Through C draw a line CE parallel to BA.

We have labelled the angles with small
letters.

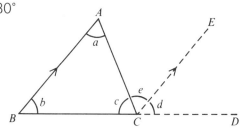

Proof

$b = d$	corresponding angles
$a = e$	alternate angles
$c + d + e = 180°$	adjacent angles

So $c + b + a = 180°$
i.e. $\angle A + \angle B + \angle C = 180°$
($\angle C$ here means $\angle ACB$)

There are slightly different ways to prove this result.
Maybe you can find one.

2   If 2 fair coins are tossed, the probability of getting 2 heads is $\frac{1}{4}$.

You can show that this statement is likely to be true by tossing 2 coins several
times and finding the probability using relative frequency.

But you can **prove** that the result is true
by using the other formula for
probability.

Probability $= \dfrac{s}{n} = \frac{1}{4}$

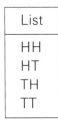

List
HH
HT
TH
TT

Or your can use the formula for independent events, as in Chapter 9. (You would have
to assume that the AND rule is true.)

Sometimes we cannot prove the statement in such a satisfactory way, but we can show
by conducting an experiment, or by showing how a pattern develops, that the statement
is likely to be true.

Example

3   If n is a whole number, then to square $n + \frac{1}{2}$, multiply n by the number which is one
larger than n and add $\frac{1}{4}$.

e.g.
$$4\tfrac{1}{2}^2 = 4 \times 5 + \tfrac{1}{4} = 20\tfrac{1}{4}$$
$$7\tfrac{1}{2}^2 = 7 \times 8 + \tfrac{1}{4} = 56\tfrac{1}{4}$$
$$99\tfrac{1}{2}^2 = 99 \times 100 + \tfrac{1}{4} = 9900\tfrac{1}{4}$$

Now you can check these results on your calculator and see that they are true. You can investigate the pattern beginning with $1\frac{1}{2}^2$, $2\frac{1}{2}^2$, $3\frac{1}{2}^2$, . . . and show how the pattern follows on.
So the statement is **likely** to be true.

But you can **prove** the statement in this way:

First, write it in symbols.
To prove that $(n + \frac{1}{2})^2 = n(n + 1) + \frac{1}{4}$

Begin with $(n + \frac{1}{2})^2$
This worked out gives $(n + \frac{1}{2})(n + \frac{1}{2}) = n^2 + n + \frac{1}{4}$
$$= n(n + 1) + \frac{1}{4},$$
so it is proved.

Here we assume that the method of multiplying out two brackets is true, and also that the rule for factorising gives $n^2 + n = n(n + 1)$

We did not use any particular number for n, so we have proved it for all numbers. (In fact, n need not be a whole number.)

Exercise 15.1

Here are some statements to be proved.

For each one, first of all do a preliminary investigation to satisfy yourself that the statement is true.
Then, try to give a satisfactory proof.
In some cases, some help is given.
If, after trying them, you cannot see how to prove them, perhaps you could ask someone to give you some help.

1. **To prove that** the sum of the angles of a quadrilateral is 360°.
    Hint: Divide the quadrilateral into 2 triangles.
    Assume that the sum of the angles of a triangle is 180°.

2. **To prove that** the angles of an equilateral triangle are each 60°.
    Assume that the sum of the angles of a triangle is 180°.
    Assume that in an isosceles triangle the angles opposite the equal sides are equal.

3. The diagram shows a semicircle.
    O is the centre of the circle.
    To prove that $\angle BAC = 90°$.
    This is called 'the angle in a semicircle'.
    Hint: Join OA.
    Assume that the sum of the angles of a
    triangle is 180°.

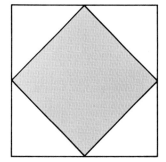

    Assume that in an isosceles triangle the angles opposite the equal sides are
    equal.

4. **To prove that** the area of a square, A cm^2, is given by the formula $A = \frac{1}{2}d^2$,
    where d cm is the length of a diagonal.
    Assume the formula $A = l^2$.
    Hint: Draw the square like the shaded
    square in this diagram.

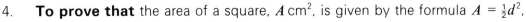

5. **To prove that** if you add any two odd numbers then the result will be an even
    number.
    Hint: An even number is a number of the form $2a$ (i.e. it has a factor 2).
    An odd number is a number of the form $2a + 1$, (there is an odd 1 added onto
    an even number).
    Let the two odd numbers be $2a + 1$ and $2b + 1$.
    Add them together and show that the sum has a factor 2.

6. **To prove that** if you multiply any two odd numbers then the result will be an
    odd number.

7. ˙ **To prove that** if n is an even number then $3n^2 - n + 1$ is an odd number.

8. **To prove that** if you toss 3 fair coins, then you are three times as likely to get
    some heads and some tails as you are to get all heads or all tails.

9. **To prove that** there is a greater chance of throwing a 6 with one die than of
    scoring a total of 6 with two dice.

10.   **To prove that** if θ is any acute angle,

then $\tan \theta = \dfrac{\sin \theta}{\cos \theta}$

Hint: Write down the ratios for $\sin \theta$ and
$\cos \theta$ and find $\sin \theta \div \cos \theta$.

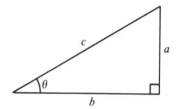

Disproving statements

In order to show that a statement is not always true, you only need to find **one**
example when it is not true.

Examples

1   Ann says that 'All birds can fly'.
Is this statement true ?

Is an emu a bird ?
Can an emu fly ?
Is it true that 'All birds can fly' ?

2   Philip said that 'All numbers which end in 3, 6 or 9 divide exactly by 3'.
Now don't get the idea that Philip is right. He is just not thinking carefully.

Does 16 end in 3, 6 or 9 ?
Does 16 divide by 3 ?
Is Philip's statement true ?

Exercise 15.2

Here are some misleading statements.
For each one, find an example to show that the statement is not true.

1.   A triangular number cannot be a square number.

2.   If $x < 4$ then $x^2 < 16$.

3.   If abc is any three-figure number which divides exactly by 11, then $a + c = b$.
e.g.   385 divides exactly by 11, and $3 + 5 = 8$,
          264 divides exactly by 11, and $2 + 4 = 6$.

4.   If a and b are any numbers then $\sqrt{a^2 + b^2}$ is equal to $a + b$.

5.   For any set of 5 numbers, the median value is always less than the mean value.

6.   6 is the only perfect number less than 100.
     (A perfect number is a whole number whose factors, except the number itself,
     add up to itself. 6 has factors 1, 2, 3 and 1 + 2 + 3 = 6.)

7.   All horizontal lines are parallel to each other.

8.   If you throw an ordinary die 6 times then you must get at least one six, because
     $P(6) = \frac{1}{6}$ and $\frac{1}{6} + \frac{1}{6} + \frac{1}{6} + \frac{1}{6} + \frac{1}{6} + \frac{1}{6} = 1$.

9.   If there are 3 numbers a, b, c and $a \times c = b \times c$, then a equals b.

10. 4199 is a prime number.

Exercise 15.3   Applications and Activities

1.   If a and b are two numbers, then $a^2 - b^2 = (a + b)(a - b)$.
     Test this statement by trying certain numbers.
     Prove the statement by starting with $(a + b)(a - b)$ and removing the brackets.
     Try to find a geometrical proof of the statement, using areas of squares and
     rectangles.

2.   People have tried to find an expression which will always give prime numbers,
     and one which has been suggested is $x^2 - x + 41$.
     By substituting $x = 1, 2, 3, \ldots, 10$, check that the expression always gives a
     prime number for these values of x.
     Does the expression always give a prime number, or can you find a value of x for
     which the expression does not give a prime number ?

3.   In a regular polygon with n sides, the size of each interior angle is $\left(180 - \frac{360}{n}\right)^{\circ}$.
     Prove this statement. There are several different ways to do this. You may wish to
     use facts about the angle sum of a triangle, or facts about isosceles triangles. You
     may also use the fact that the sum of the exterior angles of a convex polygon is
     360°.

4. **To prove that 1 equals 2**

Let $x = y$
Then multiply both sides by x
$x^2 = xy$
Subtract y^2 from both sides
$x^2 - y^2 = xy - y^2$
Factorise both sides. $x^2 - y^2 = (x + y)(x - y)$ from the proof in question 1,
$xy - y^2 = y(x - y)$

So $(x + y)(x - y) = y(x - y)$
Divide both sides by $x - y$
$x + y = y$
Let $x = 1$, then $y = 1$ also
$1 + 1 = 1$
i.e. $2 = 1$

What is wrong with this proof ?

Pythagoras' theorem

In a triangle ABC, if $\angle A = 90°$, then $BC^2 = AB^2 + AC^2$.

There are many ways of proving this theorem.
Try to complete this proof which uses similar triangles.
The sides have been labelled using small letters.

$\angle A = 90°$
You are trying to prove that
$a^2 = b^2 + c^2$, where $a = p + q$.

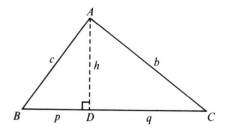

Explain why $\triangle ABC$ and $\triangle DBA$ are similar.

Using these triangles complete $\dfrac{a}{c} = \dfrac{b}{\ldots} = \dfrac{c}{\ldots}$

From these equations, $c^2 = \ldots$

Repeat using $\triangle ABC$ and $\triangle DAC$, getting $b^2 = \ldots$

So $b^2 + c^2 = \ldots$
$\qquad\quad = \ldots$ (factorising)
$\qquad\quad = \ldots$

6.   For any three consecutive whole numbers, their product divides exactly by 6.
      Is this statement likely to be true ? If so, prove it.
      Hint: To divide by 6, one of the numbers must divide by 3 and one of the
      numbers must divide by 2.

      Investigate the product of four consecutive whole numbers, and see if there is a
      similar statement which you can prove.
      You can also investigate the product of five consecutive whole numbers.

7.   A circle is divided into regions, as shown. How many regions are there for the
      hexagon ?

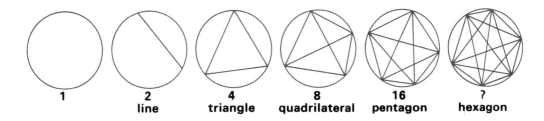

| 1 | 2 | 4 | 8 | 16 | ? |
| | line | triangle | quadrilateral | pentagon | hexagon |

      The pattern is 1, 2, 4, 8, 16, so, without counting, it seems reasonable to suppose
      that there are 32 regions in the hexagon diagram. Is this statement true ?

8.   Here is a number trick. Ask a friend to write down
      any two numbers in a column and then continue the
      column by always adding the last two numbers
      together, until there are 10 numbers altogether.
      Then say you will add them all up.
      But instead, you can find the total more easily by
      multiplying the 7th number by 11.
      In the example the 7th number is 123 and
      $123 \times 11 = 1353$, and that is the total.

      Check whether the trick works if you begin with
      other numbers.
      Then, try to prove whether it will always work, by
      beginning with numbers a and b. (The next number
      will be $a + b$ and the one after that, $a + 2b$.)

Example
7
11
18
29
47
76
123
199
322
521
1353

Miscellaneous Section C

Aural Practice

These aural exercises, C1 and C2, should be read to you, probably by your teacher or a friend, and you should write down the answers only, doing any working out in your head. You should do the 15 questions within 10 minutes.

Exercise C1

1. If $2y + 9 = 3$, what is the value of y ?

2. The area of a rectangular lawn is $85\,m^2$. If it is $10\,m$ long, how wide is it ?

3. What is the value of $49^{\frac{1}{2}}$?

4. A train starts at 9.15 am and reaches the next town at 9.45 am. If it travels at 50 miles per hour, how far is it between the towns ?

5. Express as simply as possible $8b^2 \div 4b$.

6. Two similar cylinders have heights in the ratio 4 : 5. The height of the smaller one is $4.8\,cm$. What is the height of the larger one ?

7. If x^2 is less than 36, what is the range of values of x ?

8. How many quarters are there in $3\frac{1}{2}$?

9. To do a job of work, 6 men would take 12 days. How long would it take if 8 men were employed ?

10. Four packets weigh $150\,g$, $200\,g$, $300\,g$, and $400\,g$. What is the median weight ?

11. Express as simply as possible, $x^3 \times x^4$.

12. A length, written in standard form, is 1.5×10^{-1} cm. What is this length written normally, in cm ?

13. If two fair dice are thrown and the numbers added together, which total is the most likely to occur ?

14. The weights of two boxes are in the ratio 3 : 5. The larger one weighs $35\,kg$. What is the weight of the smaller one ?

15. What is the value of s, if $s = a + 7d$, and $a = -6$ and $d = 1$?

Exercise C2

1. If 25 Swiss francs are worth £10, what is the value of 35 francs ?

2. What is the value of $p - q$ if $p = -2$ and $q = -5$?

3. What word is used for a straight line which just touches the circumference of a circle ?

4. What is the value of $x^{\frac{1}{3}}$ when $x = 27$?

5. What are the coordinates of a point on the graph of $y = x^2 - 1$, when $x = 5$?

6. One triangle has sides 3 cm, 4 cm and 5 cm, and another has sides 6 cm, 8 cm and 10 cm. Are the triangles similar ?

7. If x is a whole number and $2x$ is greater than 12, also $x + 5$ is less than 13, what is the value of x ?

8. A town has a population of 320 000. Write down this number in standard form.

9. What must be added to $\frac{1}{3}$ to make $\frac{1}{2}$?

10. Express as simply as possible, $b^4 \div b^4$.

11. If a coin is tossed 4 times in succession, what is the chance of getting 4 heads ?

12. Write in factor form the expression $\pi r^2 + \pi r h$.

13. £5 is increased in the ratio 6 : 5. What is the new amount ?

14. If a frequency distribution has an upper quartile of 350 kg and a lower quartile of 210 kg, what is the interquartile range ?

15. Transform the formula $y = mx + c$, to write it in terms of c.

Exercise C3   Revision

1. A water tank is $\frac{1}{3}$ full. After another 200 litres are poured in it is $\frac{1}{2}$ full. How many litres does the tank hold ?

2. A formula used with number sequences is $s = \dfrac{a}{1 - r}$.

   1 Write the formula in terms of a.
   2 Write the formula in terms of r.
   3 Find the value of r when $s = 45$ and $a = 13.5$.

3. Use your calculator to work out these calculations. Express the answers in standard form, correct to 3 significant figures.

    1 $(2.51 \times 10^4) \times (1.23 \times 10^{-6})$
    2 $(1.82 \times 10^3) \div (1.3 \times 10^8)$
    3 $(9.5 \times 10^{-5}) \div (7.3 \times 10^{-2})$

4. If the probability that a certain train will be late on any day is $\frac{1}{10}$, and the lateness or otherwise is independent of what happened on previous days, what is the probability that the train
    1   will be late on 3 consecutive days,
    2   will be on time on at least one of the 3 consecutive days ?

5. Solve the equation $\dfrac{2(x + 1)}{3} - \dfrac{3x}{5} = 0.8$

6. On a map a distance of 8 km is represented by a line of 3.2 cm. What is the scale of the map, in ratio form ?

7. Simplify the expression $4a + b - 5c + 5a - 7b + 8c$ and factorise it.
    What is the value of the expression when $3a - 2b + c$ equals 5 ?

8. Find
    1   the height of the tower,
    2   the angle of elevation of the top of the tower from B.

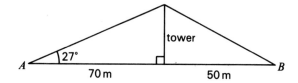

9. **1**   What is the value of n if $3^n \times 5 = 405$?
    2   What is the value of n if $2^n = 64$?
    3   What is the value of n if $10^n = 1$?

10. The extension of a spring is proportional to the weight hanging on it.
    Draw a sketch graph showing the relationship between the weight and the total length of the spring.

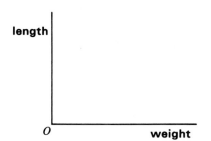

11. The sides of a triangle are of length 5 cm, $(6 + x)$ cm and $(7 + 2x)$ cm. Find the range of possible values of x. Use the fact that the sum of the lengths of any two sides of a triangle is greater than the length of the third side.

12. There are some coloured beads in a bag, either red or blue.
    When picking a bead at random, the probability that it is red is 0.7.
    If a bead is always replaced before another bead is drawn, show the results of two successive drawings on a probability tree-diagram or in a table, and find the probabilities that, in two drawings,
    1   both beads are red,
    2   both beads are blue,
    3   one bead is red and one is blue.

13. Here are 2 maps of the same field.

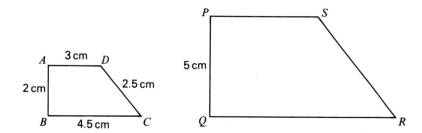

    Find the lengths of **PS**, **QR** and **SR**.
    If the map **ABCD** is drawn to a scale of 1 : 5000, what is the perimeter of the actual field, in metres ?

14. The wavelength w metres of a radio broadcast is inversely proportional to the frequency f kHz of the broadcast.
    Express this statement as an equation, using a constant k.
    One station broadcasts on a wavelength of 1200 m at a frequency of 250 kHz.
    What is the frequency of another station which broadcasts on a wavelength of 1250 m ?

15. A ship sailed from a port P on a bearing of 122° until it had gone 25 km. It then sailed due west until it was due south of P. How far was it then from P ?

16.   Identify the shaded regions in these diagrams.

1

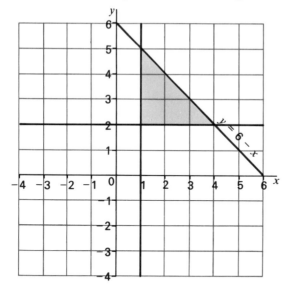

2

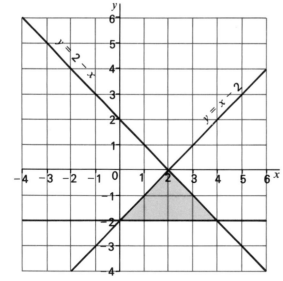

17.   On squared paper or graph paper draw the x-axis from 0 to 6 and the y-axis from 0 to 12, using equal scales on both axes.

Plot the points A, with position vector $\begin{pmatrix} 4 \\ 2 \end{pmatrix}$ and B, with position vector $\begin{pmatrix} 3 \\ 12 \end{pmatrix}$.

C is a point such that $\overrightarrow{AC} = \frac{1}{2}\overrightarrow{OA}$. Plot the point C.

D is a point such that $\overrightarrow{OD} = \frac{2}{3}\overrightarrow{OB}$. Plot the point D.

State the vectors $\overrightarrow{AD}$ and $\overrightarrow{CB}$.

What can you say about the lines AD and CB?

18.   The birth weights of 80 babies are recorded in this table.

Weight in lb	·Number of babies
4.5 to just under 5.5	3
5.5 to just under 6.5	9
6.5 to just under 7.5	22
7.5 to just under 8.5	28
8.5 to just under 9.5	16
9.5 to just under 10.5	2

Make a cumulative frequency table of the data.
Draw a cumulative frequency graph.
Use the graph to find
1   the median weight,
2   the upper and lower quartile weights and the interquartile range.

19.   The speed of light is 1.86×10^5 miles/second. The Sun is 9.3×10^7 miles from the Earth. How many minutes does it take light from the Sun to reach the Earth ?

20.   Mr Davies wants to enclose a rectangular plot of $12 \, m^2$ in his garden, to keep chickens in.
If the plot is x m wide, what is its length, in terms of x ?
Mr Davies must fence round 3 sides, as shown, the hedge making the 4th side.

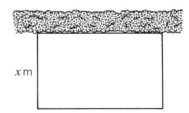

If he needs y m of fencing, show that $y = 2x + \dfrac{12}{x}$.

Copy and complete this table of values for the function $y = 2x + \dfrac{12}{x}$.

x	1	2	2.4	3	4	5	6
$2x$							
$\dfrac{12}{x}$							
y							

Draw axes with x from 0 to 6 and y from 0 to 14.
Plot the points given by the table. Draw the graph of the function for x from 1 to 6.
Mr Davies has only 10 m of fencing. Will this be sufficient ?
If so, what range of widths for the plot can he choose from ?

Exercise C4   Revision

1.   Here are the weekly attendances at a club over 7 weeks:

   21, 20, 23, 26, 22, 21, 28.

   Find
   1   the mean attendance,
   2   the median attendance.

2.   Factorise $n^2 + 3n$ and explain why the value of this expression is always even, if *n* is a positive whole number.

3.   A manufacturer sold a bicycle to a retailer at a profit of $33\frac{1}{3}\%$ of his costs, and the retailer sold the bicycle at a profit of 25% of his cost price, for £240.
   Find
   1   the profit made by the retailer,
   2   the cost of the manufacture of the bicycle.

4. $\overrightarrow{OA} = \begin{pmatrix} 3 \\ 7 \end{pmatrix}$, $\overrightarrow{OB} = \begin{pmatrix} 2 \\ 3 \end{pmatrix}$, $\overrightarrow{OC} = \begin{pmatrix} 5 \\ 5 \end{pmatrix}$ and $\overrightarrow{OD} = \begin{pmatrix} 6 \\ 9 \end{pmatrix}$.

   Draw the lines given by these vectors on squared paper or graph paper.
   State the vectors $\overrightarrow{BA}$ and $\overrightarrow{CD}$.
   What sort of figure is *ABCD* ?

5.   A small particle is in the shape of a cuboid with length 8×10^{-2} mm, breadth 6×10^{-2} mm and height 5×10^{-2} mm.
   Find, giving the answers in standard form,
   1   its surface area,
   2   its volume.

6.   A formula used to find the solutions of quadratic equations is

   $$x = \frac{-b + \sqrt{b^2 - 4ac}}{2a} \quad \text{or} \quad x = \frac{-b - \sqrt{b^2 - 4ac}}{2a}$$

   If $a = 10$, $b = -31$ and $c = -14$,

   1   find the value of $\sqrt{b^2 - 4ac}$,
   2   find the two values of *x*.

7. A vertical radio mast is 280 m high, and it is supported by a wire from the top of the mast to the ground, making an angle of 66° with the horizontal ground. How long is the wire ?

8. Mrs Parsons bought x stamps at 24p each and y stamps at 18p each.
   Express these facts as mathematical statements:
   1 Altogether she bought 30 stamps.
   2 The number of 24p stamps she bought was more than twice the number of 18p stamps she bought.
   3 The total cost of the stamps was less than £6.70.

9. A fair die is thrown and a pack of 52 cards is cut.
   What is the probability of getting
   1 a six on the die, and a diamond,
   2 a number other than six on the die, and a card other than a diamond ?

10. Solve the equation $\dfrac{x + 1}{2} - \dfrac{x}{6} = \dfrac{7}{12}$

11. A carpet to cover a floor of area 21 m² costs £252. How much would it cost for a similar carpet to cover a floor which is rectangular, 4 m long by 3.5 m wide ?

12. A formula connected with the distances of the object and the image from a lens is $\dfrac{1}{f} = \dfrac{1}{u} + \dfrac{1}{v}$.
   Find the value of f when $u = 6$ and $v = 4.5$, giving the answer correct to 3 significant figures.

13. In the right-angled triangle ABC, $AB = 6$ cm, $BC = x$ cm, and AC is 5 cm longer than BC.
   Using Pythagoras' theorem, write down an equation involving x, simplify it and solve it to find x.
   What are the lengths of BC and AC ?

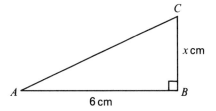

14. A coastguard on the top of a vertical cliff 80 m high sees a lifeboat out at sea, at an angle of depression of 28°.
   Find how far away the boat is from the foot of the cliff.

15. There were three famous mathematical problems of the ancient world. It is now known that these problems cannot be solved geometrically by a construction of straight lines and circles, but you can calculate the answers.

   1   To square a circle

   The aim was to find the length of the side of a square equal in area to that of a given circle.
   If a circle has radius 10 cm, what is the length of the side of a square with the same area as the circle ?

   2   The duplication of the cube

   The aim was to find the length of a cube whose volume is twice that of a given cube.
   If a cube has edge 10 cm, what is the length of the edge of a cube with twice the volume of the first cube ?

   (The third problem was to trisect an angle.)

16. Simplify these expressions:

   1 $a^2b^3c^4 \times a^2bc^3$ **4** $24h^4 \div 6h^2$
   2 $3d^2e \times 4de^3$ **5** $(2j^2k)^3$
   3 $\dfrac{21f^3g^4}{7f^2g}$

17. In the diagram, explain why the triangles ABC and APQ are similar.
   Find
   1   the length of AC,
   2   the length of PQ.

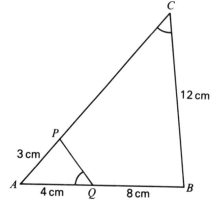

18. For the function $y = x^2 - x - 3$, make a table of values for $x = -3, -2, -1,$ 0, 1, 2, 3, 4.
   Draw the graph of the function for x from -3 to 4. (Label the y-axis from -4 to 9.)
   What is the equation of the axis of symmetry of the curve ?

19. A regular tetrahedron has each face painted a different colour. These are red, blue, green and yellow. When thrown, it lands with one of the coloured faces in contact with the floor, and it is just as likely to land on one face as another.

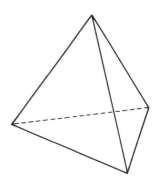

What are the probabilities that
1   the red face can be seen after one throw,
2   the red face can be seen after each of two throws,
3   the red face has not been seen after each of three throws ?

20. The distribution of marks in an examination is shown in this table.

Mark	1–10	11–20	21–30	31–40	41–50	51–60	61–70	71–80	81–90	91–100
f	6	7	7	10	15	17	18	11	6	3

Make a cumulative frequency table of the data.
Draw a cumulative frequency graph.
Use the graph to find
1   the median mark,
2   the quartile marks, and the interquartile range.
3   The pass mark for the examination is 45%. Estimate how many candidates passed.

Exercise C5   Activities

1.   Estimations

Often, in life, we do not need exact answers to our calculations. For instance, if the Gas Bill is usually about £50 per quarter, then this is about £4 per week (£50 ÷ 13), and the householder can plan to put this money aside to pay the next bill when it comes.

There are also times when we do a quick estimation to get a general idea of the cost. If a family is planning a holiday, they perhaps estimate that the hotel and travel cost will be £350 per adult and £250 for a child. For father, mother and 3 children this means a cost of about £1500. To this must be be added money for daily expenses while on holiday, and other expenses such as some new clothes. If they plan to spend £200 on clothes, and allow daily expenses of £30, for 14 days, and allow £100 for other unforseen expenses, this brings the cost of the holiday up to about £2200. Then father and mother must decide whether they can afford that much. If they have already saved £1000 and if there are 5 months left before the holiday then they would need to save about £60 each week from then onwards.

Also, it is useful to be able to make good estimates of weights and measures.

Lengths

Do you know the measurements of your thumb as far as the knuckle, the width of your hand across four fingers, the length of your hand-span, the length of your foot with a shoe on, your height, the distance you can reach with your arms stretched out sideways, the height you can reach on tiptoe, and so on ?
Use a measured distance of 100 m to find the length of your pace when you walk normally, and the length of a stride.
You can estimate other lengths by comparing them with known lengths.

Time

The microwave clock is useful for learning how to estimate seconds, as it counts down. If you have to estimate a few minutes, count how many breaths you take. How many breaths do you normally take in 1 minute ? You know how long your lessons last, and this may help you to estimate longer times.

Weight

Get used to the weight of 1 kg (a bag of sugar) and 2.5 kg (a bag of potatoes). Find your own weight in kg and the weight of a small child. Estimate other weights by comparing them with these known weights.

Capacity

Estimate how much water various containers hold and check by using a measuring jug, a litre bottle (or a pint bottle for British measures). A bucket or a watering can may have measuring lines marked on it. It is useful to remember that 1 litre of water weighs 1 kg. In British measures 1 gallon of water weighs 10 lb.

Find estimations for the following:

1   The cost of bus fares and/or school lunches for the term.

2   The cost of a year's cigarettes for someone who smokes 20 a day.

3   The cost of a year's petrol for a motorist who drives 10 000 miles a year.

4   The cost of supplying textbooks, exercise books and other stationery to your class, for the year.

5   The length and breadth of this textbook.

6   The length and breadth of your classroom, or the school hall.

7   The height of the church tower or steeple, or another tall object.

8   The distance you travel to school.

9   The distance from school to Stratford-upon-Avon.

10 The time taken to run 100 m.

11 The time taken to knit a sweater, or to paint a room.

12 The time taken to go by coach from your school to Stratford-upon-Avon.

13 The weight of this textbook.

14 The weight of rubbish a household throws away in a year.

15 The amount of water used by a household in a year.

Give estimated answers to these questions.

16 The mileage readings of a car, recorded on the MOT test certificates in 2 successive years, were 13 495 and 29 307. How far did the car travel in the year ?

17 The numbers of children in 5 schools in a district are 227, 686, 824, 792, 523. What is the total number of children ?

18 The diagram shows the distances in miles between places reached by the M1/M6 motorways.

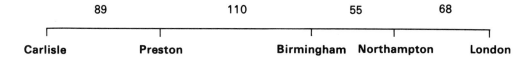

How far is it from London to Carlisle, and from Preston to Northampton ?

19 Last Saturday the attendance at a football match was 22 760. The match before it was 17 940. What was the increase in attendance ?

20 A gas fire burns 1 therm of gas in 6 hours. How many therms will it burn in a year if used for 8 hours a day for 20 weeks in the year, 5 hours a day for 15 weeks and 2 hours a day for the rest of the year ? What will be the cost of the gas used, at 48p per therm ?

2.   **A pendulum**

Make a simple pendulum and investigate the connection between the length of the string and the time for a complete swing.

A simple pendulum consists of a weight tied on the end of a string. The other end of the string is fastened to a fixed point and the string will then hang vertically.

The weight is now pulled to one side so that the string makes a small angle with the vertical (not more than about 30°) and then the weight is let go.
The pendulum should swing freely from side to side.

Begin with a pendulum with string 1.6 m long. Use a watch giving time in seconds and find out how long it takes to make 50 complete swings. A complete swing is forwards and backwards. Divide the time by 50 to find the time of one swing, and give it in seconds, to 2 decimal places.
Repeat the experiment with other lengths, 1.4 m, 1.2 m, 1.0 m, etc.
Show your results in a table.
l = length of string, in cm,
T = time of 1 complete swing, in seconds.

l	0	20	40	. . .
T	0	. . .	. . .	. . .

Draw a graph of the results with length l on the horizontal axis and T on the vertical axis.

If the points plotted appear to lie nearly on a curve, draw a smooth curve going as near to the points as possible.
Comment on the shape of the graph.

Make a new table showing the values of l and T^2, with T^2 correct to 3 decimal places.
Draw a graph with l on the horizontal axis and T^2 on the vertical axis.
Comment on its shape.

If the plotted points lie approximately on a straight line, draw a line of best fit passing through the origin.
Find the gradient of this line.
If the gradient is k, then the equation connecting T and l is $T^2 = kl$.
This is equivalent to $T = \sqrt{k}\,\sqrt{l}$.
Thus the time of swing is proportional to the square root of the length of the string.

The actual equation, worked out mathematically, is $T = 2\pi\sqrt{\dfrac{l}{g}}$.

g cm/s^2 is the acceleration due to gravity.

Now we can use the gradient to find the value of g.

$$\sqrt{k} = \frac{2\pi}{\sqrt{g}}$$

This gives $g = \dfrac{4\pi^2}{k}$

Using your value of k, find an approximate value for g.

g varies at different parts of the world, and at different heights, but it is around 980 cm/s^2.
How accurate is your result ?

1   If $l = 250$ and $g = 980$, find the value of T.   What time is taken for a complete swing on a pendulum with length 2.5 m ?

2   By squaring both sides of the equation for T, find an equation for l in terms of T. If $T = 2$ and $g = 980$, find the value of l. How long do we need to make a pendulum so that it does a **half-swing** every second ?

3. **Find the key**

You need 4 players for this game, and an extra person to be the umpire and keep a list of winners.

You need 4 similar pieces of cardboard to represent 4 doors A, B, C, D. You can draw doors on them, and label them.

You need 4 other similar pieces of cardboard to represent 4 keys for the doors A, B, C, D. You can draw keys on them and label them.

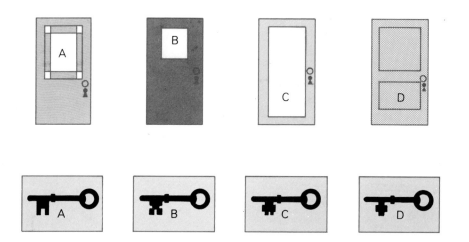

You need 2 bags or boxes, one for the doors and one for the keys. You should be able to mix up the cards in them and pick one out without looking at it.

You must decide on the order of play and you must always keep to the same order. We will call the players Number 1, Number 2, Number 3 and Number 4.

The umpire picks a card from the bag containing doors.
Then Number 1 picks a card from the bag containing keys. If the key is the right one to match the door, Number 1 wins and the game ends.

If the key is not the right one, it is the turn of Number 2 to pick a card. (Do not put the first key back yet.) If Number 2 picks the right key, he wins and the game ends.

If that key is not the right one, it is then the turn of Number 3 to pick a card. If his card matches the door, he wins, and the game ends.

If that key is not the right one, then Number 4 gets his turn.
Since there is only one card left by now, it must be the right one and he wins.

The umpire records who has won. He replaces the door card in its bag and mixes the cards up. He replaces the key cards in their bag and mixes them up.

Then you are ready to play the game again. Remember that the players must always keep to the same order, starting with Number 1.

Before you start playing, answer questions **1, 2, 3**.

1   Do you think the game is fair ?

2   Has each player an equal chance of winning ?

3   If so, what is the probability of any one person winning ? If you think that the game is not a fair one, which player do you think has the best chance of winning, who has the next best chance, who comes next, and who has least chance of winning ?

4   Play several games, at least 40 games if you have time, and record the winners.

5   Draw a bar chart showing the number of games won by each person.

6   Do the results you have got agree with your answers to questions **1, 2, 3** ?

7   Draw a probability tree-diagram to show the various outcomes, and use it to calculate the probability of each person winning.

4.   **A video film**

Nowadays, many people have video cameras, and you might have one in your school.
If there is a video camera that you will be allowed to use, then you can make plans to produce a mathematical film.
You will probably work with a group of friends.
First you must decide on what your film is about. We suggest that trigonometry would be a suitable subject, but your teacher may agree to you choosing another topic.
You can have some scenes showing people doing practical work, and some scenes showing work in the classroom. You may be able to film other people using the topic in their work.
You probably need to write a script, so that people will know what to say when they are being filmed. You may have a commentator who will explain what is going on.
When you have made all the plans, go ahead and make the film.
You may be able to edit your film. That means taking out unsuitable parts to improve it.
When your film is made, you can show it to other classes, and it can be kept in school for use in future years.

5.   **The Parabola**

This is such an interesting geometrical curve that you can make a booklet or poster about it. As well as the ideas given here you can look in library books for further details.

All quadratic functions produce graphs which are parabolas.
We have already mentioned that a parabola is the path taken by a cricket ball which is thrown into the air at an angle. Other objects moving freely under gravity can move in parabolic paths.
Notice the jets of water from a fountain.

The parabola is called a **conic** because it can be formed by slicing a cone.
Maybe you can make a cone, of wax or something similar, and slice it along a plane which is parallel to one of the lines from the vertex to the cirumference of the base. (Planes in other directions give other sorts of conics.)

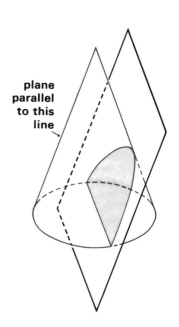

plane parallel to this line

The parabola can be defined as a locus.
It is the locus of a point which moves so that its distance from a fixed point, called the focus, is equal to its distance from a fixed line, called the directrix.

On graph paper, draw the x-axis from -2 to 6, and the y-axis from -10 to 10, using scales of 1 cm to 1 unit. Draw the line AB with equation $x = -2$ for the directrix, and mark the point S (2, 0) for the focus.

The origin lies on the locus as it lies 2 units from S and 2 units from AB.
Mark this point.

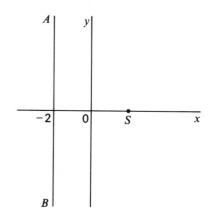

With compasses, use centre S and radius 2.2 units. Notice the line shown on the graph paper which is parallel to AB and 2.2 units from it, i.e. the line $x = 0.2$. There is no need to draw it.
Draw arcs to cut this line at 2 points. Mark these points.

Repeat using a radius 2.4 units and a line 2.4 units from AB.
Continue finding pairs of points which are the same distance from S as from AB, until no more will fit on the paper.
Join the points with a smooth curve, which is a parabola.
You will notice that it is sideways on, compared to the graphs you have drawn of quadratic functions.

The parabola as an envelope

An envelope is an outline of a curve, produced by drawing straight lines.

If you have done curve-stitching or string art you will have probably made the envelope of a parabola.
If not, copy this diagram with points at 1 cm intervals from A. The two lines can meet at any angle.
With your ruler, join 1 to 1, 2 to 2, ..., 10 to 10.
The curve formed is a parabola.
You could design a picture using curve-stitiching or string art, involving these envelopes.

If a mirror is made in a parabolic shape, then light from the focus will be reflected along rays parallel to the axis of the parabola.
These mirrors are used in searchlights, car headlights and torches.

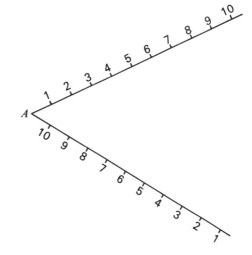

This property in reverse means that parallel beams of light will be reflected onto the focus. This property is used in reflecting telescopes.

The radio-telescope at Jodrell Bank gathers radio waves from far away and concentrates them at the focus.

A parabolic-shaped panel can gather solar heat and concentrate it at the focus.

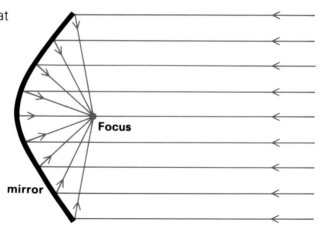

The cables supporting a suspension bridge are fixed in a parabolic shape, and the roadways of modern bridges are also of parabolic shape.

Look around you for other examples of parabolic shapes. Make a collection of drawings or photographs for your poster or booklet.

A lighthouse lamp of around 1763, with a parabolic reflector.

6.   **Fermat's Little Theorem,** continued from page 190.

Pierre Fermat (1601–1665) was a lawyer at Toulouse, who helped to develop
mathematics in several ways.

His little theorem was written in a letter of 1640, and states that if p is a prime
number, and a is prime to p, then $a^{p-1} - 1$ is divisible by p.

This can be re-written as $a^p - a$ is divisible by p, if p is prime.

This is the investigation from page 190. Did you discover that all the values of
$a^p - a$ were divisible by p ?

For over 300 years, the theorem had little practical use.

But nowadays, using the latest large computers, it can be used to test whether
large numbers are prime numbers. If L is a large odd number which may or may
not be prime, then the value of $2^L - 2$ can be divided by L, and if it does not
divide exactly, then L is not a prime number.

The other way of testing whether a number L is prime is to use the Sieve of
Eratosthenes, testing in turn whether L divides by 2, 3, 5, 7, 11, . . . up to the
prime number just less than $\sqrt{L}$. But with very large numbers, e.g. numbers of
50 digits, even a computer would take millions of years to test them in that way.

Until recently, the search for large prime numbers was of little practical
importance, but within the last 20 years a method using large numbers has been
developed for use in sending secret messages in code. To break the code, an
enemy would have to establish that a 200-digit number was not prime, and then
go on to find its factors.

So after all this time, Fermat's little theorem is being used to test for prime
numbers, for a practical purpose.

PUZZLE

47.   Copy these 12 pieces on cardboard and fit them together to form a chessboard.
      (This is quite difficult to solve, but it can be worked out logically. However, a friend who
      picked up the pieces at random found the solution within ten minutes.)

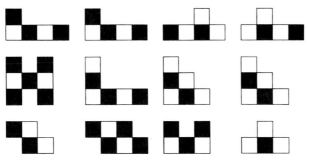

Index

Answers

Some answers have been given corrected to reasonable degrees of accuracy, depending on the questions.
There may be variations in answers where questions involve drawings or graphs.
Sometimes it will not be possible to give answers to the same degree of accuracy, depending on the scale used.

Page 4   **Exercise 1.1**

1. **1** $\frac{1}{6}$ **5** $\frac{2}{3}$ **8** $\frac{3}{20}$
   2 $\frac{3}{4}$ **6** $\frac{1}{5}$ **9** $\frac{5}{8}$
   3 $\frac{7}{16}$ **7** $\frac{3}{8}$ **10** $\frac{4}{5}$
   4 $\frac{2}{5}$

2. **1** $\frac{14}{18}$ **5** $\frac{8}{12}$ **8** $\frac{28}{44}$
   2 $\frac{18}{21}$ **6** $\frac{24}{27}$ **9** $\frac{24}{30}$
   3 $\frac{15}{40}$ **7** $\frac{10}{20}$ **10** $\frac{6}{24}$
   4 $\frac{6}{36}$

3. **1** $\frac{25}{4}$ **5** $\frac{31}{6}$ **8** $\frac{41}{12}$
   2 $\frac{19}{10}$ **6** $\frac{27}{11}$ **9** $\frac{62}{9}$
   3 $\frac{11}{3}$ **7** $\frac{32}{7}$ **10** $\frac{45}{8}$
   4 $\frac{14}{5}$

4. **1** $1\frac{3}{8}$ **5** $4\frac{3}{8}$ **8** $1\frac{1}{3}$
   2 $4\frac{1}{5}$ **6** $6\frac{1}{3}$ **9** $5\frac{3}{11}$
   3 $3\frac{3}{10}$ **7** $3\frac{5}{12}$ **10** $1\frac{1}{4}$
   4 $1\frac{5}{6}$

5. **1** $\frac{3}{4}$ **5** $3\frac{7}{8}$ **9** $2\frac{4}{5}$
   2 $\frac{9}{20}$ **6** $5\frac{19}{20}$ **10** $5\frac{5}{24}$
   3 $3\frac{1}{2}$ **7** $1\frac{3}{8}$ **11** $8\frac{1}{20}$
   4 $\frac{11}{12}$ **8** $1\frac{5}{12}$ **12** $7\frac{9}{10}$

6. **1** $\frac{1}{5}$ **5** $\frac{5}{24}$ **9** $\frac{5}{14}$
   2 $\frac{5}{12}$ **6** $1\frac{5}{8}$ **10** $2\frac{41}{50}$
   3 $\frac{13}{16}$ **7** $2\frac{1}{3}$ **11** $1\frac{15}{16}$
   4 $1\frac{1}{2}$ **8** $2\frac{3}{4}$ **12** $5\frac{2}{3}$

7. **1** $\frac{17}{24}$ **4** $1\frac{7}{12}$
   2 $\frac{19}{32}$ **5** $12\frac{21}{40}$
   3 $6\frac{1}{6}$ **6** $7\frac{6}{7}$

Page 8   **Exercise 1.2**

1. **1** $\frac{1}{4}$ **5** $\frac{7}{20}$ **9** $\frac{5}{12}$
   2 $\frac{5}{16}$ **6** $\frac{16}{21}$ **10** $13\frac{1}{2}$
   3 $\frac{2}{9}$ **7** $12\frac{1}{2}$ **11** 5
   4 20   **8** $23\frac{1}{3}$ **12** 1

2. **1** $\frac{4}{5}$ **5** $9\frac{7}{9}$ **9** $\frac{10}{27}$
   2 $1\frac{1}{7}$ **6** $\frac{2}{27}$ **10** $2\frac{1}{3}$
   3 6   **7** $\frac{3}{4}$ **11** $1\frac{1}{4}$
   4 $\frac{6}{7}$ **8** $1\frac{3}{8}$ **12** $\frac{1}{4}$

3. **1** $\frac{4}{9}$ **4** $\frac{1}{4}$
   2 $5\frac{1}{3}$ **5** $2\frac{3}{4}$
   3 $9\frac{1}{6}$ **6** 1

4. **1** $1\frac{1}{3}$ **4** $5\frac{1}{4}$
   2 $\frac{3}{10}$ **5** 28
   3 $\frac{19}{40}$ **6** 31

5. **1** $\frac{7}{10}$ **4** $\frac{3}{8}$
   2 $\frac{3}{100}$ **5** $\frac{5}{12}$
   3 $\frac{4}{9}$

6. **1** 96p   **4** $1.4\,\ell$
   2 160 m   **5** 1.25 kg
   3 50 min

Page 12   **Exercise 1.3**

1. **1** 0.55   **5** 0.083   **8** 0.727
   2 0.75   **6** 0.222   **9** 0.833
   3 0.125   **7** 0.767   **10** 0.429
   4 0.8

2. **1** $\frac{9}{10}$ **4** $\frac{1}{200}$
   2 $\frac{14}{25}$ **5** $\frac{7}{40}$
   3 $\frac{7}{20}$

3. **1** $\frac{4}{5}, \frac{7}{8}, \frac{9}{10}$ **4** $\frac{7}{12}, \frac{13}{21}, \frac{9}{14}$
   2 $\frac{4}{15}, \frac{2}{5}, \frac{5}{12}$ **5** $\frac{5}{11}, \frac{7}{13}, \frac{3}{5}$
   3 $\frac{5}{24}, \frac{1}{4}, \frac{1}{3}$

4. **1** 2.8   **5** 2.5   **8** 11.25
   2 3.2   **6** $3\frac{1}{3}$ **9** 6
   3 24   **7** 36   **10** 4.5
   4 38.5

5. **1** $\frac{1}{18}$ **4** 72
   2 $\frac{1}{3}$ **5** $\frac{1}{3}$
   3 $\frac{7}{9}$

6. **1** 195   **4** 4
   2 $\frac{3}{4}$ **5** 40
   3 2

Page 15   Exercise 1.4

1. **1** 20 : 7   **6** 7 : 4 : 2
   2 2 : 3   **7** 5 : 3 : 7
   3 3 : 8   **8** 7 : 5 : 8
   4 1 : 9   **9** 3 : 5 : 4
   5 11 : 6   **10** 5 : 10 : 19

2. **1** 3.6 cm, 8.4 cm
   2 £4, £48
   3 67.5 ha, 52.5 ha
   4 £2.88, 32p
   5 5.5 cm, 2.0 cm
   6 4 cm, 14 cm, 16 cm
   7 12 kg, 24 kg, 44 kg
   8 £54, £66, £120
   9 6.0ℓ, 4.5ℓ, 3.0ℓ, 1.5ℓ
   10 4 m, 12 m, 20 m, 24 m

3. **1** £20   **4** 9.9ℓ
   2 40 kg   **5** 120 m
   3 £1.04

4. **1** £7.50   **4** 25ℓ
   2 1 h 40 min   **5** 5 g
   3 8.8 kg

Page 17   Exercise 1.5

1. 95 p   4. 7.7 tons

2. 5.4 tonnes   5. 30 days

3. 21   6. 12 days

7. 36 kg   10. 4 hours

8. 52   11. 0.056 m³

9. £550   12. 15 (days)

Page 19   Exercise 1.6

1. $5\frac{3}{4}$ inches   7. 8 days

2. 26 mph   8. 7 : 4 : 2;   2.1 kg copper,
                        1.2 kg nickel, 0.6 kg
                        zinc

3. 30

4. 10.8 g   9. 200 m, 75 m, 125 m,
                        100 m

5. £1.60   10. A £175, B £210, C £315

6. 9

Page 26   Exercise 2.1

1. **1** −6   **5** −13   **8** −8
   2 2   **6** −3   **9** −2
   3 −3   **7** 0   **10** −7
   4 −6

2. **1** −1   **5** 0   **8** −5
   2 11   **6** 2   **9** 3
   3 3   **7** 18   **10** 0
   4 −1

3. **1** −6   **5** 6   **8** 4
   2 −12   **6** 7   **9** 6
   3 56   **7** 0   **10** −28
   4 −8

4. **1** −14   **5** 1   **8** $-\frac{2}{3}$
   2 −23   **6** 0   **9** 18
   3 0   **7** 7   **10** $-1\frac{1}{2}$
   4 $-\frac{1}{2}$

Page 28   Exercise 2.2

1. **1** −4   **5** −4   **8** $-2\frac{3}{5}$
   2 30   **6** 50   **9** $-4\frac{1}{2}$
   3 20   **7** 49   **10** 6
   4 13

2. **1** -8 **5** -64 **8** 0
   2 -15 **6** $1\frac{1}{4}$ **9** -15
   3 4   **7** 7   **10** -4
   4 $-\frac{1}{2}$

3. **1** 2   **5** -20 **8** 8
   2 -36 **6** -8 **9** -34
   3 1500   **7** 1   **10** 1
   4 115

Page 29   Exercise 2.3

1. **1** 10
   2 36 m

3. y values: 34, 15, 2, -5, -6, -1, 10
   2nd table,
   y values: -2, -6, -8, -8, -6, -2, 4

4. **1** 10
   2 13 units

5. **1** $-2°C$
   2 -2 cm, 1.38 m
   3 0.99 tonnes

Page 37   Exercise 3.1

1. **1** $x = 10.5$, $y = 9.9$
      (lengths 10.5 cm, 9.9 cm)
   2 $x = 25.2$, $y = 3.5$
   3 $x = 2.4$, $y = 14.4$
   4 33 cm
   5 9.3 cm

2. **1** 13.5 cm
   2 21 cm
   3 $x = 5.4$, $y = 4.8$
   4 1.8 cm
   5 $x = 35$, $y = 26$

Page 44   Exercise 3.2

1. **1** Yes;
      AB, FD; AC, FE; BC, DE;
      $\angle A = \angle F$
   2 Yes;
      AB, LK; AC, LM; BC, KM;
      $\angle A = \angle L$, $\angle B = \angle K$, $\angle C = \angle M$

3. Yes;
   AB, PQ; AC, PR; BC, QR;
   $\angle A = \angle P$, $\angle C = \angle R$

4. Yes;
   AB, TS; AC, TU; BC, SU;
   $\angle B = \angle S$, $\angle C = \angle U$

5. Not similar.

2. $PR = 5$ cm, $QR = 8$ cm

3. $\angle D = 63°$, $\angle E = 59°$, $\angle F = 58°$

4. $\angle A = \angle Z$, $AB = 4.5$ cm

5. $\angle A = \angle P$, $\angle B = \angle Q$, $\angle C = \angle R$

6. $BC : DF = 3 : 4$; $\angle B = \angle F$, $\angle C = \angle D$

Page 46   Exercise 3.3

1. 12.5 cm

2. 22 km

3. 6 cm

4. 4.9 cm

5. 42 m

6. AB, DE; AC, DC; BC, EC; $AB = 5.6$ cm,
   $CE = 10.5$ cm

7. $BC : DE = 2 : 3$;
   $\angle B = \angle D$

8. $\angle A = \angle D$, $\angle B = \angle E$, $\angle ACB = \angle DCE$

10. 27 m

11. 35 m

12. $PW = 1.6$ m, $QX = 2.2$ m, $RY = 2.8$ m,
    $SZ = 3.4$ m

13. **1** 2.4 cm
    2 $2\frac{1}{4}$, 225%
    3 $\frac{9}{40}$, 22.5%, 1.8 cm

14. **1** length 20 cm, width 16 cm
    2 846 cm^2, 1504 cm^2, 9 : 16
    3 1620 cm^3, 3840 cm^3, 27 : 64
    4 3 : 4

Page 54   Exercise 4.1

1. **1** $x > 6$ **6** $x < 9\frac{1}{3}$
  2 $x < 1$ **7** $x > -2$
  3 $x \leqslant 5\frac{1}{2}$ **8** $x \leqslant \frac{2}{3}$
  4 $x \geqslant -10$ **9** $x \geqslant 2$
  5 $x > 3$ **10** $x > 20$

2. **1** $x > 7$ **6** $x < -2\frac{1}{3}$
  2 $x \leqslant 2$ **7** $x \geqslant 7$
  3 $x < 10$ **8** $x \leqslant -2$
  4 $x \leqslant 0$ **9** $x < -1$
  5 $x \leqslant -2\frac{1}{4}$ **10** $x < 11$

Page 55   Exercise 4.2

1. **1** $-4 < x < 4$
  2 $x < -1$ or $x > 1$
  3 $-9 \leqslant x \leqslant 9$
  4 $-1\frac{1}{2} < x < 1\frac{1}{2}$
  5 $x \leqslant -\frac{1}{3}$ or $x \geqslant \frac{1}{3}$

2. **1** $-5 \leqslant x \leqslant 5$
  2 $x < -10$ or $x > 10$
  3 $x < -8$ or $x > 8$
  4 $-7 < x < 7$
  5 $-6 < x < 6$

3. **1** 1, 2, 3, 4, 5   **4** 7, 8, 9, 10
  2 8, 9, 10   **5** 5, 6
  3 1, 2, 3

Page 58   Exercise 4.3

2. **1** 5; (0, −2)   **4** −1; (0, 8)
  2 $\frac{1}{2}$; (0, 4)   **5** 3; (0, 0)
  3 −2; (0, 3)

3. (2, 2)

4. $(2\frac{1}{4}, 4\frac{1}{4})$

Page 63   Exercise 4.4

1. **1** $A\colon x < 3$; $B\colon x > 3$
  2 $A\colon y > 2x$; $B\colon y < 2x$
  3 $A\colon y < -x - 1$; $B\colon y > -x - 1$
  4 $A\colon y < 6 - 2x$; $B\colon y > 6 - 2x$

3. **1** $2 < x < 5$
  2 $x > 3$, $y > 2$
  3 $x < 1$, $y > -1$
  4 $x > -3$, $y < -2$

5. **1** $y > 0$, $y < x$
  2 $y < 0$, $y > 4 - 2x$
  3 $x < 2$, $y > 4 - x$
  4 $x > -3$, $y < x - 3$

Page 68   Exercise 4.5

1. **1** $x > -1$, $y > -2$, $y < -\frac{1}{2}x$
  2 $x > 2$, $y < 3$, $y > \frac{1}{2}x$
  3 $x > -3$, $y > 0$, $y < 2 - x$
  4 $y < -1$, $y > -x - 4$, $y > 2x - 4$

Page 70   Exercise 4.6

1. **1** $x < 0$ or $x > 0$
  2 all values of x
  3 no values of x
  4 $x > 3$
  5 $x < -2$

2. 10°C
lower: temperatures less than 10°C,
higher: temperatures greater than 10°C

3. **5** 200 m

4. $y > x$, $y < 2x$, $30 < x < 60$,
$x + y < 130$;
widths greater than 38 cm, less than
54 cm;
width 46.9 cm

5. $30x + 40y \leqslant 1200$, $y \geqslant 2x$,
$x + y \geqslant 30$
  1 20
  2 10

6. $(70x + 30y)$ pence;
$x + y \geqslant 80$, $y \leqslant 64$;
dearer sweets: between 5 lb and
9 lb inclusive

Page 86   Exercise A1

1. 16
2. 3
3. £60
4. -24
5. £18
6. $80°$
7. 23 (min)
8. 10 cm
9. £15
10. $\frac{5}{16}$
11. 9 cm
12. 150 miles
13. 400 m
14. $x > 9$
15. 24

Page 87   Exercise A2

1. £2.35
2. 9; 2 over
3. 5 cm
4. 300 m²
5. 20%
6. 15 years
7. no
8. $-2, -5$
9. $3 : 20$
10. £1.20
11. $x > 0$
12. £2.40
13. radius
14. £5.75
15. 12 days

Page 88   Exercise A3

1. 210
2. **1** $-1, -4$
   2 $\frac{1}{125}, -\frac{1}{625}$
   3 $-0.4, 0.4$
3. 1130 m (to nearest 10 m)
4. cost = £$(3x + 120)$;
   15 adults, 9 children
5. 23
6. $\frac{7}{10}$
7. 25 cm
8. **1** 24 cm²
   2 480 cm³

9. $3x$ cm
10. **1** 19
    2 28
11. **1** $x < 1$
    2 $x > 6\frac{1}{2}$
    3 $x < -2$
12. 4
13. **1** 355 km
    2 71 km/h
14. B: height 60 cm
    C: radius 27 cm
15. 1
16. **1** 14
    2 4
    3 9
    4 5
17. 175 mℓ tube
18. **1** $18°$
    2 $81°$
19. **1** $18x + 24y \leqslant 150$, $x \geqslant 2$,
        $y \geqslant 1$, $x + y \leqslant 7$
    4 4
20. **1** 3.5
    2 3

Page 108   Exercise 6.1

1. **1** $9a$ **5** 0   **8** $4e - 8f$
   2 $5b^2$ **6** $8a$ **9** $-g$
   3 c **7** 0   **10** $2h^3$
   4 $3d^2$

2. **1** $10a^2 - a$ **6** $a^2 + 7a + 3$
   2 $3b - c$ **7** $5 + 14b - b^2$
   3 $5d + 5e$ **8** $c + 3d + cd + 2$
   4 $16f - 9$ **9** $3e - 4$
   5 $7g$ **10** $4f + 3f^2$

4. **1** $2x^2 + 11x + 12$
   2 $x^2 + x - 2$
   3 $3x^2 - 19x + 28$
   4 $2x^2 + 7x - 15$

5 $x^2 - 9$
6 $x^2 - 4x + 4$
7 $4x^2 - 25x + 6$
8 $x^2 + 12x + 36$
9 $2x^2 + x - 6$
10 $1 + 7x + 12x^2$

5. **1** $4x^2 + 8x - 5$
   2 $2x^2 + 9x + 9$
   3 $2x^2 - 9x - 5$
   4 $x^2 - 10x + 25$
   5 $1 - 7x + 10x^2$
   6 $8x^2 + 34x + 21$
   7 $x^2 + 6x - 16$
   8 $8x^2 + 10x - 3$
   9 $12x^2 - 31xy + 7y^2$
   10 $2x^2 - 5xy - 12y^2$

6. **1** $x^2 + 6xy + 8y^2$
   2 $x^2 + xy - 6y^2$
   3 $x^2 + 2xy + y^2$
   4 $2x^2 + 11xy - 6y^2$
   5 $3x^2 - 7xy - 40y^2$
   6 $4a^2 + 12a + 5$
   7 $5 + 9b - 2b^2$
   8 $8c^2 + 22c - 21$
   9 $d^2 - 6de - 16e^2$
   10 $f^2 - 4fg + 4g2$

Page 114   Exercise 6.2

1. **1** $20a^2$ **5** $4e^2$ **8** $\dfrac{k}{2}$
   2 $56b^2$ **6** $2fg$
   3 $9c$ **7** $12j^2$ **9** $36\,m^2$
   4 $45d^3$ **10** $4p^2$

2. **1** $4(3 - a)$ **6** $x(x - 10)$
   2 $b(2b - 9)$ **7** $7(2x + 5y)$
   3 $5(c^2 + 3d^2)$ **8** $x(1 + x)$
   4 $7e(1 + 4f)$ **9** $3x^2(3x - 5)$
   5 $3g(g - 2h)$ **10** $\pi r(2 + r)$

3. **1** $a(a + 4)$ **6** $3f^2(3 - 8f)$
   2 $9b(2b - 1)$ **7** $5(3g + 1)$
   3 $2c(c + 4d)$ **8** $7x(x + 3y)$
   4 $4(3 + d^2)$ **9** $3y(4 - 5y)$
   5 $e(e - 16)$ **10** $x(2x^2 + x + 1)$

4. **1** $\dfrac{5a}{6}$ **5** $\dfrac{e}{2}$ **8** $\dfrac{h}{2}$
   2 $\dfrac{5b}{4}$ **6** $\frac{1}{24}f$ **9** $\frac{11}{30}j$
   3 $\frac{19}{20}c$ **7** $\dfrac{g}{4}$ **10** $\dfrac{k}{6}$
   4 $\dfrac{5d}{8}$

5. **1** $\dfrac{a^2}{2}$ **5** $\dfrac{3j}{2k^2}$ **8** $\frac{1}{12}$
   2 $\dfrac{3b^2}{c}$ **6** 4 **9** $1\frac{1}{2}$
   3 $\dfrac{2d^2}{3}$ **7** $\dfrac{p^2q^2}{16}$ **10** xy
   4 $5g^2$

6. **1** $x = 6$ **4** $x = 5$
   2 $x = \frac{1}{5}$ **5** $x = 2$
   3 $x = 7$

7. **1** $x = 8$ **4** $x = -7$
   2 $x = 1\frac{1}{2}$ **5** $x = 6$
   3 $x = 42$

8. **1** $x = \pm 9$ **9** $x = 4.5$
   2 $x = 4$ **10** $x = 1$
   3 $x = \pm 1$ **11** $x = 1.44$
   4 $x = \pm 1.1$ **12** $x = \pm 0.71$
   5 $x = 4.64$ **13** $x = 512$
   6 $x = \pm 6.32$ **14** $x = 100$
   7 $x = 25$ **15** $x = 3.90$
   8 $x = 8$

Page 118   Exercise 6.3

1. **1** $A = ab + cd$ **4** $A = 2ar + \frac{1}{2}\pi r^2$
   2 $A = ax + bx$ **5** $A = \frac{1}{2}ab + 2a^2$
   3 $A = \frac{1}{2}(a + b)h$

2. $h = \dfrac{2A}{b}$

3. $d = \dfrac{C}{\pi}$

4. $x = \dfrac{y - c}{m}$

5. $t = \dfrac{s}{v}$

6. $S = n\bar{x}$

7. **1** $u = v - ft$

    2 $t = \dfrac{v - u}{f}$

8. **1** $m = dv$

    2 $v = \dfrac{m}{d}$

9. $M = \frac{20}{17}P$

10. $T = \dfrac{100I}{PR}$

Page 120   Exercise 6.4

1. **1** $y = kx$
    2 $k = 4$
    3 $y = 60$
    4 $x = 25$

2. **3** $y = 48$

3. **3** $y = 22\frac{1}{2}$

4. **3** $y = 42$

5. **3** $y = 4\frac{1}{2}$

6. **1** $12\frac{1}{2}$ **4** 6
    2 $13\frac{1}{2}$ **5** 1.8
    3 $6\frac{2}{3}$

Page 121   Exercise 6.5

1. Frank 18, Derek 24

2. $x = 16\frac{5}{8}$

3. $\dfrac{5b}{24}$ hours

4. **4** $BC = 15\,\text{cm}$, $AB = 17\,\text{cm}$

5. **1** $x(x + y)$
    2 9800   **4** 262
    3 370   **5** 22 700

6. 11

7. **1** 8
    2 20

8. **1** $h = \dfrac{3V}{\pi r^2}$

    2 $r = \sqrt{\dfrac{3V}{\pi h}}$

    3 6 cm

9. **1** $(2\pi rh + \pi r^2)\,\text{cm}^2$
    2 $\pi r(2h + r)\,\text{cm}^2$
    3 $31.4\,\text{cm}^2$

10. $AP^2 + PB^2 = (2x^2 - 10x + 33)\,\text{cm}^2$,
    $DP = 1\,\text{cm}$ or $4\,\text{cm}$

11. **1** $600\,\text{cm}^3$
    2 5 kg
    3 1.6 ohms

Page 130   Exercise 7.1

1. **1** 0.213   **4** 8.144
    2 2.050   **5** 0.105
    3 0.767

2. **1** 67.4°   **4** 37.6°
    2 31.9°   **5** 67.8°
    3 75.5°

3. **1** 1.78 cm   **5** 13.2 cm   **8** 24.1 cm
    2 6.66 cm   **6** 4.13 cm   **9** 1.16 cm
    3 9.39 cm   **7** 6.33 cm   **10** 6.84 cm
    4 6.49 cm

4. **1** $\angle A = 24.0°$, $\angle C = 66.0°$
    2 $\angle B = 56.3°$, $\angle A = 33.7°$
    3 $\angle C = 58.8°$, $\angle B = 31.2°$
    4 $\angle A = 22.6°$, $\angle B = 67.4°$
    5 $\angle B = 61.3°$, $\angle C = 28.7°$
    6 $\angle C = 61.2°$, $\angle A = 28.8°$
    7 $\angle B = 36.2°$, $\angle C = 53.8°$
    8 $\angle A = 17.9°$, $\angle C = 72.1°$
    9 $\angle A = 23.1°$, $\angle C = 66.9°$
    10 $\angle B = 47.5°$, $\angle C = 42.5°$

Page 134   Exercise 7.2

1. 740 m

2. 31 m

3. 385 m

4. **1** 290 m
    2 200 m
    3 90 m

5. **1** 1.1 m
    2 69°

6. 28.2 km

7. 1.21 km

8. 4 km, 634 m, 2060 m

Page 142   Exercise 8.1

1. **1** 5^4 **5** 9^4 **8** 6
    2 7^3 **6** 10   **9** 2^3
    3 6^4 **7** 4^{12} **10** $3^{\frac{1}{2}}$
    4 8^{15}

2. **1** 5^2 **4** 7^4
    2 $6^{\frac{1}{3}}$ **5** $5^{\frac{1}{3}}$
    3 $3^{\frac{1}{2}}$

3. **1** 64   **5** 343   **8** 1
    2 64   **6** 11   **9** 0.5
    3 4   **7** 243   **10** 6
    4 10

4. **1** 1730   **5** 4.64   **8** 0.118
    2 6.35   **6** 14.1   **9** 0.368
    3 1.35   **7** 1.26   **10** 1.61
    4 6 770 000

Page 145   Exercise 8.2

1. **1** 2.07×10^2 **6** 5×10^6
    2 5.178×10^3 **7** 2.379×10^4
    3 9.106×10^1 **8** 1.51×10^1
    4 8.5×10^3 **9** 2.56×10^5
    5 6.04×10^4 **10** 1.7×10^9

2. **1** 162   **6** 7600
    2 40 000   **7** 1 100 000
    3 5 700 000   **8** 80 000
    4 803   **9** 62 315 000
    5 10 050   **10** 999 000

3. **1** 1.288×10^9 **6** 3.1×10^3
    2 1.23×10^{11} **7** 2.5×10^5
    3 4×10^4 **8** 2.56×10^6
    4 3.025×10^9 **9** 3.5×10^3
    5 5.673×10^{10} **10** 7.4×10^4

Page 148   Exercise 8.3

1. **1** 5.6×10^{-2} **6** 6.2×10^{-3}
    2 2.8×10^{-4} **7** 4.1×10^{-7}
    3 9×10^{-6} **8** 9.307×10^{-2}
    4 1.57×10^{-1} **9** 2×10^{-5}
    5 2.38×10^{-4} **10** 1.03×10^{-1}

2. **1** 0.41   **6** 0.076
    2 0.0000523   **7** 0.003
    3 0.086   **8** 0.61
    4 0.104   **9** 0.00027
    5 0.0002981   **10** 9.99

3. **1** 6.08×10^{-3} **7** 8×10^{-3}
    2 6.5×10^0 **8** 3.46×10^4
    3 1.2662×10^{-4} **9** 2×10^6
    4 5.329×10^{-5} **10** 1.7×10^{-2}
    5 3.3×10^{-8} **11** 5.65×10^{-3}
    6 1.105×10^3 **12** 8.4×10^{-1}

Page 149   Exercise 8.4

1. **1** 2   **5** $\frac{1}{2}$ **8** $\frac{1}{3}$
    2 6   **6** 3   **9** $\frac{1}{2}$
    3 4   **7** $\frac{1}{2}$ **10** -2
    4 5

2. **1** 75 000 000
    2 6 600 000, 6 500 000
    3 130 000 000
    4 21 000
    5 500 000 000 000 000

3. **1** 8.99×10^{-4} g
    2 2×10^{-9} K
    3 7×10^{-7} m
    4 5.334×10^{-1} g
    5 1×10^{-10} m

4. 1.5×10^6 ℓ

5. 3.3×10^{20} tonnes

6. 800, $n = 100 \times 2^t$, 140 (141), 1.7×10^9

7. 3.1 m, 1.5×10^{-4} s

8. 9.6×10^{-2} mm

9. 4.1×10^{13} km

10. 5.6×10^{-2} mm

11. £965, £(8.35×10^6)

12. 8.3×10^{-8} cm

Page 157   Exercise 9.1

1. $\frac{1}{32}$

2. 0.343, 0.027

3. **1** $\frac{1}{512}$
    2 $\frac{49}{512}$

4. $\frac{1}{50}$, $\frac{49}{2500}$

5. **1** $\frac{1}{8}$
    2 $\frac{1}{8}$
    3 $\frac{1}{8}$

6. $\frac{15}{64}$

7. **1** $\frac{6}{25}$
    2 $\frac{1}{625}$

8. **1** $\frac{1}{8}$
    2 $\frac{3}{169}$

9. **1** $\frac{16}{625}$
    2 $\frac{1}{16}$
    3 $\frac{1}{16}$

10. **1** $\frac{1}{20}$
     2 $\frac{3}{20}$

Page 163   Exercise 9.2

1. **1** $\frac{2}{5}$
    2 $\frac{3}{5}$
    3 $\frac{2}{15}$

2. $\frac{1}{7}$
    1 $\frac{1}{49}$
    2 $\frac{40}{49}$

3. **1** $\frac{1}{24}$
    2 $\frac{7}{12}$
    3 $\frac{5}{16}$

4. **1** $\frac{25}{64}$
    2 $\frac{5}{16}$
    3 $\frac{15}{32}$

5. $\frac{1}{6}$, $\frac{5}{36}$, $\frac{25}{216}$, $\frac{125}{216}$

Page 165   Exercise 9.3

1. 0.00000357, 3.57×10^{-6}

2. **1** $\frac{1}{6}$, $\frac{1}{216}$
    2 $\frac{5}{6}$, $\frac{125}{216}$
    3 0, $\frac{1}{18}$, $\frac{1}{12}$, $\frac{1}{9}$, $\frac{1}{6}$, $\frac{5}{6}$

3. **1** $\frac{1}{64}$
    2 $\frac{27}{64}$

Page 171   Exercise 10.1

1. $(2, -4)$; $x = 0$ or $x = 4$

2. $x = 2\frac{1}{2}$; $x = 0.4$ or $x = 4.6$

3. $(0, 10)$; $x = -3.2$ or $x = 3.2$

5. $(1, 8)$

Page 176   Exercise 10.3

1. $67\,cm^3$

2. $k = 60$, pressure = 0.8 units

3. speed $2\frac{1}{2}$ revs/s, friction 5.75 units

4. $y = x$, $y = -x$

5. $x = 3$; 3 cm by 3 cm by 1.5 cm.

Page 180   Exercise B1

1. 0.75

2. 42

3. £140

4. $6a^3$

5. 4.3×10^4

6. $b = \dfrac{A}{l}$

7. $x < 5$

8. $60\,cm^2$

9. $\frac{1}{12}$

10. 8

11. 5

12. 28 cm

13. 60

14. y^3

15. 25 cm

Page 181   Exercise B2

1. 25 (min)
2. 6
3. 2 m
4. a^6
5. 110°
6. $\frac{3}{8}$
7. £1.80
8. $x > 48$
9. 37 000 ℓ
10. $x(x - 2)$
11. £2
12. 2
13. $\frac{4}{25}$
14. 0
15. 10.5 cm

Page 182   Exercise B3

1. £60

2. $r = \sqrt{\dfrac{S}{3\pi}}$

3. 306 m

4. **1** -5
    2 10
    3 -153

5. 127°

6. 16

7. £600

8. $6.0 \times 10^5 \ \ell$

9. **1** $\dfrac{x}{5}$

    2 $\dfrac{7a^2c}{5b^2}$

    3 $6d^2e$

10. $-\frac{4}{3}$

11. **1** $-7 \leqslant x \leqslant 7$
    2 $x \leqslant -3$ or $x \geqslant 3$
    3 $4 < x < 6$

12. **1** $\frac{1}{2}$
    2 $\frac{3}{10}$
    3 $\frac{7}{20}$
    4 $\frac{1}{400}$

13. **1** 6^{14}
    2 5^2, 25
    3 $\frac{1}{6}$

14. 50p

15. $x^2 + 4xy + 4y^2$; 100

17. $S = \pi r (r + l)$; 990 cm²

18. **1** 4.3×10^{-4} m
    2 2×10^{-5} Pa
    3 3×10^{-7} m

19. **1** $AC = 20$ cm, $AX = 10$ cm
    2 16 cm to 20 cm, inclusive

20. 6.3 $(6\frac{1}{4})$

Page 187   Exercise B4

4. **1** volume
    2 length
    3 area
    4 length
    5 area
    6 area
    7 volume
    8 area
    9 length
    10 area
    11 length
    12 area
    13 length
    14 length
    15 length
    16 km/h
    17 g/cm³
    18 m, s
    19 g, cm³

Page 200   Exercise 11.1

1. **1** 0.292
    2 0.934
    3 0.537
    4 0.988
    5 0.070

2. **1** 0.990
    2 0.087
    3 0.777
    4 0.399
    5 0.934

3. **1** 64.2°
    2 39.2°
    3 22.8°
    4 33.7°
    5 46.5°

4. **1** 36.9°
    2 65.2°
    3 78.2°
    4 23.6°
    5 73.2°

5. **1** 1.95 cm
    2 4.82 cm
    3 3.76 cm
    4 5.83 cm
    5 7.13 cm
    6 4.02 cm
    7 AB = 7.41 cm, AC = 5.79 cm
    8 AB = 6.76 cm, BC = 1.81 cm
    9 AB = 3.92 cm, BC = 1.51 cm
    10 AB = 5.87 cm, AC = 6.29 cm

6. **1** $\angle A$ = 23.7°, $\angle C$ = 66.3°
    2 $\angle B$ = 52.1°, $\angle A$ = 37.9°
    3 $\angle C$ = 58.2°, $\angle B$ = 31.8°
    4 $\angle A$ = 34.8°, $\angle B$ = 55.2°
    5 $\angle B$ = 60.0°, $\angle C$ = 30.0°
    6 $\angle C$ = 76.2°, $\angle A$ = 13.8°
    7 $\angle B$ = 39.6°, $\angle C$ = 50.4°
    8 $\angle A$ = 12.3°, $\angle C$ = 77.7°
    9 $\angle A$ = 19.1°, $\angle C$ = 70.9°
    10 $\angle B$ = 50.9°. $\angle C$ = 39.1°

Page 204   Exercise 11.2

1. **1** 12.9 cm   **5** 15.4 cm   **8** 6.91 cm
    2 3.73 cm   **6** 14.9 cm   **9** 13.9 cm
    3 8.97 cm   **7** 11.5 cm   **10** 9.83 cm
    4 8.56 cm

2. **1** 2.15 cm   **5** 3.82 cm   **8** 1.26 cm
    2 30.5 cm   **6** 26.3 cm   **9** 33.8 cm
    3 7.41 cm   **7** 4.68 cm   **10** 14.2 cm
    4 9.15 cm

3. **1** $\angle A$ = 41.4°, $\angle B$ = 48.6°
    2 $\angle C$ = 26.6°, $\angle B$ = 63.4°
    3 $\angle A$ = 51.9°, $\angle B$ = 38.1°
    4 $\angle B$ = 75.0°, $\angle C$ = 15.0°
    5 $\angle A$ = 55.2°, $\angle C$ = 34.8°
    6 $\angle B$ = 57.5°, $\angle A$ = 32.5°
    7 $\angle B$ = 64.2°, $\angle A$ = 25.8°
    8 $\angle A$ = 24.2°, $\angle B$ = 65.8°
    9 $\angle C$ = 19.7°, $\angle B$ = 70.3°
    10 $\angle C$ = 62.2°, $\angle A$ = 27.8°

Page 206   Exercise 11.3

1. 6.2 m

2. 8.6°

3. 15.4 km

4. 52 m

5. 2.7 cm

6. 113 m

7. 67 m, 42°

8. **1** 51.3°
    2 4.7 m

9. 6.5 m

10. 9.2 m

11. **1** 26.8 km
    2 29.7 km
    3 16.6°
    4 107°

12. **1** $\angle A$ = 44.0°, $\angle B$ = 68.0°,
        $\angle C$ = 68.0°
    2 6.6 cm
    3 16.2 cm
    polygon: AB = 7.1 cm

Page 216   Exercise 12.1

Cumulative frequencies:

1. 0, 4, 13, 31, 68, 118, 141, 147, 150

2. 0, 7, 50, 123, 185, 240, 283, 300

3. 0, 4, 19, 81, 164, 259, 324, 372, 394, 399, 400

4. 0, 5, 14, 24, 36, 51, 67, 79, 90, 96, 100

5. 0, 25, 68, 133, 184, 232, 250

Page 223   Exercise 12.3

Median, lower quartile, upper quartile, interquartile range, in order:

1. 155.5 cm, 151 cm, 159.5 cm, 8.5 cm

2. 61.5 mm, 56 mm, 68 mm, 12 mm

3. 73 kg, 69.5 kg, 77 kg, 7.5 kg

4.   49, 31, 67, 36

5.   3.9 kg, 2.9 kg, 5.1 kg, 2.2 kg

6.   45, 33, 56, 23

Page 223   Exercise 12.4

1.   Cumulative frequencies:
     0, 14, 39, 69, 131, 176, 194, 199, 200;
     Median, lower quartile, upper quartile,
     interquartile range:
     50.00 cm, 49.89 cm, 50.09 cm, 0.20 cm;
     15 rods to be filed down.

2.   Cumulative frequencies:
     0, 6, 16, 28, 42, 59, 78, 94, 108, 116,
     120;
     Median, lower quartile, upper quartile,
     interquartile range: 51, 31, 68, 37;
     Over 75: 19 candidates

3.   Cumulative frequencies:
     0, 200, 550, 1470, 2640, 3690, 4540,
     5170, 5630, 5880, 6000;
     Median, lower quartile, upper quartile,
     interquartile range: 9.3 years, 8.0 years,
     11.0 years, 3 years;
     Over $12\frac{1}{2}$ years old: 10%

4.   Cumulative frequencies:
     0, 31, 66, 105, 149, 173, 195, 200
     Median, lower quartile, upper quartile,
     interquartile range:
     5.7 years, 3.1 years, 8.1 years, 5 years;
     152 cars to be tested.

Page 230   Exercise 13.1

2.   **1 D**   **2 A**   **3 B**   **4 C**

3.   **1 C**   **2 A**   **3 B**   **4 D**

Page 234   Exercise 13.2

1.   Going, against the current;
     Returning, with the current.

5.   **1**   Timbuktu
     2   Sydney
     3   Reykjavic
     4   London

Page 240

Example

$$\overrightarrow{AC} = \begin{pmatrix} 1 \\ 3 \end{pmatrix}, \ \overrightarrow{CA} = \begin{pmatrix} -1 \\ -3 \end{pmatrix}, \ \overrightarrow{CE} = \begin{pmatrix} 6 \\ 0 \end{pmatrix}$$

Page 241   Exercise 14.1

1. $\overrightarrow{AB} = \begin{pmatrix} 4 \\ 2 \end{pmatrix}, \ \overrightarrow{BC} = \begin{pmatrix} 2 \\ 3 \end{pmatrix}, \ \overrightarrow{AC} = \begin{pmatrix} 6 \\ 5 \end{pmatrix}$

2. $\overrightarrow{AB} = \begin{pmatrix} 5 \\ 2 \end{pmatrix}, \ \overrightarrow{BC} = \begin{pmatrix} -1 \\ 3 \end{pmatrix}, \ \overrightarrow{AC} = \begin{pmatrix} 4 \\ 5 \end{pmatrix}$

3. $\overrightarrow{AB} = \begin{pmatrix} -2 \\ -4 \end{pmatrix}, \ \overrightarrow{BC} = \begin{pmatrix} -2 \\ 2 \end{pmatrix}, \ \overrightarrow{AC} = \begin{pmatrix} -4 \\ -2 \end{pmatrix}$

4. $\overrightarrow{AB} = \begin{pmatrix} 0 \\ -4 \end{pmatrix}, \ \overrightarrow{BC} = \begin{pmatrix} 4 \\ 6 \end{pmatrix}, \ \overrightarrow{AC} = \begin{pmatrix} 4 \\ 2 \end{pmatrix}$

5. $\overrightarrow{AB} = \begin{pmatrix} -3 \\ -4 \end{pmatrix}, \ \overrightarrow{BC} = \begin{pmatrix} 6 \\ 0 \end{pmatrix}, \ \overrightarrow{AC} = \begin{pmatrix} 3 \\ -4 \end{pmatrix}$

6. $\overrightarrow{PR} = \begin{pmatrix} 5 \\ -1 \end{pmatrix}$

7. $\overrightarrow{PR} = \begin{pmatrix} 5 \\ 0 \end{pmatrix}$

8. $\overrightarrow{PR} = \begin{pmatrix} 7 \\ -3 \end{pmatrix}$

9. $\overrightarrow{PR} = \begin{pmatrix} -5 \\ -2 \end{pmatrix}$

10. $\overrightarrow{AB} = \begin{pmatrix} 6 \\ -3 \end{pmatrix}, \ \overrightarrow{BC} = \begin{pmatrix} 0 \\ 6 \end{pmatrix}, \ \overrightarrow{DC} = \begin{pmatrix} 2 \\ -1 \end{pmatrix},$

       $\overrightarrow{AD} = \begin{pmatrix} 4 \\ 4 \end{pmatrix}$

Page 244   Exercise 14.2

1. $\overrightarrow{AB} = \begin{pmatrix} 1 \\ 5 \end{pmatrix}$, $\overrightarrow{BC} = \begin{pmatrix} -7 \\ -3 \end{pmatrix}$,

$\overrightarrow{CD} = \begin{pmatrix} -4 \\ -10 \end{pmatrix}$, $\overrightarrow{DA} = \begin{pmatrix} 10 \\ 8 \end{pmatrix}$,

$\overrightarrow{DE} = \begin{pmatrix} 14 \\ 6 \end{pmatrix}$, $\overrightarrow{EF} = \begin{pmatrix} 2 \\ 10 \end{pmatrix}$;

AB is parallel to *EF*, *BC* is parallel to *ED*;
$\overrightarrow{EF} = 2\overrightarrow{AB}$, $\overrightarrow{BC} = -\tfrac{1}{2}\overrightarrow{DE}$

3. $\begin{pmatrix} 5 \\ -1 \end{pmatrix}$, $\begin{pmatrix} -5 \\ 1 \end{pmatrix}$

4. **1** $\mathbf{a} = \begin{pmatrix} 7 \\ -1 \end{pmatrix}$, $\mathbf{b} = \begin{pmatrix} 4 \\ -2 \end{pmatrix}$, $\mathbf{c} = \begin{pmatrix} -8 \\ 2 \end{pmatrix}$,

$\mathbf{d} = \begin{pmatrix} -7 \\ 1 \end{pmatrix}$, $\mathbf{e} = \begin{pmatrix} 6 \\ -9 \end{pmatrix}$, $\mathbf{f} = \begin{pmatrix} 4 \\ 0 \end{pmatrix}$,

$\mathbf{g} = \begin{pmatrix} 8 \\ -4 \end{pmatrix}$, $\mathbf{h} = \begin{pmatrix} 1 \\ 4 \end{pmatrix}$, $\mathbf{j} = \begin{pmatrix} 2 \\ -3 \end{pmatrix}$,

$\mathbf{k} = \begin{pmatrix} 6 \\ -2 \end{pmatrix}$, $\mathbf{m} = \begin{pmatrix} 1 \\ 4 \end{pmatrix}$, $\mathbf{n} = \begin{pmatrix} 0 \\ -5 \end{pmatrix}$

  2 $\mathbf{h} = \mathbf{m}$
  3 $\mathbf{g} = 2\mathbf{b}$
  4 $\mathbf{a} = -\mathbf{d}$
  5 $\mathbf{j} = \tfrac{1}{3}\mathbf{e}$

5. $\overrightarrow{AB} = \begin{pmatrix} -3 \\ 1 \end{pmatrix}$; D, $\begin{pmatrix} -4 \\ 3 \end{pmatrix}$

6. $\overrightarrow{PQ} = \begin{pmatrix} -1 \\ 5 \end{pmatrix}$; S, $\begin{pmatrix} 2 \\ -2 \end{pmatrix}$; rhombus

7. D, $\begin{pmatrix} 3 \\ -1 \end{pmatrix}$; E, $\begin{pmatrix} 5 \\ 2 \end{pmatrix}$; F, $\begin{pmatrix} 7 \\ -3 \end{pmatrix}$

Page 246   Exercise 14.3

1. D (5, 2), E (6, 6); $\overrightarrow{CD} = \overrightarrow{DE} = \begin{pmatrix} 1 \\ 4 \end{pmatrix}$

2. **1** $\overrightarrow{AD} = \begin{pmatrix} 10 \\ 2 \end{pmatrix}$, $\overrightarrow{DC} = \begin{pmatrix} 2 \\ 6 \end{pmatrix}$;

$\overrightarrow{AE} = \overrightarrow{EC} = \begin{pmatrix} 6 \\ 4 \end{pmatrix}$,

$\overrightarrow{BE} = \overrightarrow{ED} = \begin{pmatrix} 4 \\ -2 \end{pmatrix}$

  2 $\overrightarrow{AD} = \begin{pmatrix} 9 \\ -3 \end{pmatrix}$, $\overrightarrow{DC} = \begin{pmatrix} -1 \\ -3 \end{pmatrix}$;

$\overrightarrow{AE} = \overrightarrow{EC} = \begin{pmatrix} 4 \\ -3 \end{pmatrix}$, $\overrightarrow{BE} = \overrightarrow{ED} = \begin{pmatrix} 5 \\ 0 \end{pmatrix}$

  3 $\overrightarrow{AD} = \begin{pmatrix} -4 \\ -7 \end{pmatrix}$, $\overrightarrow{DC} = \begin{pmatrix} 8 \\ 1 \end{pmatrix}$;

$\overrightarrow{AE} = \overrightarrow{EC} = \begin{pmatrix} 2 \\ -3 \end{pmatrix}$,

$\overrightarrow{BE} = \overrightarrow{ED} = \begin{pmatrix} -6 \\ -4 \end{pmatrix}$

  4 $\overrightarrow{AD} = \begin{pmatrix} 3 \\ 5 \end{pmatrix}$, $\overrightarrow{DC} = \begin{pmatrix} -5 \\ 3 \end{pmatrix}$;

$\overrightarrow{AE} = \overrightarrow{EC} = \begin{pmatrix} -1 \\ 4 \end{pmatrix}$,

$\overrightarrow{BE} = \overrightarrow{ED} = \begin{pmatrix} 4 \\ 1 \end{pmatrix}$

3. D (-5, -1), E (-6, 4), F (0, 1);
    G (0, -5), H (-1, 0), J (5, -3);
    $\begin{pmatrix} -2 \\ -6 \end{pmatrix}$

Page 258   Exercise C1

1. −3

2. 8.5 m

3. 7

4. 25 miles

5. 2b

6. 6 cm

7. −6 < x < 6

8. 14

9. 9 days

10. 250 g

11. x^7

12. 0.15 cm

13. 7

14. 21 kg

15. 1

Page 259   Exercise C2

1. £14

2. 3

3. tangent

4. 3

5. (5, 24)

6. yes

7. 7

8. 3.2 × 10⁵

9. $\frac{1}{6}$

10. 1

11. $\frac{1}{16}$

12. $\pi r(r + h)$

13. £6

14. 140 kg

15. $c = y - mx$

Page 259   Exercise C3

1. 1200 ℓ

2. **1** $a = s(1 - r)$

   2 $r = \dfrac{s - a}{s}$ $\left(\text{or } r = 1 - \dfrac{a}{s}\right)$

   3 0.7

3. **1** 3.09 × 10⁻²
    2 1.40 × 10⁻⁵
    3 1.30 × 10⁻³

4. **1** $\frac{1}{1000}$
    2 $\frac{999}{1000}$

5. $x = 2$

6. 1 : 250 000

7. $3(3a - 2b + c)$, 15

8. **1** 35.7 m
    2 35.5°

9. **1** $n = 4$
    2 $n = 6$
    3 $n = 0$

11. $-2\frac{2}{3} < x < 4$, (if x is positive, $0 < x < 4$)

12. **1** 0.49
     2 0.09
     3 0.42

13. PS = 7.5 cm, QR = 11.25 cm,
     SR = 6.25 cm; perimeter = 600 m

14. $w = \dfrac{k}{f}$, 240 kHz

15. 13.2 km

16. **1** $x > 1$, $y > 2$, $y < 6 - x$
     2 $y > -2$, $y < x - 2$, $y < 2 - x$

17. $\overrightarrow{AD} = \begin{pmatrix} -2 \\ 6 \end{pmatrix}$, $\overrightarrow{CB} = \begin{pmatrix} -3 \\ 9 \end{pmatrix}$

18. Cumulative frequencies:
     0, 3, 12, 34, 62, 78, 80
     1 7.7 kg
     2 upper quartile 8.4 kg,
     lower quartile 6.9 kg,
     interquartile range 1.5 kg

19. 8.3 min ($8\frac{1}{3}$ min)

20. length = $\dfrac{12}{x}$ m;

     yes, widths 2 m to 3 m

Page 264   Exercise C4

1. **1** 23
    2 22

2. $n(n + 3)$

3. **1** £48
    2 £144

4. $\vec{BA} = \vec{CD} = \begin{pmatrix} 1 \\ 4 \end{pmatrix}$

5. **1** 2.36×10^{-2} mm^2
    2 2.4×10^{-4} mm^3

6. **1** 39
    2 $x = 3.5$ or -0.4

7. 306 m

8. **1** $x + y = 30$
    2 $x > 2y$
    3 $24x + 18y < 670$

9. **1** $\frac{1}{24}$
    2 $\frac{5}{8}$

10. $x = \frac{1}{4}$

11. £168

12. 2.57

13. $x = 1.1$; $BC = 1.1$ cm, $AC = 6.1$ cm

14. 150 m

15. **1** 17.7 cm
    2 12.6 cm

16. **1** $a^4 b^4 c^7$ **4** $4h^2$
    2 $12d^3 e^4$ **5** $8j^6 k^3$
    3 $3fg^3$

17. **1** 16 cm
    2 3 cm

18. $x = \frac{1}{2}$

19. **1** $\frac{3}{4}$
    2 $\frac{9}{16}$
    3 $\frac{1}{64}$

20. Cumulative frequencies:
    0, 6, 13, 20, 30, 45, 62, 80, 91, 97, 100
    1 53
    2 upper quartile 67, lower quartile 35,
         interquartile range 32.
    3 63